D0982383

The Life and Adventures of
Nicholas Nickleby

PR
6055
.D44
L5
1982b

WITHDRAWN

The Life and Adventures of
NICHOLAS NICKLEBY

By Charles Dickens

Adapted for the Stage by
David Edgar

Nelson Doubleday, Inc.   Garden City, New York

© Copyright, 1982, by David Edgar

CAUTION: Professionals and amateurs are hereby warned that THE LIFE AND ADVENTURES OF NICHOLAS NICKLEBY is subject to a royalty. It is fully protected under the copyright laws of the United States of America, and of all countries covered by the International Copyright Union (including the Dominion of Canada and the rest of the British Commonwealth), and of all countries covered by the Pan-American Copyright Convention and the Universal Copyright Convention, and of all countries with which the United States has reciprocal copyright relations. All rights, including professional, amateur, motion picture, recitation, lecturing, public reading, radio broadcasting, television, and the rights of translation into foreign languages, are strictly reserved. Particular emphasis is laid upon the question of readings, permission for which must be secured from the author's agent in writing.

All inquiries concerning rights (other than amateur rights in the United States and Canada) should be addressed to Michael Imison Playwrights Ltd., Somerset House, Penthouse D, 150 West 47th Street, New York, N.Y. 10036.

The amateur production rights in THE LIFE AND ADVENTURES OF NICHOLAS NICKLEBY, in the United States and Canada, are controlled exclusively by the DRAMATISTS PLAY SERVICE, INC., 440 Park Avenue South, New York, N.Y. 10016. No amateur performance of the play may be given without obtaining in advance the written permission of the DRAMATISTS PLAY SERVICE, INC., and paying the requisite fee.

SPECIAL NOTE ON MUSIC

The incidental music and lyrics composed by Stephen Oliver for the original production of THE LIFE AND ADVENTURES OF NICHOLAS NICKLEBY are copyrighted by Novello and Company Ltd., Borough Green, Sevenoaks, Kent TN15 8DT, England. Sole distributor for the United States is Theodore Presser Company, Presser Place, Bryn Mawr, PA 19010. Terms quoted on request.

© Copyright, 1981, by Novello and Company Limited
(PAu 352-229)
Lyrics reprinted by permission
Photographs Copyright © 1981 Martha Swope
Design by Jeanette Portelli

The Royal Shakespeare Company production of THE LIFE AND ADVENTURES OF NICHOLAS NICKLEBY was presented by James M. Nederlander, The Shubert Organization, Elizabeth I. McCann and Nelle Nugent at the Plymouth Theatre, in New York City, on October 4, 1981. It was directed by Trevor Nunn and John Caird (assisted by Leon Rubin); the designers were John Napier and Dermot Hayes; costumes were by John Napier; and the lighting was by David Hersey. The American production was designed in association with Neil Peter Jampolis (sets and costumes); Beverly Emmons (lighting); and Richard Fitzgerald (sound). The music and lyrics were by Stephen Oliver; and the musical director was Donald Johnston.

"The Life and Adventures of Nicholas Nickleby"
is set in England in the first half of the Nineteenth Century.

CAST
(in order of appearance)

THE NICKLEBY FAMILY
NICHOLAS NICKLEBY	*Roger Rees*
KATE NICKLEBY	*Emily Richard*
RALPH NICKLEBY	*John Woodvine*
MRS. NICKLEBY	*Priscilla Morgan*

LONDON
NEWMAN NOGGS	*Edward Petherbridge*
HANNAH	*Hilary Townley*
MISS LA CREEVY	*Rose Hill*
SIR MATTHEW PUPKER	*David Lloyd Meredith*
MR. BONNEY	*Andrew Hawkins*

IRATE GENTLEMAN	*Patrick Godfrey*
FLUNKEY	*Timothy Kightley*
MR. SNAWLEY	*William Maxwell*
SNAWLEY MAJOR	*Janet Dale*
SNAWLEY MINOR	*Hilary Townley*
BELLING	*Stephen Rashbrook*
WILLIAM	*John McEnery*
WAITRESSES	*Sharon Bower, Sally Nesbitt*
COACHMAN	*Clyde Pollitt*
MR. MANTALINI	*John McEnery*
MADAME MANTALINI	*Thelma Whiteley*
FLUNKEY	*Richard Simpson*
MISS KNAG	*Janet Dale*
RICH LADIES	*Sharon Bower, Shirley King*
MILLINERS	*Suzanne Bertish, Sharon Bower, Lucy Gutteridge, Cathryn Harrison, Ian East, William Maxwell, Sally Nesbitt, Stephen Rashbrook, Hilary Townley*

YORKSHIRE

MR. SQUEERS	*Alun Armstrong*
MRS. SQUEERS	*Lila Kaye*
SMIKE	*David Threlfall*
PHIB	*Sally Nesbitt*
FANNY SQUEERS	*Suzanne Bertish*
YOUNG WACKFORD SQUEERS	*Ian McNeice*
JOHN BROWDIE	*Bob Peck*
TILDA PRICE	*Cathryn Harrison*
Boys	
TOMKINS	*William Maxwell*
COATES	*Andrew Hawkins*
GRAYMARSH	*Alan Gill*
JENNINGS	*Patrick Godfrey*
MOBBS	*Christopher Ravenscroft*
BOLDER	*Mark Tandy*
PITCHER	*Sharon Bower*
JACKSON	*Nicholas Gecks*
COBBEY	*John McEnery*
PETERS	*Teddy Kempner*

| SPROUTER | *Lucy Gutteridge* |
| ROBERTS | *Ian East* |

LONDON AGAIN

MR. KENWIGS	*Patrick Godfrey*
MRS. KENWIGS	*Shirley King*
MORLEENA KENWIGS	*Hilary Townley*
MR. LILLYVICK	*Timothy Kightley*
MISS PETOWKER	*Cathryn Harrison*
MR. CROWL	*Ian East*
GEORGE	*Alan Gill*
MR. CUTLER	*Jeffery Dench*
MRS. CUTLER	*Janet Dale*
MRS. KENWIGS' SISTER	*Sharon Bower*
LADY FROM DOWNSTAIRS	*Rose Hill*
MISS GREEN	*Priscilla Morgan*
BENJAMIN	*Teddy Kempner*
PUGSTYLES	*Roderick Horn*
OLD LORD	*Richard Simpson*
YOUNG FIANCEE	*Lucy Gutteridge*
LANDLORD	*Jeffery Dench*

PORTSMOUTH

MR. VINCENT CRUMMLES	*Christopher Benjamin*
MRS. CRUMMLES	*Lila Kaye*
THE INFANT PHENOMENON	*Hilary Townley*
MASTER PERCY CRUMMLES	*Teddy Kempner*
MASTER CRUMMLES	*Mark Tandy*
MRS. GRUDDEN	*Rose Hill*
MISS SNEVELLICCI	*Suzanne Bertish*
MR. FOLAIR	*Clyde Pollitt*
MR. LENVILLE	*Christopher Ravenscroft*
MISS LEDROOK	*Lucy Gutteridge*
MISS BRAVASSA	*Sharon Bower*
MR. WAGSTAFF	*Alun Armstrong*
MR. BLIGHTEY	*Jeffery Dench*
MISS BELVAWNEY	*Janet Dale*
MISS GAZINGI	*Sally Nesbitt*
MR. PAILEY	*William Maxwell*
MR. HETHERINGTON	*Andrew Hawkins*
MR. BANE	*Stephen Rashbrook*

MR. FLUGGERS	*Richard Simpson*
MRS. LENVILLE	*Shirley King*
MR. CURDLE	*Hubert Rees*
MRS. CURDLE	*Emily Richard*
MR. SNEVELLICCI	*John McEnery*
MRS. SNEVELLICCI	*Thelma Whiteley*
SCALEY	*Ian McNeice*
TIX	*Teddy Kempner*
SIR MULBERRY HAWK	*Bob Peck*
LORD FREDERICK VERISOPHT	*Nicholas Gecks*
MR. PLUCK	*Teddy Kempner*
MR. PYKE	*Mark Tandy*
MR. SNOBB	*Christopher Ravenscroft*
COLONEL CHOWSER	*Timothy Kightley*
BROOKER	*Clyde Pollitt*
MR. WITITTERLEY	*Roderick Horn*
MRS. WITITTERLEY	*Janet Dale*
ALPHONSE	*Stephen Rashbrook*
OPERA SINGERS	*Sharon Bower, Andrew Hawkins, John Woodvine*
CHARLES CHEERYBLE	*David Lloyd Meredith*
NED CHEERYBLE	*Hubert Rees*
TIM LINKINWATER	*Richard Simpson*
THE MAN NEXT DOOR	*Patrick Godfrey*
KEEPER	*Alan Gill*
FRANK CHEERYBLE	*Christopher Ravenscroft*
NURSE	*Thelma Whiteley*
ARTHUR GRIDE	*Jeffery Dench*
MADELINE BRAY	*Lucy Gutteridge*
WALTER BRAY	*Christopher Benjamin*
PEG SLIDERSKEW	*Suzanne Bertish*
HAWK'S RIVAL	*Edward Petherbridge*
CAPTAIN ADAMS	*Andrew Hawkins*
WESTWOOD	*Alan Gill*
CROUPIER	*Ian McNeice*
CASINO PROPRIETOR	*Patrick Godfrey*
SURGEON	*Timothy Kightley*
UMPIRE	*Roderick Horn*
POLICEMEN	*Andrew Hawkins, Mark Tandy*
MRS. SNAWLEY	*Janet Dale*
YOUNG WOMAN	*Hilary Townley*

UNDERSTUDIES

Understudies never substitute for listed players unless a
specific announcement for the appearance is made
at the time of the performance.

Catherine Brandon, Wilfred Grove, Katherine Levy

MUSICIANS

Donald Johnston	*Musical Conductor/Piano*
Mel Rodnon	*Flute*
Seymour Press	*Clarinet*
Ethan Bauch	*Bassoon*
Lowell Hershey	*Trumpet*
Robert Zittola	*Trumpet*
Christine Snyder	*French Horn*
Daniel Repole	*Trombone*
Sandra Billingslea	*Violin*
Karen Ritscher	*Viola*
Doc Solomon	*Bass*
Bruce Yuchitel	*Banjo*
Jack Jennings	*Percussion*

Wedding Anthem sung by Choristers from
St. Paul's Cathedral. Master of the Choir Barry Rose.

The first performance of THE LIFE AND ADVENTURES OF
NICHOLAS NICKLEBY was on June 6, 1980 at the Royal Shakespeare Company's Aldwych Theatre, in London.

AUTHOR'S INTRODUCTION

On November 19, 1979, a group of about 50 people sat down in a large circle in a rehearsal room in Stratford-upon-Avon, to discuss the possibility of turning Charles Dickens' vast, panoramic novel *Nicholas Nickleby* into a theatrical entertainment. This group consisted of a large number of actors and actresses, two directors, an assistant director, four stage managers, and a writer. Over the following months, this line-up changed: some actors left, others joined, the team acquired two designers, an assistant designer, a composer and lyricist, a musical director, a band, a script assistant, a lighting director, lighting and sound technicians, dressers and stage-hands. During this period, the performers had experimented, improvised and completed 20 research projects into aspects of early Victorian life; the directors had overseen these exercises, had discussed, organised and undertaken rehearsals; the writer had written. By January 1980 it had become clear that early hopes of a one-evening project had to be jettisoned; if we were to tell the entire Dickens' story (as we were determined to do) then we would need two evenings: as Spring approached it became clear that these would be very long evenings indeed. And by our opening night, June 5, 1980, we had two vast plays: the first lasting four hours, the second four and a half.

The opening of the play, at the Royal Shakespeare Company's London theatre, was not the end of the story. After a short run in the summer of 1980, the production was brought back into the company's repertoire on two occasions; the show was adapted for television and recorded in the summer of 1981; the stage production transferred to New York in the fall of that year. Each revival and transfer saw cast changes, the production developed, and the script was rewritten and (I hope) improved.

This is not the place for a history of the way *Nickleby* came about (there is a good one, written by Leon Rubin, called *The Nicholas Nickleby Story*). But it is important to give some impression of the process, for two reasons. The first is a matter of simple justice. Most scripts are developed and improved by the directors and performers who work on them, but *Nickleby* was perhaps unique as a collaborative venture. The original idea came from the directors, John Caird and Trevor Nunn; the style and texture of the adaptation was created by the performers; the set and the score helped to define not just how the show looked and sounded, but the basic method of storytelling as well. The script published here is thus a collective possession, in a very real sense: it was created over nearly two years by the best part of a hundred people.

The second point concerns the extent to which it has been possible to produce an acting edition in the conventional sense. While I have tried to make clear, in the notes that follow this introduction and in the text, how the show was and thus could be costumed, set and staged, many of these decisions resulted from the specific conditions in which we worked (and indeed from our personnel). It is open to future companies to make their own decisions, based on their own resources.

Two further things should be said by way of introduction. The first is that *Nicholas Nickleby,* Parts One and Two, tells the entire story of a huge Dickens novel. One can imagine all sorts of good reasons for doing one part but not the other, or even for doing versions of the play which contain some plots but not others. But I would nonetheless beg producers to consider attempting the whole, because one of the unique things about our adaptation was that, unlike every Dickens film and stage adaptation (and most of the television serialisations as well), we did it all, because we felt strongly that the only way to represent Dickens' achievement was to display it in its entirety.

Finally, I am aware that the notes and stage directions in this text may seem woefully inadequate to companies used to the excellent documentation provided in most acting editions. I hope they will understand that in order to present such detail in a show in which at least 39 performers play round about 123 speaking parts in 95 scenes would require a book of at least twice this size. Luckily, however, producers are able to purchase, at most good bookshops, a companion volume which contains the most comprehensive acting, costuming, staging and setting instructions, and a lot else besides. It is called *The Life and Adventures of Nicholas Nickleby,* and it was written by the English novelist Charles Dickens in the early years of the 19th Century.

Part One

ACT ONE

Scene One

As the audience come in, the Company mingles with them, welcoming them to the show. Eventually, the whole company assembles on stage. Each member of the company takes at least one of the lines of opening narration:

NARRATION.
There once lived in a sequestered part of the county of Devonshire, one Mr. Godfrey Nickleby, who, rather late in life, took it into his head to get married.

And in due course, when Mrs. Nickleby had presented her husband with two sons, he found himself in a situation of distinctly shortened means,

Which were only relieved when, one fine morning, there arrived a black-bordered letter, informing him that his uncle was dead and left him the bulk of his property, amounting in all to five thousand pounds.

And with a portion of this property, Mr. Godfrey Nickleby purchased a small farm near Dawlish,

And on his death some fifteen years later, he was able to leave to his eldest son three thousand pounds in cash, and to his youngest, one thousand and the farm.

The younger boy was of a timid and retiring disposition, keen only to attach himself to the quiet routine of country life.

The elder son, however, resolved to make much use of his father's inheritance.

For young Ralph Nickleby had commenced usury on a limited scale even at school, putting out at interest a small capital of slate pencil and marbles,

And had now in adulthood resolved to live his life by the simple motto that there was nothing in the world as good as money.

And while Ralph prospered in the mercantile way in London, the young brother lived still on the farm,

And took himself a wife,

Who gave birth to a boy and a girl,

And by the time they were both nearing the age of twenty, he found his expenses much increased and his capital still more depleted.

Speculate. His wife advised him.

Think of your brother, Mr. Nickleby, and speculate.

And Mr. Nickleby did speculate,

But a mania prevailed,

A bubble burst,

Four stockbrokers took villa residences at Florence,

Four hundred nobodies were ruined,

And one of them was

Mr. Nickleby.

And Mr. Nickleby took to his bed,

Apparently resolved to keep that, at all events.

Cheer up, sir!

Said the apothecary.

You mustn't let yourself be cast down, sir.

Said the nurse.

Such things happen every day,

Remarked the lawyer,

And it is very sinful to rebel against them,

Whispered the clergyman,

And what no man with a family ought to do,

Added the neighbours.

But Mr. Nickleby shook his head,

And he motioned them all out of the room

And shortly afterwards his reason went astray,

And he babbled of the goodness of his brother and the merry times they'd had at school,

And one day he turned upon his face,

Observing that he thought that he could fall asleep.

And so, with no-one in the world to help them but Ralph Nickleby,

(*Mrs. Nickleby, Kate and Nicholas are emerging from the crowd.*)

MRS. NICKLEBY. The widow,
KATE/NICHOLAS. And her children,
NARRATOR. Journeyed forth to—LONDON!

(*And immediately, the company becomes the population of London, jostling and bustling round, past and through the Nicklebys, until we can see them no more, and the next scene has emerged.*)

Scene Two

The London Tavern. A public meeting. On stage, some seated, some standing, are the organisers of the meeting: Sir Matthew Pupker, Mr. Bonney, a Flunkey, several gentlemen, and, sitting a little apart, Ralph Nickleby. In and around the audience are representatives of the lower classes: in particular, a large number of Muffin-boys, who distribute muffins to the audience from the trays they carry round their necks. There are also a few policemen to keep public order, and, as we shall discover, an Irate Gentleman and a Furious Gentleman as well. The Flunkey bangs his staff for silence.

FLUNKEY. My lords, ladies and gentlemen. Pray give silence for Sir Matthew Pupker, Honourable Member of the Commons of England in Parliament assembled. (*Applause. The odd catcall. The Police finger their truncheons.*)
SIR MATTHEW. Good morning. It falls to me today to announce the opening of a public meeting to discuss the propriety or otherwise of petitioning Parliament in urgent condemnation of the appalling, deplorable, and generally heinous state of the Hot Muffin Baking and Delivery Industry. (*The Irate Gentleman shouts from the audience.*)
IRATE GENTLEMAN. Crumpets. (*Polite applause.*)
SIR MATTHEW. Ladies and gentlemen, in troubled times like these, when naked riot stalks the frightened streets at home, and overseas the Russian bear is pawing at the very vitals of the Empire, there could not be a greater nor a nobler task than this we face today. (*Applause. To stop it, Sir Matthew raises his hand.*) So, Mr. Bonney will now read the resolution. (*Bonney stands, coughs, and reads.*)

BONNEY. The Resolution. That this meeting views with alarm and apprehension, the present state of the Muffin trade.

IRATE GENTLEMAN. (*Shouts.*) And crumpet trade.

BONNEY. . . . that it considers the present constitution of the Muffin Boys—

IRATE GENTLEMAN. (*Shouts.*) And crumpet boys!

SOME. Order—shh—

BONNEY. (*After a slight pause.*) . . . wholly undeserving of the confidence of the public, and that it deems the whole Muffin System—

IRATE GENTLEMAN. Crumpet! (*Bonney turns to Sir Matthew in frustration.*)

SIR MATTHEW. Now, what—(*The Irate Gentleman has marched up on to the stage.*)

IRATE GENTLEMAN. Sir, I must protest.

SIR MATTHEW. I beg your pardon?

IRATE GENTLEMAN. Sir, I must protest and I must insist. I must insist and I must demand.

SIR MATTHEW. Yes? What?

IRATE GENTLEMAN. And crumpets, sir. And *crumpets*. Not just muffins. Crumpets. (*Pause.*)

SIR MATTHEW. Is that an amendment?

IRATE GENTLEMAN. It's a demand. And an amendment, too.

SIR MATTHEW. I see. Well, then. All those in favour?

ALMOST EVERYONE. Aye! (*One Furious Man, however, shouts.*)

FURIOUS MAN. No, no, a thousand times, no! You'll rue the day. (*And he strides out.*)

SIR MATTHEW. The ayes appear to have it. Mr. Bonney.

BONNEY. And it deems the whole Muffin and Crumpet system prejudicial to the best interests of a great mercantile community. (*Applause.*) My lords, ladies, and gentlemen: I must state that I have visited the houses of the poor, and have found them destitute of the slightest vestige of a muffin, or a crumpet, which there appears to be much reason to believe some of these persons to not taste from year's end to year's end. (*Boos and expressions of shock and horror: "It's a scandal", "This must stop", "Fancy that".*) It is this melancholy state of affairs that the company proposes to correct. (*During the following a certain amount of protest develops among those sectors of the audience who are in fact muffin and crumpet sellers themselves, and have thus far been sympathetic to the emotional description of their sad and miserable lot.*) . . . firstly, by prohibiting under dire penalties all private muffin and crumpet trading of every description; (*Applause—dies down, and we hear Muffineers.*)

1st MUFFINEER. Eh?

2nd MUFFINEER. What's he saying?

BONNEY. . . . and secondly, by ourselves providing the public generally, with muffins and crumpets of first quality at reduced prices— (*Applause—dies down, we hear Muffineers.*)

1st MUFFINEER. He must be joking.

2nd MUFFINEER. It's our livelihood!

BONNEY. . . . and it is with this object that a bill has been introduced into Parliament; (*The Muffineers are striding up towards the stage.*) . . . it is this bill that we have met to support;

1st MUFFINEER. What about the muffin boys! (*Some Muffineers have reached the stage. Others are throwing their muffins on to the stage. Some disreputable members of the audience probably join in too.*)

MUFFINEERS. So what about the Muffin Boys
So what about the Muffin Boys
So what about the— (*The Muffineers are roundly truncheoned by the Police for this anarchic display, and are ejected, as Bonney:*)

BONNEY. . . . and, finally, it is the supporters of this bill who will confer undying brightness and splendour upon England, under the name of the United Metropolitan Improved Hot Muffin and Crumpet Baking and Punctual Delivery Company! Capital five millions, in five hundred thousand shares of Ten—Pounds—Each! (*Wild applause. Bonney accepts hand-shakes from supporters and wipes his brow. Eventually, the applause dies.*)

SIR MATTHEW. Well, thank you, Mr. Bonney. (*Pause. Something should have happened. Sir Matthew looks to Ralph Nickleby, who has sat, impassively, throughout the proceedings.*) Mr. Nickleby?

RALPH. Seconded.

SIR MATTHEW. All those in favour?

EVERYONE. Aye!

SIR MATTHEW. Carried by an acclamation! Meeting closed. (*And suddenly, Sir Matthew, Mr. Bonney, the gentlemen, and everyone else disperse, and Ralph walks forward.*)

Scene Three

Ralph Nickleby is greeted by his clerk Newman Noggs, a sallow-faced man in rusty-brown clothes. Noggs carries a letter. We suppose we are in the street, outside the meeting.

RALPH. Noggs.

NOGGS. That's me.

RALPH. What is it?

NOGGS. It's a letter.

RALPH. Oh. The Ruddles mortgage, I suppose?

NOGGS. No. Wrong.

RALPH. What *has* come, then?

NOGGS. I have.

RALPH. (*Irritated.*) What else?

NOGGS. (*Handing over the letter.*) This. Postmark Strand, black wax, black border, woman's hand, C.N. in the corner.

RALPH. Black wax. I know the hand, too. Newman, I shouldn't be surprised if my brother was dead. (*He opens the letter and reads.*)

NOGGS. I don't think you would.

RALPH. (*Reading.*) Why not, sir?

NOGGS. You never are surprised at anything, that's all.

RALPH. (*Folding the letter.*) It's as I thought. He's dead.

NOGGS. Children alive?

RALPH. Yes, well, that's the point. They're both alive.

NOGGS. Both?

RALPH. And a widow too, and all three of 'em in London, damn 'em. (*Slight pause. Ralph looks at Noggs, who is looking neutral. Enter Mr. Bonney.*)

NOGGS. (*Unconvincingly.*) Terrible. (*Slight pause.*)

RALPH. Go home. (*Bonney coughs. Ralph turns to Bonney. Noggs does not go.*) Ah, Bonney. Put me down for 500, would you?

BONNEY. They'll nearly double in a three-month, Mr. Nickleby.

RALPH. I'm sure of it.

BONNEY. And when they have . . . You'll know just what to do with 'em. (*Slight pause. Embarrassingly confidential.*) Back quietly out, at just the right time, eh?

RALPH. Indeed. (*He notices Noggs is still there.*) I told you to go home.

NOGGS. I'm going. (*Noggs snaps his knuckles and goes out.*)

BONNEY. What a very remarkable man that clerk of yours is.

RALPH. Kept his own hounds and horses, once. But squandered everything, borrowed at interest, took to drinking . . . I'd done a little business with him, as it happens, and he came to me to borrow more, I needed to employ a clerk . . .

BONNEY. Yes, yes, just so.

RALPH. So, then—five hundred, Bonney. (*Bonney goes. Ralph waves the letter. To himself.*) What are they to me? I've never even seen 'em. Damn 'em! (*And he too turns to go.*)

Scene Four

Outside and inside a house in the Strand. Ralph walks round the stage, as narrators describe his journey:

NARRATORS.

And so Ralph Nickleby proceeded to the Strand . . .

And found the number of the house . . .

And stopped,

And gave a double-knock, (*Someone bangs a stick twice on the floor.*)

And waited for an answer. (*A dirty-faced servant, Hannah, appears.*)

HANNAH. Yes?

RALPH. Mrs. Nickleby at home?

HANNAH. La Creevy.

RALPH. Beg you pardon?

HANNAH. Name, in't what you said. It's Miss La Creevy.

RALPH. (*Waving the letter.*) But— (*A female voice from off.*)

MISS LA CREEVY. Who is it, Hannah?

HANNAH. There's a man here, wanting something. (*Enter Miss La Creevy, a small lady of 50 in a yellow bonnet, carrying a paintbrush.*)

MISS LA CREEVY. Who? And wanting what? (*Hannah shrugs, nods at Ralph.*) Oh, sir—

RALPH. Madam, to whom—

MISS LA CREEVY. Oh, sir, I'm Miss La Creevy, sir, I am a painter of portraiture in miniature, sir, and if I may presume to speak such, you have a very strongly marked countenance for such a purpose, sir, should that be your—

RALPH. Is there a widow lodging here? A Mrs. Nickleby?

MISS LA CREEVY. Oh, you're for Mrs. Nickleby?

RALPH. That's right. I am Mr. Ralph Nickleby.

MISS LA CREEVY. Oh, Hannah, what a stupid thing you are. Why, sir, yes, they have their apartments just across the hall from mine, just there, sir, and I must say what an extremely affable lady she is, though of course very low in her spirits, and the children too, most pleasant—

RALPH. Over here, you say?

MISS LA CREEVY. That's right, sir, but may I remark, that if you should ever wish to have a miniature . . . (*Ralph turns back looks darkly at Miss La Creevy, who retains sufficient composure to produce a small card.*) Perhaps you will have the kindness to take a card of terms. (*Ralph takes the card. With a humourless smile.*)

RALPH. Of course.

MISS LA CREEVY. Now, Hannah, go on, and announce Mr. Nickleby to Mrs. Nickleby.

RALPH. I thank you. (*Miss La Creevy goes out, as Nicholas, Kate and Mrs. Nickleby come forward. Nicholas carries a chair, on which Mrs. Nickleby sits. Hannah leads Ralph to them. Hannah tries to make a proper announcement.*)

HANNAH. Uh, Mrs. Nickleby, here's . . . Mr. Nickleby. (*Hannah withdraws.*)

RALPH. Ah, young Nicholas, I suppose. Good morning sir. And, Kate.

MRS. NICKLEBY. That is correct, sir. These are my— (*Unable to get out the word "children", Mrs. Nickleby bursts into tears.*)

RALPH. Well, ma'am, how are you? You must bear up against sorrow, ma'am, I always do. You didn't mention how he died.

MRS. NICKLEBY. The doctors could attribute it to no particular disease. We have no reason to fear that he died of a broken heart.

RALPH. Hm. What?

MRS. NICKLEBY. I beg your pardon?

RALPH. I don't understand. A broken leg or head, I know of them, but not a broken heart.

NICHOLAS. Some people, I believe, have none to break.

RALPH. What's that? How old is this boy, ma'am?

MRS. NICKLEBY. Nineteen.

RALPH. And what's he mean to do for bread?

NICHOLAS. To earn it, sir. And not look for anyone to keep my family, except myself.

RALPH. I see. Well, ma'am, the creditors have administered, you say, and you spent what little was left, coming all the way to London, to see me.

MRS. NICKLEBY. I hoped . . . It was my husband's wish, I should appeal to you—

RALPH. I don't know why it is. But whenever a man dies with no property, he always thinks he has the right to dispose of other people's. If my brother had been acquainted with the world, and then applied himself to make his way in it, then you would not now be in this—in your situation. I must say it, Miss Nickleby: my brother was a thoughtless, inconsiderate man, and no-one, I am sure, can feel that fact more keenly than you do.

MRS. NICKLEBY. Well, well. That may be true. I've often thought, if he had listened to me . . . Yes. It may well be true. (*Nicholas and Kate give an uncertain glance at each other. Ralph clocks this.*)

RALPH. So, what's your daughter fit for, ma'am?

MRS. NICKLEBY. Oh, Kate has been well-educated, sir.

KATE. I'm willing to try anything that will give me home and bread.

RALPH. (*Slightly affected by Kate.*) Well, well. (*To Nicholas, briskly.*) And you, sir? You're prepared to work?

NICHOLAS. Yes, certainly. (*Ralph takes a newspaper cutting from his pocket.*)

RALPH. Then read that. Caught my eye this morning. (*Nicholas takes the cutting and reads.*)

NICHOLAS. Education. The Master of the Academy, Dotheboys Hall, near Greta Bridge in Yorkshire, is in town, and attends at the Saracen's Head, Snow Hill. Able assistant wanted. Annual salary five pounds. A Master of Arts would be preferred.

RALPH. Well. There.

MRS. NICKLEBY. But he's not a Master of Arts.

RALPH. That I think can be got over.

KATE. And the salary is so small, uncle, and it is so far away—

MRS. NICKLEBY. Hush, Kate, your uncle must know best.

RALPH. And I'm convinced that he will have you, if I recommend it. (*Pause.*) Ma'am, if he can find another job, in London, now, which keeps him in shoe leather . . . He can have a thousand pounds. (*Pause.*)

KATE. We must be separated, then, so soon?

NICHOLAS. Sir, if I am appointed to this post, what will become of those I leave behind?

RALPH. If you're accepted, and you take it, they will be provided for. That will be my care. (*Pause.*)

NICHOLAS. Then, uncle, I am ready to do anything you wish.

RALPH. That's good. And, come, who knows, you work well, and you'll rise to be a partner. And then, if he dies, your fortune's made.

NICHOLAS. Oh, yes? (*To his family, to cheer them up, but becoming convinced himself.*) Oh, yes, to be sure. Oh, Kate, and who knows, perhaps there will be some young nobleman or other, at the school, who takes a fancy to me, and then I'll become his travelling tutor when he leaves . . . And when we get back from the continent, his father might procure me some handsome appointment, in his household, or his business. Yes? And, who knows, he might fall in love with Kate, and marry her . . . (*To Ralph.*) Don't you think so, uncle?

RALPH. (*Unconvincingly.*) Yes, yes, of course. (*Kate goes to Ralph.*)

KATE. Uncle. We're a simple family. We were born and bred in the country, we have never been apart, and we are unaquainted with the world.

RALPH. Well, then, my dear—

KATE. It will take time for us to understand it, to apply ourselves to make our way in it, and to bear that separation which necessity now forces on us. I am sure you understand. (*Pause.*)

RALPH. Oh, yes, indeed I do. (*Nicholas embraces his mother and sister.*) Now, sir . . . Shall we go? (*Nicholas follows Ralph out one way, as Mrs. Nickleby and Kate leave the other.*)

Scene Five

The coffee house of the Saracen's Head. A table, on which Wackford Squeers is sitting, reading a newspaper. Near him is a little trunk, on which a small boy, Belling is sitting. This scene is set up during the following narration:

NARRATOR. And so the uncle, and his nephew, took themselves with all convenient speed towards Snow Hill, and Mr. Wackford Squeers. (*The narration is carried on by William, a waiter at the Saracen's Head. Two maids enter, and stare at Mr. Squeers.*)

WILLIAM. And in Snow Hill, near to the jail and Smithfield, is the Saracen's Head, and outside the Saracen's Head are two stone heads of Saracen's, both fearsome and quite hideously ugly, and inside, on this January afternoon, stood Mr. Squeers, whose appearance was not much more prepossessing. (*Squeers lowers the newspaper. We see him as the two maids describe him to each other.*)

1st MAID. He's only got one eye.

WILLIAM. While the popular prejudice runs in favour of two.

2nd MAID. And, look, the side of his face is all wrinkled and puckered.

WILLIAM. Which gave him a highly sinister appearance, especially when he smiled.

1st MAID. And the eye he's got's a very funny colour.

WILLIAM. Which indeed it was, a kind of greenish grey, in shape resembling the fanlight of a street-door, through which Mr. Squeers was glaring at a tiny boy, who was sitting on a tiny trunk, in front of him. (*And indeed Squeers and Belling are looking at each other. Belling sneezes as William and the maids withdraw.*)

SQUEERS. Hallo, sir! What's that, sir? (*The maids withdraw.*)

BELLING. Nothing, please, sir.

SQUEERS. Nothing, sir?

BELLING. Please, sir, I sneezed, sir.

SQUEERS. (*Taking the boy by the ear.*) Sneezed? You Sneezed? Well, that's not nothing, is it?

BELLING. No, sir.

SQUEERS. Wait till Yorkshire, my young gentleman. And then I'll give you something to remember. (*Belling is crying. Reenter William.*)

WILLIAM. Mr. Squeers, there's a gentleman who's asking for you.

SQUEERS. Show him in, William, show him in. (*William goes out. Squeers looks at Belling, who is still sniffing. Belling cringes at this look, and is somewhat surprised when Squeers sits on the bench, and puts his arm round the tiny boy.*) Now, dear child, why are you weeping? All people have their trials, but what is yours? You are losing your friends, that is true, but you will have a father in me, my dear, and a mother in Mrs. Squeers. (*William admitting Snawley, a sleek, flat-nosed man in sombre garments, and two little Snawley boys.*) At the delightful village of Dotheboys, near Greta Bridge in Yorkshire, where youth are boarded, clothed, booked, furnished with pocket-money, provided with all necessaries, (*Snawley checks Squeers' speech against a newspaper advertisement he carries. It is the same.*) . . . instructed in all languages, living and dead, mathematics, orthography, geometry, astronomy, trigonometry, the use of the globes, algebra, single stick (if required), writing, arithmetic, fortification, and every other branch of classical literature. Terms, 20 guineas per annum, no extras, no vacations, and diet unparalleled, why good day, sir, I had no idea . . . (*And Squeers has turned to Snawley and extended his hand.*)

SNAWLEY. Mr. Squeers?

SQUEERS. The same, sir.

SNAWLEY. My name is Snawley. I'm in the oil and colour way.

SQUEERS. Well, how do you do, sir? (*To the little Snawleys.*) And how do *you* do, young sirs?

SNAWLEY. Mr. Squeers, I have been thinking of placing my two boys at your school.

SQUEERS. Sir, I do not think you could do a better thing.

SNAWLEY. At—£20 per annum?

SQUEERS. Guineas.

SNAWLEY. Pounds for two, perhaps? They're not great eaters.

SQUEERS. Then we will not be great feeders, sir. I am sure that we can reach accommodation.

SNAWLEY. And this is another boy, sir?

SQUEERS. Yes, sir, this is Belling, and his luggage that he's sitting on. Each boy requires two suits of clothes, six shirts, six pairs of stockings, two nightcaps, two pocket hankerchiefs, two pairs of shoes, two hats and a razor.

SNAWLEY. Razor? Sir, whatever for?

SQUEERS. To Shave With. (*Pause. Snawley takes Squeers aside. The little boys look at each other.*)

SNAWLEY. Sir, up to what age . . . ?

SQUEERS. As long as payment's regularly made.

SNAWLEY. I see. (*Slight pause.*)

SQUEERS. Sir, let us understand each other. Are these boys legitimate?

SNAWLEY. They are.

SQUEERS. They are?

SNAWLEY. But I am not their father. (*Slight pause.*)

SQUEERS. Go on.

SNAWLEY. I'm the husband of their mother. (*Slight pause.*) And as it's so expensive, keeping boys . . . And as she has so little money of her own . . . (*Slight pause.*) And hearing of a school, a great distance off, where there are none of those ill-judged comings-home three times a year, that do unsettle the children so . . . (*Pause.*)

SQUEERS. And payments regular, and then, no questions asked. (*Slight pause.*)

SNAWLEY. I should . . . I should want their morals particularly attended to. (*William brings in Ralph and Nicholas.*)

SQUEERS. Well, you've come to the right shop for morals, sir. I think we do, now, understand each other.

RALPH. Mr. Squeers.

SQUEERS. Yes? What is it?

RALPH. A matter of business, sir. My name is Ralph Nickleby. Perhaps you recollect me.

SQUEERS. Why, yes, sir . . . Did you not pay me a small account for some years . . . on behalf of parents of a boy named Dorker who . . .

RALPH. That's right. Who died, unfortunately, in Yorkshire.

SQUEERS. Yes, sir, I remember well. (*Snawley looking at Squeers.*) And I remember too, how Mrs. Squeers nursed the boy . . . Dry toast and warm tea when he wouldn't swallow, and a candle in his bedroom on the night he died, a dictionary to lay his head upon . . .

RALPH. Yes, yes. So, shall we come to business? You have advertised for an able assistant, and here he is. (*Squeers looks at Nicholas.*) My nephew Nicholas, hot from school, with everything he learnt there fermenting in his head, and nothing fermenting in his pocket. (*Pause.*) His father lies dead, he is wholly ignorant of the world, he has no resources whatever, and he wants to make his fortune.

SQUEERS. Well . . .

NICHOLAS. I fear, sir, that you object to my youth, and my not being a Master of Arts?

SQUEERS. Well, the absence of a college degree *is* an objection . . .

RALPH. And if any caprice of temper should induce him to cast aside this golden opportunity, I shall consider myself absolved from extending any assistance to his mother and sister. Now the question is, whether, for some time to come, he won't exactly serve your purposes. (*Pause. Squeers a little gesture. He and Ralph withdraw a little.*)

SNAWLEY. (*To convince himself.*) A fine gentleman, sir. That Mr. Squeers, a gentleman of virtue and morality.

NICHOLAS. (*To convince himself.*) I'm sure of it. (*Ralph and Squeers back.*)

RALPH. Nicholas, you are employed.

NICHOLAS. (*Delighted.*) Oh, sir—

SQUEERS. The coach leaves eight o'clock tomorrow morning, Mr. Nickleby—and you must be here a quarter before.

NICHOLAS. I shall be. Surely.

RALPH. And, your fare is paid. (*Squeers takes Snawley aside, taking money from and inserting something in a ledger. Noggs enters.*)

NICHOLAS. Well, thank you, uncle. I will not forget this kindness.

RALPH. See you don't.

SQUEERS. Mr. Snawley . . . (*Squeers, Snawley, the little Snawleys and Belling withdraw as Ralph and Nicholas meet Noggs D.*)

RALPH. Noggs.

NOGGS. (*Hands Ralph a letter.*) Mortgage letter's come. And Mr. Bonney says—
RALPH. (*Taking the letter and opening it.*) Oh, yes. I know what Mr. Bonney says. A matter of investment. (*He opens the letter and reads. Noggs is looking fixedly at Nicholas. Nicholas doesn't quite know what to do. After a few moments, to break the silence.*)
NICHOLAS. Um, I'm—
NOGGS. Yes, I know. (*Ralph pocketing the letter.*)
RALPH. And we're late. You'd best go home and pack, sir. Early in the morning, you heard Mr. Squeers. (*Exit Ralph and Noggs.*)

Scene Six

The Nicklebys' rooms. Mrs. Nickleby and Kate, carrying a suitcase, books and clothes, enter to Nicholas as he speaks:

NICHOLAS. And there was so much to be done,
KATE. And so little time to do it in, (*The Nicklebys quickly packing Nicholas' suitcase.*)
MRS. NICKLEBY. So many kind words to be spoken,
KATE. And so much bitter pain to be suppressed,
NICHOLAS. That the preparations for the journey were mournful indeed.
KATE. (*Putting a book in the suitcase.*) A hundred things deemed indispensible for his comfort, Nicholas left behind,
NICHOLAS. (*Taking the book out again.*) As they might prove convertible into money if required. (*As Kate puts the book back into the suitcase.*)
MRS. NICKLEBY. A hundred affectionate contests on such points as these took place;
NICHOLAS. And as they grew nearer and nearer to the close of their preparations,
KATE. Kate grew busier and busier, and wept more silently. (*During the following, Kate and Mrs. Nickleby leave Nicholas, alone with his suitcase.*)
NICHOLAS. And bed at last, and at six the next morning, Nicholas rose up, and wrote a few lines in pencil to say goodbye, and resolved that, come what may, he would bear whatever might be in store for him, for the sake of his mother and his sister, and giving his uncle no excuse to desert them in their need. (*And by now, the Saracen's Head has reappeared behind him.*)

Scene Seven

The Saracen's Head. Squeers sitting at the table with a plate of eggs and ham. The two Snawleys and Belling sitting with nothing. A maid stands next to William, carrying a tray, on which is a jug of water, and a plate of one piece of bread and butter. Squeers is holding up a mug of milk. Nicholas stands apart, watching.

SQUEERS. This is two penn'orth of milk, is it, William?

WILLIAM. S'right, sir.

SQUEERS. What a rare article milk is in London, to be sure. Now fill it up with water, will you?

WILLIAM. To the top, sir?

SQUEERS. (*Starting to eat.*) That's correct.

WILLIAM. But, sir, you'll drown the milk.

SQUEERS. Well, serve it right for being so expensive. Now. Where's bread-and-butter?

WILLIAM. Here, sir. (*He puts the bread-and-butter on the table. The little boys quickly reach for it.*)

SQUEERS. Wait! (*The boys freeze. Their hands go back. William goes away. Squeers divides the slice of bread into three, as Nicholas approaches.*) Good morning, Nickleby. Sit down. We're breakfasting.

NICHOLAS. Good morning, sir.

SQUEERS. Now, boys, when I say 'One', young Snawley takes a drink of milk and eats his bread. When I say 'two', the older Snawley, and then three is Belling. Clear?

BOYS. Oh, yes, sir.

SQUEERS. (*Eating.*) Right. Now, wait. Subdue your appetites, my dears, you've conquered human nature. One! (*Snawley Jnr. eats and drinks.*) Say 'thank you',

SNAWLEY JNR. (*Eating.*) 'Ank 'ou. (*Pause. Squeers eats.*)

SQUEERS. Two! (*Snawley Snr. eats and drinks.*) Well?

SNAWLEY SNR. Thank you, sir. (*Squeers finishes his food.*)

SQUEERS. And—(*He is interrupted by the blowing of a horn.*) Oh, dear Belling, there's the horn. You've missed your turn. Come, my dears, let's bustle. (*And at once there is tremendous bustle, and, during the following dialogue, one of two things occurs: if there is a mobile truck available, it is brought on, and the company build on it, out of skips, tables, chairs and luggage, a representation of an early Victorian stagecoach; or the sudden, noisy entrance of coachmen, passengers, porters, flower- and newspaper-sellers and passers-by gives the impression that the coach has arrived offstage and is nearly ready to go. Either way, everything suddenly becomes totally busy and confusing, as Squeers marshalls the little boys, and Nicholas is collared by Noggs, who appears out of the crowd.)*

NOGGS. Psst.

NICHOLAS. I'm sorry? Mr. Noggs!

NOGGS. *(Handing him a letter.)* Hush. Take it. Read it. No-one knows. That's all. *(He is going. Mrs. Nickleby and Kate appear.)*

NICHOLAS. Stop!

NOGGS. No. *(Exit Noggs.)*

NICHOLAS. But—

MRS. NICKLEBY. Nicholas!

NICHOLAS. Oh, mother, Kate—you shouldn't.

KATE. How could we just let you go . . . *(Squeers, dragging Belling, comes to Nicholas.)*

SQUEERS. Now Nickleby, I think you'd better ride behind. I'm feared of Belling falling off, and there goes 20 pounds a year.

NICHOLAS. Right, I, uh—

SQUEERS. *(Dragging Belling away.)* And, dear Belling, if you don't stop chattering your teeth and shaking, I'll warm you with a severe thrashing in about half a minute's time. Come Nickleby!

KATE. Oh, Nicholas, who is that man? What kind of place can it be that you're going to?

NICHOLAS. Well, I suppose—that Yorkshire folk are rather rough and uncultivated—

SQUEERS. *(Calling.)* Nickleby, God damn you! *(If the coach is onstage, it is complete, and its passengers are clambering on to it, with the Coachman sitting up front with his whip, the horn-blower beside him; or it is clear from waving passers-by and exiting passengers that its departure is imminent.)*

NICHOLAS. Goodbye, mother. To our meeting, one day soon. And goodbye, Kate.

KATE. You'll write?

NICHOLAS. Of course I will.

COACHMAN. Stage leaving! Stage leaving! Everyone for the stage, up and sit fast! *(And Nicholas climbs up on to the back of the coach, next to Belling; or he runs out past the waving passers-by. Narrators speak to the audience.)*

NARRATORS.
And a minute's bustle,

And a banging of the coach doors,

A swaying of the vehicle,

A cry of all right,

A few notes from the horn—

(*The horn sounds. The coach departs, everyone on and off it waving. If we imagine the coach, then there is a further line of narration:*)

NARRATOR. And the coach was gone, and rattling over the stones of Smithfield. (*And one way or another, everyone except Kate is gone.*)

Scene Eight

Miss La Creevy's house: Miss La Creevy with her painting equipment in front of her on a little table: opposite a chair on a little platform. This is set up as Kate speaks to the audience:

KATE. And on the second morning after Nicholas' departure, Kate found herself sitting in a very faded chair, raised upon a very dusty throne, in Miss La Creevy's room, giving that lady a sitting for a portrait. (*Kate sits on the other chair, and poses. Miss La Creevy painting.*)

MISS LA CREEVY. Well, I think I have caught it now. And it will be the sweetest portrait I have ever done, certainly.

KATE. It will be your genius that makes it so, I'm sure.

MISS LA CREEVY. Well, my dear, you are right, in the main: though I don't allow that it's of such great importance in the present case. Ah! The difficulties of art, my dear, are very great.

KATE. I have no doubt.

MISS LA CREEVY. They are beyond anything you can form the faintest perception of. What with bringing out eyes and keeping down noses, and adding to heads, and taking away teeth altogether, you have no idea of the trouble one little miniature can be.

KATE. The remuneration can scarcely repay you.

MISS LA CREEVY. Well, it does not, and that's the truth. And then sitters are so dissatisfied and unreasonable, that nine times out of ten there's no pleasure in painting them. Sometimes they say, "Oh, how very serious you have made me look, Miss La Creevy", and at others, "La, Miss La Creevy, how very smirking!", when the very essence of a good portrait is that it must be either serious or smirking, or it's no portrait at all.

KATE. Indeed! And which, dear Miss La Creevy, which am I? (*Miss La Creevy beckons Kate, who goes to look at the portrait.*) Oh!

MISS LA CREEVY. Dear, now what's the matter?

KATE. Oh, it's just, the shade. Is my face, really, that—

MISS LA CREEVY. Oh, that's my salmon pink, my dear. Originally, I hit upon it for an officer. But it went down so well, among my patrons, that I use it now for almost everything. It is considered, in the art world, quite a novelty.

KATE. (*Returning and sitting.*) I am convinced of it.

MISS LA CREEVY. (*Continuing to paint.*) And now, my dear, when do you expect to see your uncle again?

KATE. I scarcely know. I'd thought to, before now.

MISS LA CREEVY. Hm. I suppose he has money, hasn't he?

KATE. I'm told he's very rich.

MISS LA CREEVY. Hm. You may depend on it, or he wouldn't be so surly.

KATE. Yes, he is a little rough.

MISS LA CREEVY. A little rough! A porcupine's a featherbed to him.

KATE. It's only his manner, I believe. I should be sorry to think ill of him unless I knew he deserved it.

MISS LA CREEVY. Well, that is very right and proper. But mightn't he, without feeling it himself, make you and your mama some nice little allowance . . . What would a hundred a year, for instance, be to him?

KATE. I don't know what it would be to him. But it would be unacceptable to me.

MISS LA CREEVY. He is your uncle, dear . . .

KATE. (*Stands.*) From anyone. Not him, particularly. Anyone. (*Pause.*) I'm sorry. I have moved.

MISS LA CREEVY. It doesn't matter, dear. (*Hannah is there. Someone knocks.*) Now, who can that be? Yes, come in. (*Hannah steps into the room.*)

HANNAH. Um . . . It's Mr.—um . . .

MISS LA CREEVY. It's who? (*Enter Ralph Nickleby.*)

RALPH. Your servant, ladies.

KATE. (*Standing.*) Uncle.

RALPH. Hm. Where's Mrs. Nickleby?

MISS LA CREEVY. Hannah. (*Exit Hannah.*)

RALPH. Is it my niece's portrait, ma'am?

MISS LA CREEVY. Well, yes it is, sir, and between you and me and the post, sir, it will be a very nice portrait too, though I say it myself as shouldn't.

RALPH. Well, don't trouble yourself to show it to me, ma'am, I have no eye for likenesses. Is it nearly finished?

MISS LA CREEVY. Why, yes. Two more sittings will—

RALPH. Have them done at once, ma'am, for she'll have no time to idle over fooleries. Have you let your lodgings, ma'am?

MISS LA CREEVY. I have not put a bill up yet, sir.

RALPH. Then do so, at once. For neither of them's going to need your rooms, or if they do, can't pay for 'em.

KATE. Uh—uncle, we are moving? Where?

RALPH. I'm not yet sure where either of you will be placed.

KATE. Oh, uncle, do you mean we're to be separated? (*Hannah admits Mrs. Nickleby.*)

MRS. NICKLEBY. Brother-in-law.

RALPH. Ma'am. I've found a situation for your daughter.

MRS. NICKLEBY. (*Sitting in Kate's chair.*) Well: This is good news. But I will say it is only what I would have thought of you. (*Ralph about to say something.*) "Depend on it", I said to Kate only yesterday at breakfast, "that after your uncle has provided in that most ready manner for Nicholas, he will not leave us until he has done at least the same for you!" (*Ralph about to say something.*) Those were my very words, as near as I can remember, Kate, my dear, why don't you thank your—

RALPH. Let me proceed, ma'am, pray.

MRS. NICKLEBY. Kate, my love, let your uncle proceed.

KATE. I am most anxious that he should, mama.

MRS. NICKLEBY. Well, if you are, you had better allow your uncle to say what he has to say, without interruption.

RALPH. I am very much obliged to you, ma'am. An absence of business habits in this family apparently leads to a great waste of words before business is arrived at at all.

MRS. NICKLEBY. (*With a sigh.*) I fear it is so, indeed. Your poor brother—

RALPH. My poor brother, ma'am, had no idea what business was.

(*Pause. Mrs. Nickleby says nothing.*) The situation that I have made interest to procure for your daughter, is with a milliner and dressmaker.

MRS. NICKLEBY. A milliner.

RALPH. Yes, and milliners in London, as I need not remind you, ma'am, are persons of great wealth and station.

MRS. NICKLEBY. Well, now, that's very true. That's very true, Kate, for I recollect when your poor papa and I came to town after we were married, that a young lady brought me home a chip cottage bonnet, with white and green trimming, and a green persian lining, in her own carriage, which drove up to the door at a full gallop—at least, I am not quite certain whether it was her own carriage or a hackney chariot, but I remember very well that the horse dropped down dead as he was turning round, and that—

RALPH. The lady's name is Madame Mantalini. She lives near Cavendish Square. If your daughter is disposed to try the situation, I'll take her there on Monday. Now, I must—

MRS. NICKLEBY. Kate, have you nothing that you wish to say? To tell your uncle?

KATE. Yes, I have. But I'd prefer to speak to him alone.

MRS. NICKLEBY. Now Kate, I'm sure—

KATE. I'll see you out then, uncle. (*She firmly gestures Ralph out of the room.*)

RALPH. Then—I'm your servant, ma'am. (*Kate and Ralph leave the room, and come downstage together. Mrs. Nickleby, Miss La Creevy and the furniture leave during this dialogue.*) So? What d'you want to say?

KATE. I must ask one question of you, uncle. Am I to live at home?

RALPH. At home? Where's that?

KATE. I must—we must, me and my mother, have some place we can call home. It may be very humble—

RALPH. "May be!" Must be. "May be" humble!

KATE. Well, then, must be. But, my question, uncle. You must answer it. (*Pause.*)

RALPH. I'd some idea . . . providing for your mother, in a pleasant district of the country . . .

KATE. Out of London?

RALPH. Yes, I'd thought so, but if you're quite determined that you want to stay with her . . .

KATE. I am.

RALPH. Yes. I had thought you would be. (*Slight pause.*) Well, I have an empty house. It's in the East End. Till it's rented, you can live in it. I'll send my clerk on Saturday to take you there. So—is that satisfactory? (*Kate is cracking.*)

KATE. I'm very much, obliged to you, dear uncle. (*Pause.*) Very much—

RALPH. Please don't begin to cry.

KATE. It's very foolish, I know, uncle.

RALPH. Yes, it is. And most affected, too. (*To Kate.*) Let's have no more of it. (*Ralph goes out. Kate goes out another way.*)

Scene Nine

Outside and inside Dotheboys Hall. A bare stage. Snow falls. Wind blows. Squeers, Nicholas, Belling, and the two Snawleys walk D. with the luggage. They stop.

NICHOLAS. Dotheboys Hall.

SQUEERS. Oh, sir, you needn't call it a hall up here.

NICHOLAS. Why not?

SQUEERS. Cos the fact is, it ain't a hall. (*As Squeers leads the party round to the side of the stage, Nicholas speaks to the audience.*)

NICHOLAS. A host of unpleasant misgivings, which had been crowding upon Nicholas during the whole journey, thronged into his mind. And as he considered the dreary house and dark windows, and the wild country round covered with snow, he felt a depression of heart and spirit which he had never experienced before.

SQUEERS. No, we call it a hall up in London, because it sounds better, but they don't know it by that name here. (*He bangs an imaginary door. Someone makes the sound.*) A man may call his house an island if he likes; there's no Act of Parliament against that, I believe?

NICHOLAS. No, I think not, sir.

SQUEERS. (*Banging.*) Well, then. Hey! Door! (*From the darkness, Smike appears. He is about 19, but bent over with lameness, and dressed in ragged garments which he has long since outgrown. He pulls open the huge door, and the wind howls as Squeers strides into the house.*) Smike. Where the devil have you been?

SMIKE. Please, sir, I fell asleep.

SQUEERS. You fell awhat?

SMIKE. Please, sir, I fell asleep over the fire.

SQUEERS. Fire? What fire? Where's there a fire? (*During the following,*

Squeers, Smike, Nicholas, and the boys with their luggage move round the stage—as if passing along corridors—as the Squeers' servant Phib brings on a big chair and then a table to centre stage. This is the Squeers' parlour, and Phib goes out again to bring on a tray of brandy, glasses and water, placing it on the table.)

SMIKE. Please, sir, Missus said as I was sitting up, I might be by the fire for a warm . . .

SQUEERS. Your missus is a fool. You'd have been a deuced deal more wakeful in the cold. (*From off, we hear the voice of Mrs. Squeers.)*

MRS. SQUEERS. (*Off.*) Squeers!

SQUEERS. (*Calls.*) My love!

MRS. SQUEERS. Squeers! (*By now Squeers is in the parlour area, the boys are standing in the corridor with their luggage, and Nicholas is between them, as if in the doorway, not knowing quite what to do.)*

SQUEERS. (*To Smike.*) There's boys. The boys, to bed. (*Smike takes the boys out, leaving their luggage, as Mrs. Squeers enters.)*

MRS. SQUEERS. Oh, Squeers. How is my Squeery, dearie. (*The Squeerses embrace.)*

SQUEERS. Well, well, my love. How are the cows?

MRS. SQUEERS. All right, every one of 'em.

SQUEERS. And the pigs?

MRS. SQUEERS. As well as they were when you went.

SQUEERS. Well, that's a great blessing. (*These sweet nothings over, Squeers leaves Mrs. Squeers and takes letters and documents from his pocket. As an afterthought.*) The boys all as they were, I suppose? (*Mrs. Squeers, taking the letters from Squeers and placing them on the table, glancing at one or two.)*

MRS. SQUEERS. Oh yes, they're well enough. But young Sprouter's had a fever.

SQUEERS. (*Taking off his greatcoat.*) No! Damn the boy, he's always at something of that sort. (*Phib takes Squeers' huge coat, and stands there, holding it. Squeers goes to the table, sits, Mrs. Squeers pours him a brandy and tops it up with water. As:*)

MRS. SQUEERS. Never was such a boy, I do believe. Whatever he has is always catching, too. I say it's obstinacy, and nothing shall ever convince me that it isn't. I'd beat it out of him, and I told you that six months ago.

SQUEERS. So you did, my love. We'll try what can be done. (*Slight pause. Mrs. Squeers nods in the direction of Nicholas, who is still standing near the door, not knowing what to do.*) Ah, Nickleby. Come, sir, come in. (*Nicholas comes a little further into the room.*) This is our new young man, my dear.

MRS. SQUEERS. (*Suspiciously.*) Oh. Is it?

SQUEERS. He can shake down here tonight, can't he?

MRS. SQUEERS. (*Looking round.*) Well, if he's not particular . . .

NICHOLAS. (*Politely.*) Oh, no, indeed.

MRS. SQUEERS. That's lucky. (*She looks at Squeers and laughs. Squeers laughs back. They laugh at each other. Meanwhile, Smike reappears. Mrs. Squeers looks at Phib, and snaps her head towards the door. Phib goes out with the big coat. Slight pause. Then, with a wink to Squeers, as if to ask if Nicholas should be given a drink.*) Another brandy, Squeers?

SQUEERS. (*Nodding back.*) Certainly. A glassful. (*Mrs. Squeers pours a large brandy-and-water for Squeers, and a smaller one for Nicholas. She takes the drink to Nicholas. Squeers is looking through the letters. Nicholas takes the drink. Smike stands, staring fixedly at the letters on the table. Mrs. Squeers goes and picks up one of the boys' bags and takes it back to the table.*) Bolder's father's short.

MRS. SQUEERS. Tt tt.

SQUEERS. But Cobbey's sister's sent something. (*Mrs. Squeers starts going through the boys' luggage, picking out the bits and pieces she fancies.*)

MRS. SQUEERS. That's good.

SQUEERS. And Graymarsh's maternal aunt has written, with no money, but two pairs of stockings and a tract.

MRS. SQUEERS. Maternal aunt.

SQUEERS. My love?

MRS. SQUEERS. More likely, in my view, that she's Graymarsh's maternal mother. (*The Squeerses look at each other. Then Squeers notices that Smike is very close, craning to see the letters.*)

SQUEERS. Yes? What's to do, boy?

SMIKE. Is there—

SQUEERS. What?

SMIKE. Is there . . . there's nothing heard . . . ?

SQUEERS. No, not a word. And never will be.

MRS. SQUEERS. (*The very idea.*) Tt. (*Pause. Squeers decides to rub it in.*)

SQUEERS. And it is a pretty sort of thing, that you should have been left here all these years and no money paid after the first six—nor no notice taken, nor no clue to who you belong to? It's a pretty sort of thing, is it not, that I should have to feed a great fellow like you, and never hope to get one penny for it, isn't it? (*Squeers looking at Smike.*)

NICHOLAS. (*Out front.*) The boy put his hand to his head, as if he was making an effort to remember something, and then, looking vacantly at his questioner, gradually broke into a smile.

SQUEERS. That's right. Now, off with you, and send the girl. (*Smike limps out. Mrs. Squeers has finished sifting the boy's bag. She looks for something on the table.*)

MRS. SQUEERS. I tell you what, Squeers, I think that young chap's turning silly.

SQUEERS. (*Wiping his mouth.*) I hope not. For he's a handy fellow out of doors, and worth his meat and drink anyway. (*He stands.*) But come, I'm tired, and want to go to bed.

MRS. SQUEERS. Oh, drat the thing.

SQUEERS. What's wrong, my dear?

MRS. SQUEERS. The school spoon. I can't find it.

SQUEERS. Never mind, my love.

MRS. SQUEERS. What, never mind? It's brimstone, in the morning.

SQUEERS. Ah, I forgot. (*He helps the search.*) Yes, certainly, it is.

NICHOLAS. Uh . . . ?

SQUEERS. We purify the boys' bloods now and then, Nickleby.

MRS. SQUEERS. (*Crossly.*) Purify fiddle-sticks. Don't think, young man, that we go to the expense of flour of brimstone and molasses just to purify them; because if you think we carry on the business in that way, you'll find yourself mistaken, and so I tell you plainly. (*Squeers is not sure this intelligence is quite discreet. Enter Phib, who tidies round the table, putting things back on the tray.*)

SQUEERS. My dear . . . should you . . .

MRS. SQUEERS. Nonsense. If the young man comes to be a teacher, let him understand at once that we don't want any foolery about the boys. They have the brimstone and treacle, partly because if they hadn't something or other in the way of medicine they'd always be ailing and giving a world of trouble, and partly because it spoils their appetites and comes cheaper than breakfast and dinner. So it does them good and us good at the same time, and that's fair enough, I'm sure. (*Squeers looking embarrassed. Mrs. Squeers shoots a glance at him.*) Now, where's the spoon? (*Phib has picked up the tray.*)

PHIB. Uh. Ma'am.

MRS. SQUEERS. What is it?

PHIB. S'round your neck. (*And indeed the spoon is round Mrs. Squeers neck. She cuffs Phib lightly for telling her.*)

MRS. SQUEERS. Why did you not say *before*.

PHIB. M'sorry, ma'am. (*Phib picks up the tray, leaving the brandy bottle, and goes out.*)

MRS. SQUEERS. (*Pleasantly.*) And so, dear Mr. Nickleby, good night. (*Mrs. Squeers goes out. Pause.*)

SQUEERS. A most invaluable woman, Nickleby.

NICHOLAS. Indeed, sir.

SQUEERS. I do not know her equal. That woman, Nickleby, is always the same: always the same bustling, lively, active, saving creature that you see her now.

NICHOLAS. I'm sure of it.

SQUEERS. (*Warming further to his theme.*) It is my custom, when I am in London, to say that she is like a mother to those boys. But she is more, she's ten times more. She does things for those boys, Nickleby, that I don't believe half the mothers going would do for their own sons.

NICHOLAS. I'm certain of it, sir.

SQUEERS. And so, goodnight, then, Nickleby. (*He tries to make a solemn exit, undermined by spotting the brandy, which he returns to pick up.*)

NICHOLAS. Goodnight, sir. (*Squeers nods gravely and goes out. Nicholas stands a moment, then takes off his coat. He sits, on the floor. He notices Noggs' letter in his coat pocket. He opens it and begins to read. Noggs himself appears, with a glass of brandy. He sits on the arm of Squeers' chair, and he speaks his letter as we see Nicholas read it.*)

NOGGS. My dear young man. I know the world. Your father did not, or he would not have done me a kindness when there was no hope of return. You do not, or you would not be bound on such a journey. If ever you want a shelter in London, they know where I live at the sign of the Crown, in Silver St., Golden Square. You can come at night. Once, nobody was ashamed—never mind that. It's all over. Excuse errors. I have forgotten all my old ways. My spelling may have gone with them.

NICHOLAS. (*Reads.*) Yours obediently, Newman Noggs.

NOGGS. P.S.: If you should go near Barnard Castle, there is a good ale at the King's Head. Say you know me, and I am sure they will not charge you for it. You may say Mr. Noggs there, for I was a gentleman then. I was indeed. (*Noggs shambles out. Nicholas crumples to the floor. He is crying. Blackout.*)

Scene Ten

Dotheboys Hall. The school bell rings, the lights come up. The parlour chair and table have gone. Squeers shouts to Nicholas, who wakes.

SQUEERS. Past seven, Nickleby! It's morning come, and well-iced already. Now, Nickleby, come, tumble up, will you?
(*Squeers, with his cane, strides round the stage. Nicholas jumps up and, pulling on his coat, follows. Mrs. Squeers enters, followed by Smike, who carries a bowl of brimstone and treacle. Squeers and Nicholas arrive at one side of the stage, Mrs. Squeers and Smike at the other. Then, through the darkness at the back of the stage, we see, approaching us, the boys of Dotheboys Hall. They are dressed in the ragged remains of what were once school uniforms. They move slowly, through lameness and sullenness and fear. Then they form themselves into a kind of line, and each boy goes to Mrs. Squeers to receive a spoonful of brimstone and treacle.*) There. This is our shop, Nickleby. (*Each boy gives his number, name, age and reason for being at the school before receiving his dose. Clearly, this is an accepted ritual.*)
TOMKINS. First boy. Tomkins. Nine. A cripple.
COATES. Second boy. Coates. Thirteen. A bastard.
GRAYMARSH. Third boy. Graymarsh. Twelve, Another bastard.
JENNINGS. Fourth boy. Jennings. Thirteen. Disfigured.
MOBBS. Fifth boy. (*Pause.*) Mobbs. Uh—'leven. (*Pause. He doesn't know what's wrong with him. Mrs. Squeers hits him on the side of the head.*)
MRS. SQUEERS. Simpleton!
MOBBS. Fifth. Mobbs. Eleven. Sim-pull-ton.
BOLDER. Sixth. Bolder. Fourteen, Orphan.
PITCHER. Seventh. Pitcher. Ten.
MRS. SQUEERS. Yes! (*Pause.*)
PITCHER. I'm very. Very. Slow.
MRS. SQUEERS. Move on. Move *on.*
JACKSON. Eighth. Johnny.
MRS. SQUEERS. Johnny?
JACKSON. Jackson. Thirteen. Illegitimate.
COBBEY. Ninth. Cobbey. Fifteen. Cripple.

PETERS. Tenth. Uh—Peters. Seven. Blind.

SPROUTER. Eleventh. Sprouter. Seven. My father killed my mother.

MRS. SQUEERS. Yes?

SPROUTER. Sent away.

ROBERTS. Twelfth. Roberts. Ten. There's something wrong—my brain. (*Squeers' young son, Wackford, well-dressed and stout, pushes forward the two Snawley boys and Belling.*)

SNAWLEY SNR. Robert Arthur Snawley.

MRS. SQUEERS. Number!

SNAWLEY SNR. I'm eleven.

MRS. SQUEERS. (*Twisting Snawley Snr.'s ear.*) Number, is thirteen.

SNAWLEY SNR. Thirteen.

SNAWLEY JNR. Uh—fourteen-th. Snawley, H. Uh—seven.

BELLING. Fifteen. Anthony Belling. Seven years of age. A classical and modern—moral, education. (*Mrs. Squeers wipes her hands on Smike. Squeers to Wackford.*)

SQUEERS. Thank you, young Wackford. Thank you, son. And what do you say? And what d'you say, to this? (*Pause.*)

BOYS. For what we have received, may the lord make us truly thankful.

SQUEERS. Amen.

BOYS. Amen.

SQUEERS. That's better. Now, boys, I've been to London, and have returned to my family and you, as strong and well as ever. (*Pause. Mrs. Squeers gestures to a boy.*)

COATES. (*Feebly.*) Hip hip.

BOYS. (*Equally feebly.*) Hooray.

COATES. Hip hip.

BOYS. Hooray.

COATES. Hip hip.

BOYS. Hooray. (*Squeers takes various letters from his pockets and wanders around among the boys as he speaks.*)

SQUEERS. I have seen the parents of some boys, and they're so glad to hear how their sons are doing, that there's no prospect at all of their going home, which of course is a very pleasant thing to reflect upon for all parties. (*He continues to perambulate.*) But I have had disappointments to contend with. Bolder's father, for an instance, was two pound ten short. Where is Bolder? (*The boys around Bolder kick him and he puts up his hand. Squeers goes to Bolder.*) Ah, Bolder. Bolder, if you father thinks that because—(*Squeers suddenly notices warts on Bolder's hand. He grabs the boy's arm.*) What do you call this, sir?

BOLDER. Warts, sir.

SQUEERS. What, sir?

BOLDER. Warts, sir.

SQUEERS. Warts?

BOLDER. I can't help it, sir. They will come . . . It's working in the garden does it sir, at least I don't know what it is, sir, but it's not my fault . . .

SQUEERS. Bolder. You are an incorrigible young scoundrel, and as the last thrashing did you no good, we must see what another will do towards beating it out of you. (*Bolder looks terrified.*) La—ter. (*He lets Bolder go and walks on, reading.*) Now, let's see . . . A letter for Cobbey. Cobbey? (*Cobbey puts his hand up. Squeers hardly acknowledges, but walks on.*) Oh. Cobbey's grandmother is dead, and his uncle John has took to drinking, which is all the news his sister sends, except eighteenpence, which will just pay for that broken square of glass. Mobbs! (*Mobbs, not sure whether this will be good or bad news, nervously puts up his hand. It is clear it is not good news when Squeers walks to him and stands near.*) Now, Mobbs' step-mother took to her bed on hearing that he would not eat fat, and has been very ill ever since. She wishes to know by an early post where he expects to go to, if he quarrels with his vittles; and with what feelings he could turn up his nose at the cow's liver broth, after his good master had asked a blessing on it. She is disconsolate to find he is discontented, which is sinful and horrid, and hopes Mr. Squeers will flog him into a happier state of mind. (*Into Mobbs' ear.*) Which—he—will. (*Long pause to let this sink in to everyone. Then.*) Right, boys. I'd like you all to meet my new assistant, Mr. Nickleby. Good morning, Mr. Nickleby.

BOYS. Good morning, Mr. Nickleby.

NICHOLAS. Good, morning.

SQUEERS. Now, this is the first class in English spelling and philosophy, Nickleby. We'll soon get up a Latin one and hand that over to you. (*Nicholas joins Squeers.*) Now, then, where's Smallpiece?

BOYS. Please, sir . . .

SQUEERS. Let any boy speak out of turn and I'll have the skin off his back! (*He points to Jennings.*)

JENNINGS. Please, sir, he's cleaning the back parlour window.

SQUEERS. So he is, to be sure. We go on the practical mode of teaching, Nickleby; C-l-e-a-n, clean—

BOYS. Clean.

SQUEERS. verb active, to make bright, to scour. W-i-n, win,—

BOYS. Win—

SQUEERS. d-e-r, der—

BOYS. der, winder—

SQUEERS. Winder, a casement. When a boy knows this out of a book, he goes and does it. It's just the same principle as the use of the globes. Where's Grinder? (*Coates puts his hand up. Squeers points to Coates.*)

COATES. Please, sir, he's weeding the garden.

SQUEERS. To be sure. So he is. B-o-t, Bot—

BOYS. Bot—

SQUEERS. T-i-n, tin—

BOYS. Tin—

SQUEERS. Bottin—

BOYS. Bottin—

SQUEERS. N-e-y, Ney—

BOYS. Ney—

SQUEERS. Bottiney—

BOYS. Bottiney—

SQUEERS. Noun substantive, a knowledge of plants. When he has learned that bottiney means a knowledge of plants, he goes and knows 'em. That's our system, Nickleby. What do you think of it?

NICHOLAS. It's a very useful one, at any rate.

SQUEERS. I believe you. Graymarsh, what's a horse?

GRAYMARSH. A beast, sir.

SQUEERS. So it is. A horse is a quadroped, and quadroped's Latin for beast, as anybody that's gone through the grammar knows, or else where's the use in having grammars at all?

NICHOLAS. Where indeed.

SQUEERS. (*To Graymarsh.*) And as you're so perfect in that, go to *my* horse, and rub him down well, or I'll rub *you* down. The rest go and draw water up till somebody tells you to leave off, for it's washing day tomorrow, and they'll want the coppers filled. (*The boys hurry out, Mobbs and Bolder hurrying more than the others.*) Except—for Mobbs and Bolder. (*Everyone stops. Some of the boys push Mobbs and Bolder forward, towards Squeers. Then the others go out, as Mrs. Squeers and Wackford go too. Smike tries to go as well.*) Stay there, Smike. They'll need taking to their beds. (*He turns to Nicholas.*) This is the way we do it, Nickleby. (*Squeers lifts his cane. Blackout. Some of the older men of the company appear in a little light. As they speak this narration, we see Nicholas sit morosely down at the side of the stage. Squeers, Smike, Mobbs, and Bolder have gone.*)

NARRATORS.

And Nicholas sat down, so depressed and self-degraded that if death could have come upon then he would have been happy to meet it.

The cruelty of which he had been an unwilling witness,

The coarse and ruffianly behaviour of Squeers,

The filthy place,

The sights and sounds about him,

All contributed to this feeling.

And when he recollected that, being there as an assistant, he was the aider and abetter of a system which filled him with disgust and indignation,

He loathed himself. (*Blackout.*)

Scene Eleven

Bare stage. Outside Dotheboys Hall. Enter Mrs. Squeers, and, from the other side, her 20-year old daughter Fanny.

FANNY. Mama! Mama, I'm home!

MRS. SQUEERS. Fanny. (*Enter Fanny's friend Tilda Price, followed by her swain John Browdie, carrying luggage.*)

FANNY. Tilda Price brought me home, mama.

MRS. SQUEERS. Miss Price.

TILDA. (*A little bob.*) Good morning, ma'am.

JOHN. Ah, 'allo, missus. How's thissen?

FANNY. And John as well.

MRS. SQUEERS. I see.

FANNY. (*Aside to Mrs. Squeers.*) Mama, do ask them in.

MRS. SQUEERS. Hm. Would you care for a glass of something, Miss Price? (*Slight pause.*) Mr. Browdie?

JOHN. Ay. We would that, certainly.

MRS. SQUEERS. Well, then—

JOHN. As soon as tied me 'orse. (*John goes out to tie his 'orse. Fanny confidentially to Mrs. Squeers.*)

FANNY. Engaged.

MRS. SQUEERS. Who is?

FANNY. She is.

MRS. SQUEERS. To who?

FANNY. To him.

MRS. SQUEERS. At her age? (*Pause.*) Well, I suppose, she is quite easy on the eye.

FANNY. And, after all, he's hardly what you'd call a gentleman. (*Re-enter John.*)

JOHN. Right then. Let's have that glass of summat, missus, and let's have it sharpish, eh? (*He and Tilda go out, as:*)

FANNY. (*To Mrs. Squeers.*) No. Certainly. Not what you'd call a gentleman, at all. (*Fanny and Mrs. Squeers follow out John and Tilda.*)

Scene Twelve

The Boys drag on a sofa to represent the Squeers' parlour. Squeers is drinking, Mrs. Squeers is trying Belling's clothes on young Wackford. Phib is in attendance.

SQUEERS. Well, my dear, so what do you think of him?

MRS. SQUEERS. Think of who? (*Fanny comes in, having just said her goodbyes to Tilda and John. She sits, knits, and listens, as:*)

SQUEERS. The new man.

MRS. SQUEERS. Oh. Young Knuckleboy.

SQUEERS. Young Nickleby.

MRS. SQUEERS. Well, if you want to know, Squeers, I'll tell you that I think him quite the proudest, haughtiest, turned-up nosediest—

SQUEERS. He is quite cheap, my dear. In fact, he's very cheap.

MRS. SQUEERS. I don't see why we need another man at all.

SQUEERS. Because it says in the advertisement quite clearly—

MRS. SQUEERS. Fiddlesticks it *says*. You *say,* in the advertisement, it's "Education by Mr. Wackford Squeers and his able assistants", but that don't mean you have to have 'em, does it? Sometimes, Squeers, you try my patience.

SQUEERS. Sometimes, you try mine.

MRS. SQUEERS. What's that?

SQUEERS. Well, my love, any slave-driver in the West Indies is allowed a man under him, to see his blacks don't run away, or get up a rebellion; and I want a man under me, to do the same with our blacks, till such time as little Wackford is able to take charge.

WACKFORD. Oh, am I?

MRS. SQUEERS. (*Impatiently.*) Am you what?

WACKFORD. Oh, am I to take charge of the school when I grow up father?

SQUEERS. Yes, of course you are.

WACKFORD. Oh. Oh. Oh, won't I give it to 'em. Won't I make 'em shriek and squeal and scream. (*The Squeerses look at each other. This exemplary attitude on the part of their son has brought them back together.*)

SQUEERS. Of course you will, my boy, of course you will.

FANNY. (*Unable to keep silence.*) Papa . . . (*Squeers and Mrs. Squeers look at Fanny.*) Who is this—person? This young man?

MRS. SQUEERS. (*Impatient again.*) Oh, he's the new assistant, and your father has got some nonsense in his head he's the son of a gentleman that died the other day.

FANNY. A gentleman.

MRS. SQUEERS. Yes, but I don't believe a word of it. If he's a gentleman's son at all, he's a fondling, that's my opinion.

SQUEERS. Foundling, and he's nothing of the kind. His father was married, *to* his mother years before he was born, and she's alive now.

MRS. SQUEERS. Well, all I say—

SQUEERS. (*Stands.*) And if you do dislike him, dear, I don't know anyone shows dislike better than you do, and if there's a touch of pride about him, then I do not believe there is a woman living that can bring a person's spirit down as quick as you.

MRS. SQUEERS. Oh, is that so.

SQUEERS. My love. (*Pause. Mrs. Squeers looks at Squeers. Then she laughs. Squeers laughs too.*)

MRS. SQUEERS. Come, Wackford. (*Mrs. Squeers, still laughing, gestures Wackford to follow her, and goes out. Squeers, laughing too, goes out. Fanny and Phib left.*)

FANNY. Well? So what's he like?

PHIB. He's lovely.

Scene Thirteen

The Boys take out the sofa and some lie down, to represent the common dormitory. Smike is sitting. Nicholas, still sitting at the side of the stage, now stands, and goes to Smike. Nicholas carries a book.

NICHOLAS. Hallo (*Smike looks up, scared, and flinches a little.*) Please, don't be frightened. (*Nicholas crouches down near Smike. He puts down his book.*) Are you cold? (*Smike shakes his head.*) You're shivering. (*Pause. Nicholas stands to go. He stops when Smike speaks.*)

SMIKE. Oh, dear. (*Nicholas turns back.*) Oh, dear, oh, dear. My heart. Will break. It will. (*Louder, more forceful.*) It *will*. I know it *will*.

NICHOLAS. (*Embarrassed, looking round.*) Shh, shh.

SMIKE. Remember Dorker, do you?

NICHOLAS. Dorker?

SMIKE. I was with him at the end, he asked for me. Who will I ask for? Who? (*Pause. Nicholas doesn't know what Smike is talking about.*)

NICHOLAS. Who will you ask for when? (*Smike back into himself again.*)

SMIKE. No One. No Hope. Hope Less. (*Slight pause.*)

NICHOLAS. (*Feebly.*) There's always hope.

SMIKE. (*To himself.*) Is there? (*Smike turns again to Nicholas. Forcefully.*) O-U-T-C-A-S-T. A noun. Substantive. Person cast out or rejected. Abject. And foresaken. Homeless. Me. (*Nicholas looks at Smike. He doesn't know what to say. Pause. Then Fanny enters, behind Nicholas. She takes in the scene.*)

FANNY. Oh—I'm sorry. (*Nicholas turns.*) I was looking for my father.

NICHOLAS. He's not here.

FANNY. I see. (*Pause.*) I beg your pardon, sir. How very awkward.

NICHOLAS. Please, please don't apologise.

FANNY. I thank you, sir. Oh . . . Sir. (*Fanny curtseys, turns, turns back, turns again and goes. Nicholas to go out too, when he realises he's left his book. He looks back to Smike, who has picked up the book and is holding it to himself. Nicholas decides to leave Smike with the book. Smike is left alone, with the sleeping boys. Blackout.*)

Scene Fourteen

Miss La Creevy's house in the Strand. Enter Kate and Hannah, with luggage, from upstage.

HANNAH. Is it the East End that you're going to, Miss?

KATE. That's right. Is that unusual, as a place to live?

HANNAH. (*Trying to avoid answering "yes."*) Well, uh . . . (*Enter Mrs. Nickleby and Miss La Creevy.*)

MISS LA CREEVY. Well, I'm still afraid that millinery is not a healthy occupation, for your dear Kate or anyone else. For I remember getting three young milliners to sit for me, and they were all very pale and sickly.

MRS. NICKLEBY. Oh, Miss La Creevy, that's not a general rule by any means. For I recall employing one to make a scarlet cloak, at the time when scarlet cloaks were fashionable, and she had a very red face—a very red face indeed.

MISS LA CREEVY. Perhaps she drank.

MRS. NICKLEBY. Well, I don't know how that may have been, but I do know she had an extremely red face, so your argument goes for nothing. (*Pause.*) And Kate, who knows, if you work well, you might be taken into partnership with Madame Mantalini. (*Pause.*) Think. Nickleby and Mantalini. How well it would sound. And, who knows, Dr. Nickleby, the headmaster of Westminister School, living in the same street . . . (*Slight pause.*) It's not impossible, at all. (*Enter Hannah, followed by Newman Noggs.*)

HANNAH. Uh—it's a gentleman. I think. (*Miss La Creevy looks peevishly at Hannah.*)

NOGGS. Name's Noggs. From Mr. Nickleby. To Thames Street.

KATE. Yes. We'll need a coach, I fear.

NOGGS. I'll get one.

MRS. NICKLEBY. Uh, Mr. Noggs . . . did not we see you on the morning when my son departed on the coach for Yorkshire?

NOGGS. Me? Oh, no.

MRS. NICKLEBY. I'm sure of it, I—

NOGGS. No. First time I've been out, three weeks. I've had the gout. You ready?

KATE. Yes. (*She turns to Miss La Creevy.*) We are sorry, very sorry, to leave you, Miss La Creevy.

MISS LA CREEVY. Oh, that's stuff. You cannot shake me off that easily. I'll see you very often, come and call, and hear how you get on. (*Kate smiles.*) And if, in all the world, there's no-one else to take an interest in your welfare, there will still be one poor, lonely heart that prays for it night and day.

NOGGS. Uh—can we go? (*And the Nicklebys leave with Mr. Noggs, Miss La Creevy and Hannah waving, the former with a handkerchief pressed to her nose.*)

Scene Fifteen

The parlour at Dotheboys Hall. Early evening. Enter Tilda and Fanny, both dressed up to the nines. Phib enters, too, setting the table with tea and a plate of bread and butter.

TILDA. Engaged!
FANNY. No, not exactly. Not exactly, as it were, engaged. But going to be, there is no question. (*They sit on the sofa.*)
TILDA. Fanny, that is *wonderful*.
FANNY. Because, you see, his very presence, coming here to live with us, beneath this roof, and under the most mysterious circumstances . . .
TILDA. Fanny, what's he said? (*Slight pause.*)
FANNY. What do you mean?
TILDA. I mean—what has he *said*? (*Pause.*)
FANNY. Don't ask me what he said, my dear. If you had only seen his look . . .
TILDA. Was it like this? (*Tilda gives a love-lorn look.*)
FANNY. Like that?
TILDA. John looked at me like that.
FANNY. Well, so did he. Like that, entirely, only rather more genteel.
TILDA. Well, then, that's it.
FANNY. That's what?
TILDA. He must mean something, if he looks like that. He must feel . . . something very strong.
FANNY. Oh, I'm so jealous of you, Tilda!
TILDA. Why?
FANNY. Because you are so fortunate. That your mama and papa are so readily agreeable to your engagement, indeed appear not to have thought twice about it, whereas my mother and my father are so bitterly opposed to my dear Nicholas; and will throw all kinds of obstacles in our way; and will force us to meet in secret, and deny our passion . . . Oh that my course of love were half as simple, quiet and smooth as yours! (*Pause.*)
TILDA. I cannot wait to see him.
FANNY. Oh, I'm shaking!
TILDA. Yes, I know just how you feel. (*Knock, knock.*)

FANNY. Oh, there he is! Oh, Tilda!

TILDA. Shh. Just say, come in.

FANNY. (*Almost silently.*) Come in! (*Tilda a glance at Phib, who looks away. Nothing.*)

TILDA. Come in! (*Nicholas comes in.*)

NICHOLAS. Good evening. I understood from Mr. Squeers that—

FANNY. Oh, yes. It's all right. Father's been called away, but you won't mind that, I dare venture.

NICHOLAS. (*Out front.*) And Nicholas opened his eyes at this, but he turned the matter off very coolly—not minding particularly about anything just then—and went through the ceremony of introduction to the miller's daughter with as much grace as he could muster. (*Bowing to Tilda.*) Your servant, ma'am.

FANNY. We are only waiting for one more gentleman.

NICHOLAS. (*Out front.*) It was a matter of equal moment to Nicholas whether they were waiting for one gentleman or twenty; and being out of spirits, and not seeing any especial reason why he should make himself agreeable, looked out of the window and sighed. (*He looks "out of the window" and sighs.*)

TILDA. Oh, Mr. Nickleby.

NICHOLAS. (*With a start.*) I'm sorry.

TILDA. Please, don't apologise. Perhaps your languor is occasioned by my presence. But, please, don't heed me. You may behave just as you would if you two were alone.

FANNY. (*Blushing.*) Tilda! I'm ashamed of you! (*The young women giggle.*)

NICHOLAS. And here the two friends burst into a verity of giggles, glancing from time to time at Nicholas, who, in a state of unmixed astonishment, gradually fell into one of irrepressible amusement.

TILDA. Come, now, Mr. Nickleby. Will you have tea?

NICHOLAS. (*Cheerfully, going over to sit.*) Oh, certainly. I'm honoured. And delighted. (*The women look at each other. Tilda a little nod, Fanny a deep breath.*)

FANNY. Some—bread-and-butter?

NICHOLAS. Please. (*Nicholas being poured tea and helping himself to bread-and-butter when there's another knock. Tilda stands, Fanny gestures to Phib, who admits John Browdie, looking scrubbed and uncomfortable in a huge collar and white waistcoat.*)

TILDA. Well, John.

JOHN. Well, lass.

FANNY. I beg your pardon, Mr. Nickleby—Mr. John Browdie.

JOHN. Your servant, sir.

NICHOLAS. Yours to command, sir.

FANNY. Please, Mr. Browdie, sit down. (*John, as he sits.*)

JOHN. Old woman gone awa, be she?

FANNY. She has.

JOHN. (*Helping himself to bread-and-butter.*) And schoolmaster as well?

FANNY. Yes, yes.

JOHN. An' just the four o' us?

FANNY. That's right. Do have some bread-and-butter. (*John, in mid-bite, grins hugely. Then, to Nicholas.*)

JOHN. Tha won't get brea-and-butter ev'ry night, eh, man? (*Nicholas a weak smile.*) In fact, I tell thee, if tha stay here long enough, tha'll end up nowt but skin and bone. (*John laughs hugely. Nicholas annoyed by this criticism of his employer. John elbows Fanny.*) Just skin and bone, eh, Fanny? (*John looks back to Nicholas. To explain.*) I tell tha, man, last teacher, 'ad 'ere, when turned sideway, couldn't tell were there! (*Nicholas suddenly to his feet.*)

NICHOLAS. Sir, I don't know whether your perceptions are quite keen enough, to enable you to understand that your remarks are highly offensive, to me and my employer, but if they are, please have the goodness to—(*Tilda stops John's response.*)

TILDA. If you say one more word, John, only half a word, I'll never speak to you again.

JOHN. Oh. Weel. I'll shut me mouth, then. Eh? (*John eats bread-and-butter and slurps his tea. Fanny, overcome, stands and runs to the side. Tilda follows. Nicholas looks alarmed.*)

TILDA. Fanny, what's the matter?

FANNY. Nothing.

TILDA. There was never any danger of an altercation, was there, Mr. Nickleby?

NICHOLAS. (*A step towards the women.*) No, none at all. (*Tilda to Nicholas, Fanny still sniffing.*)

TILDA. Say something kind to her.

NICHOLAS. Why, what—

TILDA. Or better, why don't John and I go off next door, and leave you two together? For a little while.

NICHOLAS. Whatever for?

TILDA. Whatever for? And her dressed up so beautifully, and looking really almost handsome. I'm ashamed of you.

NICHOLAS. My dear girl, what is it to me how she is dressed, or how she looks? It's hardly my concern. (*Tilda quickly to the table.*)

TILDA. Don't call me a dear girl, or Fanny will be saying it's my fault. We will play cards. Phib, dear, please clear the table. (*Phib clears the table, Tilda whispers to Fanny, and John finishes the bread-and-butter, as Nicholas speaks out front.*)

NICHOLAS. And all of this was completely unintelligible to Nicholas, who had no other distinct impression, than that Miss Squeers was an ordinary-looking girl, and her friend Miss Price a pretty one, and that he had been called to join in a game of Speculation. (*Fanny and Tilda both standing near the chair opposite John.*)

TILDA. So, who's to partner whom?

NICHOLAS. (*Obviously, moving to a chair opposite an empty chair.*) I'll partner you, Miss Price.

TILDA. Oh, *sir.*

NICHOLAS. (*Taking this response as meaning assent.*) It will be my great pleasure. (*Tilda glances at Fanny, and sits opposite the chair beside which Nicholas is standing. Fanny sits opposite John. Nicholas tearing up cards for chips.*)

FANNY. (*Hysterically.*) Well, Mr. Browdie, it appears we're to be partners.

JOHN. (*Dumbfounded.*) Aye.

NICHOLAS. I'll deal?

FANNY. Oh, please, do deal. (*Nicholas deals five cards to each player. They look at their cards.*) Well, Mr. Browdie?

JOHN. (*Pushing two chips into the centre.*) Two on spades.

NICHOLAS. Miss Price?

TILDA. (*Three chips.*) Bid three. On hearts.

FANNY. (*Putting one chip in.*) I'll—pass.

NICHOLAS. (*Putting one chip in.*) Then hearts it is. (*Fanny a sharp intake of breath. The hand is played out in total silence. The principle is the same as whist, with each player laying a card for each trick, hearts being trumps. Tilda and Nicholas win.*) Well, then. We've won.

FANNY. And Tilda something that she'd not expected to win, I think.

TILDA. (*Ingenuously.*) Oh, only seven, dear. (*John dealing another hand.*)

FANNY. (*To Tilda.*) How dull you are.

TILDA. Oh, no, indeed. I am in excellent spirits. It was thinking *you* seemed out of sorts.

FANNY. Oh, me? Why, no.

TILDA. Your hair's coming out of curl, dear.

FANNY. Pray, dear, don't mind me. You'd better attend to your partner.

NICHOLAS. Thank you for reminding her. She had. (*John looking black.*)

TILDA. One diamond.

FANNY. Two clubs.

NICHOLAS. Two diamonds.

JOHN. Three clubs.

TILDA. Pass.

FANNY. Pass.

NICHOLAS. Pass. (*John looks round. Nicholas and Tilda indicate they have no further bid. The hand is played, and, surprisingly, Nicholas and Tilda win again, on the last trick, with Nicholas's king of clubs. Nicholas pulls in the chips. Tilda deals again during:*)

TILDA. Well, I never had such luck. It's all you, Mr. Nickleby, I'm sure. I should like to have you for a partner always.

NICHOLAS. Well, I wish you had.

TILDA. Though if you win at cards, of course, you'll have a bad wife, sure as sure.

NICHOLAS. Not if your wish is gratified, Miss Price. (*He picks up his cards. Aware of the silence of the others.*) We have all the talking to ourselves, it seems.

FANNY. Oh, but you do it so well, Mr. Nickleby. It would be quite an outrage to interrupt you, wouldn't it? Two hearts.

NICHOLAS. Pass. (*Pause.*)

TILDA. John, dear, your bid.

JOHN. My what?

TILDA. Your bid.

JOHN. (*Throwing down his cards.*) Well, damn me if I'm going to take this longer. (*Pause. The young women very shocked.*)

NICHOLAS. Erm . . .

JOHN. (*Stands.*) And you are coming home with me, now, Tilda, and him o'ert there can look sharp for a broken head next time he comes near me.

TILDA. Mercy on us, what is all this?

JOHN. Home! Home, now, home! (*Fanny crying.*)

TILDA. And here's Fanny in tears, now. What can be the matter?

FANNY. Oh, don't you bother, ma'am. Oh, don't you trouble to enquire.

TILDA. Well, you are monstrous polite, ma'am.

FANNY. Well, I shall not come to you to take lessons in the art, ma'am.

TILDA. And you need not take the trouble to make yourself plainer than you are, ma'am, because it's quite unnecessary.

FANNY. Oh! Oh, I can thank God that I haven't the boldness of some people!

TILDA. (*Standing.*) And I can thank God I haven't the envy of others. While wishing you a good night, ma'am, and pleasant dreams attend your sleep.

FANNY. Tilda, I hate you! (*Tilda sweeps out, followed by John, with a dark look at Nicholas. Fanny, weeping, thumps Phib. Nicholas, out front:*)

NICHOLAS. This is one consequence, thought Nicholas, of my cursed readiness to adapt myself to any society into which chance carries me. If I had sat mute and motionless, as I might have done, this would not have happened. (*Pause. End of reportage. Nicholas flails.*) What did I do? What did I do? (*Nicholas withdraws.*)

FANNY. Oh, I swear that there is no-one in the world more miserable than I. And never has been. And never will be. (*Pause.*)

PHIB. (*Carefully.*) Well, I can't help saying, miss, if you were to kill me for it, that I never saw anyone look so vulgar as Miss Price this night.

FANNY. Oh, Phib, how you do talk. (*Pause.*)

PHIB. And I know it's very wrong of me to say so, Miss, Miss Price being a friend of yours and all, but she do dress herself out so, and go on in such a manner to get noticed: well, if people only saw themselves.

FANNY. Now, Phib, you know you mustn't talk like that.

PHIB. So vain. And so, so plain.

FANNY. And I will hear no more of this. It's true, Miss Price has faults, has many, but I wish her well. And above all, I wish her married. And I think it desirable—most desirable, from the nature of her failings—that she is married as soon as possible.

PHIB. Yes, miss. (*A knock.*)

FANNY. Who's that? Come in. (*Enter Tilda. Phib exit.*)

TILDA. Well, Fanny. (*Slight pause.*) Well, Fanny, you see I have come back to see you. Although we had bad words.

FANNY. I bear no malice, Tilda. I am above it.

TILDA. Don't be cross, please, Fanny. I have come to tell you something.

FANNY. What may that be, Tilda?

TILDA. Well . . . Well, this. After we left here, John and I had the most dreadful quarrel. But after a great deal of wrangling, and saying we would never speak again, we made it up, and John has promised that first thing tomorrow morning he'll put our names down in the church, and I give you notice to get your bridesmaid's frock made now. There!

FANNY. Oh, *Tilda*. Oh, dear Tilda. (*And the two women burst into tears and embrace each other.*) Oh, I'm so *happy*. (*Tilda decides to strike while the iron is cool.*)

TILDA. But, now, Fanny, there's the matter of young Mr. Nickleby.

FANNY. Oh, him. He's nothing to me.

TILDA. Oh, come, now, Fanny, that's not true.

FANNY. It Is. I hate him. And I wish that he was dead. And me as well.

TILDA. Now, dear. You know you'll think very differently in five minutes, and wouldn't it be much nicer to take him back in favour?

FANNY. Oh, Tilda. How could you have acted so mean and dishonourable. I wouldn't have believed it of you.

TILDA. Now, Fanny, you're talking as if I murdered someone.

FANNY. Very near as bad.

TILDA. Oh, don't be silly. It's not my fault I've got enough good looks to make some people civil. Persons don't make their own faces, and it's no more my fault if mine is a good one than it is other people's fault if their's is not.

FANNY. (*In horror.*) Oh, *Tilda*.

TILDA. Fanny, I don't mean—

FANNY. Now, go. Go back home at once.

TILDA. Oh, Fanny—

FANNY. Now, at once, d'you hear me?

TILDA. Very well, but—

FANNY. NOW. (*Fanny turns firmly away. Tilda to the exit. She turns back. Fanny turns slowly to Tilda. Tilda gives a little, shruggy, affectionate gesture, as if to apologise. Pause. Then Fanny runs to her friend, crying.*) Oh, I'm so *happy* for you, Tilda.

Scene Sixteen

The Boys clear the Dotheboys Hall furniture and set two meagre, broken chairs and a threadbare carpet. The Nicklebys' new house in Thames St. Mrs. Nickleby, Kate and Noggs—who carries their luggage—enter during the narration.

NARRATION.

And at that very moment, Kate and Mrs. Nickleby arrived at their new home.

Around, the squalid slums of the East End of London—

And behind, a wharf that opened to the river—

And nearby, an empty kennel, and some bones of animals—

Past which they quickly walked,

And went inside.

NOGGS. (*Putting down the luggage.*) Well, here it is.
KATE. I see.
NOGGS. It's not, of course . . . There are some bits of furniture. And there's a fire made up. I'm sure, although it looks a little gloomy, it can be made, quite . . .
KATE. Yes. (*Pause.*)
MRS. NICKLEBY. Well, well, my dear. Is it not thoughtful and considerate of your kind uncle? To provide us with . . .
NOGGS. Your uncle, yes. (*Noggs picks up the luggage and takes it to another room in the house.*)
KATE. Oh, mama, this house is so depressing. I—one could imagine that some dreadful—that some awful thing had—
MRS. NICKLEBY. Lord, dear Kate, don't talk like that, you'll frighten me to death.
KATE. It's just a foolish fancy.
MRS. NICKLEBY. Well, Kate, I'll thank you to keep your foolish fancies to yourself, and not wake up my foolish fancies to keep them company.
KATE. Yes, I'm sorry. (*The two women look at each other. Then, quite suddenly, they embrace. Noggs enters.*) Mr. Noggs, we need detain you no longer.
NOGGS. Is there nothing more?
KATE. No, nothing, really. Thank you.
MRS. NICKLEBY. (*Fumbling in her purse.*) Perhaps, dear, Mr. Noggs would like to drink our healths.
KATE. I think, mama, you'd hurt his feelings if you offered it. (*Noggs bows and withdraws. The women sit.*)

NARRATION.

Gloomy and black in truth the old house was—

No life was stirring there—

And everything said coldness, silence and decay.

Scene Seventeen

Outside Dotheboys Hall. Day. Enter Nicholas.

NICHOLAS. And so it happened that, the next day, during the short daily interval that was suffered to elapse between what was pleasantly called the dinner of Mr. Squeers' pupils and their return to the pursuit of useful knowledge, Nicholas was engaged in a melancholy walk, and brood, and listless saunter. (*Nicholas perambulates as Tilda and Fanny enter, arm-in-arm.*)

TILDA. And Miss Price, who had stayed the night with Miss Squeers, was at that same being taken by her best friend at least as far home as the second turning of the road.

FANNY. (*Seeing Nicholas.*) Ah! Him!

TILDA. Oh, Fanny, shall we turn back? He hasn't seen us yet.

FANNY. No, Tilda . . . It is my duty to go through with it, and so I shall. (*Nicholas walks straight past Tilda and Fanny.*)

NICHOLAS. (*As he passes.*) Good morning.

FANNY. (*Nudging Tilda violently.*) He's going. I shall faint.

TILDA. Oh, Mr. Nickleby, come back!

FANNY. (*Staggering slightly, and needing to be supported by Tilda.*) I know I shall—

TILDA. Oh, Mr. Nickleby— (*Nicholas turns back, and comes to Tilda and Fanny.*)

NICHOLAS. Um, what's the—

TILDA. Just, please, help— (*Nicholas to hold Fanny, when that young lady expertly twists and falls backwards into his arms. For a moment, they stand there, and then Nicholas, unable to prevent himself, falls over backwards, Fanny on top of him.*)

NICHOLAS. Miss Squeers . . .

FANNY. (*Coming around.*) Oh, dear, this foolish faintness—

TILDA. It's not foolish, dear. You have no reason to feel shamed. It's others, who provoke it, who should—

NICHOLAS. Ah. I understand. (*Nicholas manhandles Fanny to a sitting position.*) You are still resolved to fix it upon me. I see. Although I told you last night it was not my fault.

TILDA. There, he says it was not his fault. Perhaps you were too jealous, or too hasty with him? He says it was not his fault. I think that is apology enough.

NICHOLAS. Um—

FANNY. All right, Tilda. You've convinced me. I forgive him. (*Fanny lies back on Nicholas again.*)

NICHOLAS. Oh, dear. This is more serious than I supposed. Allow me— (*He dislodges Fanny, and stands. Fanny stands with Tilda.*) May I speak? (*The two women look at him with eager anticipation.*) I must say—that I am very sorry—truly and sincerely so—for having been the cause of any difference among you last night. I reproach myself most bitterly for having been so unfortunate as to cause the dissention that occurred, although I did so, I assure you, most unwittingly and heedlessly. (*Pause.*)

TILDA. Well, that's not all you have to say, surely.

NICHOLAS. No, it is not, I fear there is something more. (*Slight pause.*) It is a most awkward thing to say, as the very mention of such a supposition makes one look like a puppy—but, still . . . May I ask if that lady supposes that I entertain . . . a sort of . . . (*Quickly.*) Does she think that I'm in love with her?

FANNY. Oh! (*Change of tack.*) Oh, answer for me, dear.

TILDA. Of course she does.

NICHOLAS. She does?

TILDA. Of course.

FANNY. And you may say, dear Tilda, that if Mr. Nickleby had doubted that, he may set his mind at rest. His sentiments are completely recipro—

NICHOLAS. Stop!

FANNY. Whatever for?

NICHOLAS. Pray hear me. This is the grossest and wildest delusion, the completest and most signal mistake, that ever human being laboured under or committed. I have scarcely seen the young lady half a dozen times, but if I had seen her sixty times, or sixty thousand, it would be and will be precisely the same. I have not one thought, wish, or hope, connected with her unless it be—and I say this, not to hurt her feelings, but to impress her with the real state of my own—unless it be the one object dear to my heart as life itself, of being one day able to turn my back on this accursed place, never to set foot in it again or to think of it—even think of it—except with loathing and disgust. (*Pause. Then Nicholas, out front.*) And with this particularly plain and straightforward declaration, Nicholas bowed slightly, and waiting to hear no more, retreated. (*Nicholas retreats.*)

TILDA. But oh, poor Fanny! Her anger, rage and vexation are not to be described.

FANNY. Refused! (*Fanny starts to push at Tilda, to make her go away, as punishment for encouraging her.*)

TILDA. (*Being pushed, and beginning to enjoy Fanny's fury, and find it amusing.*) Refused by a teacher picked up by advertisement at an annual salary of five pounds payable at indefinite periods . . . (*Really taunting now.*) . . . and this too in the presence of a little chit of a miller's daughter of eighteen,

FANNY. (*Pushing and shoving.*) . . . who was going to be married, to a man who had gone down on his very knees to ask her! (*And, with a little, dismissive gesture, Fanny turns, runs to the side and weeps, while Tilda, still laughing, dances out the other way, and Nicholas speaks out front.*)

NICHOLAS. And it may be remarked, that Miss Squeers was of the firm opinion that she was prepossessing and beautiful, and that her father was, after all, master, and Nicholas man, and that her father had saved money and Nicholas had none, all of which seemed to her conclusive arguments why the young man should feel only too honoured by her preference, and all too grateful for her deep affection . . . (*And Nicholas turns and sees Fanny. She has composed herself now, but this has the effect of making her look even more crumpled. She marches to Nicholas, with an effort at dignity, but then breaks down.*)

FANNY. Sir . . . I pity you. (*She turns and runs back, as Mrs. Squeers and Smike appear, as if from the house.*) You're right, mama.

MRS. SQUEERS. Right? What about?

FANNY. (*Crying.*) About that Knuckleboy. (*She runs out, as if into the house.*)

MRS. SQUEERS. (*To Nicholas.*) You, sir!

NICHOLAS. Yes, ma'am?

MRS. SQUEERS. You've been wanted in the classroom for ten minutes.

NICHOLAS. Certainly. (*He goes towards Mrs. Squeers, as if into the house.*)

MRS. SQUEERS. Not through the house, sir. Round that way. (*Pause.*

Then Nicholas turns his collar up against the cold, and goes out an-other way. Smike makes to follow him.) Smike! (Smike turns back to Mrs. Squeers.) In here. You haven't finished. (She cuffs Smike on the head as he passes her into the house.)

Scene Eighteen

The dormitory at Dotheboys Hall. Night. The boys enter and lie down, on the bare stage. Smike enters and sits, with Nicholas' book. Nicholas enters with a candle, to see Smike trying to read the book. Smike can't work out what to do.

SMIKE. Can't do it. With the book. Can't do it, with the book, at all.
NICHOLAS. Oh, please. Don't try. (*Smike crying.*) Don't. For God's sake. I cannot bear it. (*Smike whimpering.*) They are more hard on you, I know. But, please . . .
SMIKE. Except for you, I die.
NICHOLAS. No, no. You'll be better off, I tell you, when I'm gone. (*Smike picks it up after a second.*)
SMIKE. You gone?
NICHOLAS. Shh. Yes.
SMIKE. You going?
NICHOLAS. I was speaking to my thoughts.
SMIKE. *Tell* me. Will you? Will you go? (*Pause.*)
NICHOLAS. I shall be driven to it. Yes. To go away. (*Pause.*)
SMIKE. Please tell me. Is away as bad as here? (*Pause.*)
NICHOLAS. Oh, no. Oh, no, there's nothing—
SMIKE. Can I meet you there? Away?
NICHOLAS. Well, yes . . . you can, of course . . .
SMIKE. Can meet you there? Away? And I will find you, in away?
NICHOLAS. You would. And, if you did, I'd try to help you. (*Pause. Nicholas moves away with the candle and sits. He takes out a paper and a pen. He is writing a letter to Kate.*) I miss you terribly, but at least I feel that if my work here prospers—I miss you terribly. (*Pause.*) I took a Latin class today. The boys are—they are not ad-vanced and there is much to do. (*Pause.*) The countryside is— (*Pause. He puts away the letter. He blows out the candle. Darkness.*)

Scene Nineteen

The same. A bell rings offstage, and then cold, morning light. The boys and Nicholas are in the same positions, but, in the blackout, Smike has slipped away.

SQUEERS. (*Off.*) Hey! Hey, you up there? Are you going to sleep all day?

NICHOLAS. We shall be down directly, sir. (*He gestures to the boys, who speed up.*)

SQUEERS. (*Off.*) Well, you'd better be, or I'll be down on some of you in less—Where's Smike? (*Nicholas goes to Smike's place, but sees he isn't there. The boys nearly fully up.*) (*Off.*) I said—where's Smike? (*Nicholas turns and calls.*)

NICHOLAS. He isn't here, sir.

SQUEERS. (*Off.*) What? Not there? (*Pause. Squeers enters, rushes to Smike's place. He sees Smike is absent.*) What does this mean? Where have you hid him?

NICHOLAS. I have not seen him since last night.

SQUEERS. Oh, no? (*Turning to the boys.*) And you? You boys? Have any of you— (*Jennings, who is obscured from Squeers by other boys.*)

JENNINGS. Please, sir . . .

SQUEERS. Yes? What's that?

JENNINGS. Please, sir, I think he's run away.

SQUEERS. Who said that?

BOYS. Jennings, sir.

SQUEERS. And, where is Jennings?

BOYS. Here, sir. (*Jennings is pushed forward by his fellows. Squeers to Jennings.*)

SQUEERS. So, you think he's run away, do you?

JENNINGS. Yes, sir. Please, sir.

SQUEERS. And what, sir, what reason have you to suppose that any boy would *want* to run away from this establishment? (*Squeers hits Jennings on the face.*) Eh, sir? (*Jennings says nothing. Squeers looks to Nicholas, who is looking away. Squeers to Nicholas.*) And you, Nickleby. I s'pose you think he's run away?

NICHOLAS. I think it's highly likely, yes.

SQUEERS. You do? Perhaps you *know* he's run away?

NICHOLAS. I do not know, sir. And I'm glad I did not, for it would then have been my duty to have warned you.

SQUEERS. Which, no doubt, you would have been devilish sorry to do.
NICHOLAS. I should indeed, sir. (*Mrs. Squeers enters.*)
MRS. SQUEERS. What's going on? Where's Smike?
SQUEERS. He's gone.
MRS. SQUEERS. (*An order, to Squeers.*) Gone? Well, then, we'll find him, stupid. We must search the roads. He hasn't any money, any food. He'll have to bed. He must be on the public road.
SQUEERS. (*Going towards the exit.*) That's true.
MRS. SQUEERS. (*Following.*) And when we catch him, oh . . . (*Squeers turns back to the boys. Slowly.*)
SQUEERS. And when we catch him, I will only stop just short of flaying him alive. So, follow your leader, boys, and take your pattern by Smike. If you dare. (*The Squeerses go out. Nicholas and the boys follow.*)

Scene Twenty

The streets of the West End of London. Early morning. During this opening narration, we set up the breakfast room of the Mantalinis: a table and two chairs on the one side, and a single chair on the other. The Narration is delivered by Kate Nickleby and four or five Milliners.

KATE. It was with a heavy heart, and many sad forebodings, that Kate Nickleby left the city when its clocks yet wanted a quarter of an hour of eight, and threaded her way, alone, amid the noise and bustle of the streets, towards the West End of London.
MILLINERS.
At this early hour many sickly girls,

Whose business, like that of the poor worm, is to produce with patient toil the finery that bedecks the thoughtless and luxurious,

Traverse our streets, making towards the scene of their daily labour,

And catching, as if by stealth, in their hurried walk,

The only gasp of wholesome air and glimpse of sunlight which cheers their monotonous existence during the long train of hours that make up the working day.

(*The milliners dispersing, as a tall, old footman enters, a little unsteadily.*)

KATE. Kate saw, in their unhealthy looks and feeble gait, but too clear an evidence that her misgivings were not wholly groundless. (*Kate goes to the Footman, as a male Narrator enters.*)

NARRATOR. She arrived at Madame Mantalini's at the appointed hour, and was admitted to a small, curtained room, by a tall, elderly footman. (*During the following, Mr. and Madame Mantalini enter to the breakfast table and sit. Madame Mantalini is a handsome, well-dressed middle-aged woman. Her husband wears a morning gown, with a green waistcoat and Turkish trousers, a pink kerchief, bright slippers, black curled whiskers and a moustache. He is younger than his wife.*)

KATE. Excuse me—Mantalini? Are they Italian?

FOOTMAN. Muntle.

KATE. I beg your pardon?

FOOTMAN. Changed his name. From Mr. Muntle. To Mr. Mantalini.

KATE. Oh, I see. (*The footman nods gravely and goes out. Kate sits on the single chair. We gather from the fact that the Mantalinis do not notice her that the room is divided by an imaginary curtain. There is a bad-tempered silence between the Mantalinis, which is broken when Mr. Mantalini speaks.*)

MANTALINI. I tell you again, my soul, that if you will be odiously, demnibly, outrageously jealous, you will make yourself most horrid miserable.

MADAME MANTALINI. (*Pouting.*) I *am* miserable.

MANTALINI. And I tell you, my fastness, that it is a pretty bewitching little countenance you have, but if it is out of humour, it quite spoils itself, and looks very much like a hobgoblin's.

MADAME MANTALINI. It's very easy to talk.

MANTALINI. Not so easy when one is eating an egg and one is provoked into a passion by demned false accusations, my jewel, for the yolk runs down the waistcoat, and yolk of egg don't match it. 'Cept, of course, a yellow waistcoat. Which this ain't. (*Pause. Madame Mantalini breaks.*)

MADAME MANTALINI. You flirted with her all night long.

MANTALINI. No, no, my love.

MADAME MANTALINI. I watched you all the time.

MANTALINI. Oh, bless the little winking eye—was on me all the time?

MADAME MANTALINI. And I say, Mantalini, that you waltz with anyone but me again, I will take poison. I will swear it, now.

MANTALINI. Take poison?

MADAME MANTALINI. Yes.

MANTALINI. You'll take demned poison on account of Mantalini, preciousness?

MADAME MANTALINI. I will.

MANTALINI. He would could have had the hands of a dowager and two countesses—

MADAME MANTALINI. *One* countess.

MANTALINI. (*Stands and goes round to his wife's side of the table.*) But who at a morning concert saw the demndest little fascinator in the world, and married it, and fiddlesticks to every countess in the world?

MADAME MANTALINI. Oh, Mantalini.

MANTALINI. Oh, my little cherub. I'm forgiven?

MADAME MANTALINI. Well . . . Oh, well.

MANTALINI. (*Moving briskly back to his seat.*) Now, tell me, sapphire, how are we for cash? For there's a horse for sale at Scrubbs, for next to nothing, and if I can raise some discount from Ralph Nickleby, a hundred guineas buys him, mane and crest and legs and tail, all of the demdest beauty. (*Kate looks up in alarm. Madame Mantalini turns her head away.*) Then I can ride him in the park, before the very chariots of the rejected countesses. (*Moving back to his wife.*) My little— princess.

MADAME MANTALINI. Oh, my—Mantalini. (*Kate coughs loudly. Mantalini stands and mimes pulling back the curtain—we hear the swish and rattle from offstage, Mantalini sees Kate.*)

MANTALINI. Well. What's this?

MADAME MANTALINI. Child, who are you?

KATE. (*Standing.*) I—I am sent here, by my uncle. I am sent here for a situation.

MANTALINI. (*Coming closer to Kate.*) And, my dear, you'll have one.

MADAME MANTALINI. Mantalini. (*Kate thrusts Ralph's letter at Madame Mantalini.*)

KATE. There's a letter. From my uncle, Mr. Nickleby.

MADAME MANTALINI. (*Taking the letter, opening it, a little tartly.*) Oh, yes.

MANTALINI. (*Trying to look at the letter.*) Ralph Nickleby?

KATE. I'm sorry, I was—I was left here, by your footman.

MANTALINI. What a rascal is that footman, dear. To keep this sweet young creature waiting—

MADAME MANTALINI. (*Folding Ralph's letter.*) Well, dear, I must say that that's your fault.

MANTALINI. My fault, my joy?

MADAME MANTALINI. Of course. What can you expect, dearest, if you will not correct the man? (*Slight pause.*)

MANTALINI. Well, then. Indeed. He shall be horsewhipped.

MADAME MANTALINI. Well, my dear. Your uncle recommends you, and we are, connected with him, in commercial matters. Now, do you speak French?

KATE. Yes, ma'am, I do.

MANTALINI. But do you speak it like a native?

MADAME MANTALINI. (*Ignoring Mr. Mantalini.*) Miss Nickleby, we have twenty young women constantly employed in this establishment.

MANTALINI. Some of them demned handsome, too. (*Mantalini a knowing smirk at Kate. Madame Mantalini clocks it.*)

MADAME MANTALINI. Of whom, I am pleased to say, Mr. Mantalini knows nothing, as he is never in their room, as I will not allow it. (*Mantalini shrugs, poutishly, and lies down on the sofa.*) Now, our hours are from nine to nine, with extra if we're busy, for which there's a little payment, and I'd think your wages would be in the region of five to seven shillings. Is that satisfactory?

KATE. Oh, yes. It's . . . Certainly.

MANTALINI. Demned satisfactory.

MADAME MANTALINI. Miss Nickleby, you will pay no attention, please, to anything that Mr. Mantalini says.

KATE. I will not, ma'am.

MADAME MANTALINI. So, then, let me take you to the workroom, now, Miss Nickleby. (*Madame Mantalini leads Kate out. Mantalini goes too.*)

Scene Twenty-One

The Mantalinis' workroom, downstage, and the showroom, upstage. The scene change is performed by Milliners. In the workroom are clothesrails, tailors' dummies, hatboxes, and uncompleted dresses and hats. In the showroom are display tailors' dummies, more hatboxes, a chaise longue and a tall mirror. For the moment, the showroom is empty, and the workroom is full of working Milliners, presided over by a short, bustling, over-dressed lady called Miss

Knag. Madame Mantalini and Kate enter. The Milliners look Kate up and down, whisper and giggle.

MADAME MANTALINI. Miss Knag?

MISS KNAG. Madame Mantalini.

MADAME MANTALINI. Ah, Miss Knag, this is the young person I spoke to you about.

MISS KNAG. Oh, good morning, miss. (*To the gawping Milliners.*) Come on, come on, no gawping, is there no work to be done? (*The Milliners set about their tasks with bad humour.*)

MADAME MANTALINI. I think, for the present, it will be better for Miss Nickleby to come into the showroom with you—

MISS KNAG. Showroom, yes.

MADAME MANTALINI. And try things on for people.

MISS KNAG. People, yes.

MADAME MANTALINI. She'll not be much use yet in any other way,

MISS KNAG. Way, no.

MADAME MANTALINI. And her appearance will—

MISS KNAG. Suit very well with mine. (*Miss Knag to Kate.*) For, yes, I see, Miss Nickleby and I are very much a pair—although I am just a little darker, and I have, I think, a slightly smaller foot. Miss Nickleby will not, I am sure, be too much offended at my saying that, as our family has always been quite celebrated for its feet—the smallness of them—ever since the family had feet at all.

MADAME MANTALINI. You'll take care, Miss Knag, that she understands her hours,

MISS KNAG. Hours,

MADAME MANTALINI. And so forth.

MISS KNAG. So forth, yes.

MADAME MANTALINI. And I'll leave her with you.

MISS KNAG. Yes, of course, dear Madame Mantalini.

MADAME MANTALINI. Good morning, ladies.

EVERYONE. Good morning, madame. (*Madame Mantalini goes out. As she leaves, she finds Mantalini skulking near the doorway. She looks at him, and shakes her head, near tears, and runs off. Mantalini, dramatically, follows.*)

MISS KNAG. Well, what a charming woman.

KATE. Yes. I'm sure she is.

MISS KNAG. And what a charming husband.

KATE. Is he?

MISS KNAG. You don't think so?

KATE. Well—

MISS KNAG. Oh, goodness gracious mercy—where's your taste? And such a dashing man, with such a head of hair and teeth.

KATE. Well, p'raps I'm very foolish—

MISS KNAG. (*With a conspiratorial look at the Milliners.*) Well, I should say you—

KATE. But as my opinion is of very little importance to him or anyone else, I think I shall keep it, just the same. (*Pause. Miss Knag slightly thrown. The odd Milliner, aware of this, giggles. Miss Knag turns to them.*)

MISS KNAG. Well, come on, girls, where are your manners? Make Miss Nickleby welcome. Take her shawl. (*The Milliners bustle round Kate.*)

1st MILLINER. Your shawl, miss?

2nd MILLINER. Can I take your bonnet?

KATE. (*Giving the Milliner her shawl.*) Oh, thank you.

1st MILLINER. Oh, *miss.* And all in black.

KATE. Well, yes, I—

3rd MILLINER. Don't you find it quite intol'r'ble hot? And dustry?

KATE. (*Almost in tears.*) Yes. I do. Oh, yes, I do. (*Embarrassed pause.*)

1st MILLINER. Was it a near relation, Miss?

KATE. My father.

MISS KNAG. (*Calls.*) For what relation?

2nd MILLINER. Father.

MISS KNAG. A long illness, was it?

2nd MILLINER. I don't know.

KATE. Our misfortune was very sudden. Or I might, perhaps, be able to support it better now. (*And the Milliners turn out front.*)

MILLINERS.

And then there came a knock at Madame Mantalini's door,

And there entered a great lady,

Well, a rich one,

Who had come with her daughter for approval of some court dresses,

Long in preparation,

Upon whom Miss Nickleby was told to wait,

(Madame Mantalini, Miss Knag, Kate, a Rich Lady and her Rich Daughter are in the showroom. The Rich Lady sits on the chaise, the Rich Daughter stands trying on a coat and hat, near the mirror.)

MADAME MANTALINI. Bonjour, madame.
1st MILLINER. With Miss Knag,
MISS KNAG. Mademoiselle—
3rd MILLINER. And officered of course by—
MILLINERS. Madame Mantalini.
KATE. *(Bustling about with clothes and hats.)* Kate's part in the pageant was humble enough—
MISS KNAG. *(Taking something from Kate.)* La, ma chere—
KATE. Her duties being limited to holding the articles of costume until Miss Knag was ready to try them on . . .
MISS KNAG. *(Taking something else.)* Ici . . .
KATE. And now and then tying a string,
MISS KNAG. Or fastening a hook and eye . . . Merci . . .
KATE. And thinking that she was beneath the reach of all arrogance and ill-humour.
MISS KNAG. *(Surveying the effect.)* Ah. Mais *oui.*
RICH LADY. *(Off-hand.)* Alors . . .
MILLINERS.
But as it happened, both the rich lady and her rich daughter were in a terrible temper,

And Miss Nickleby came in for a considerable share of their displeasure.

(Kate steps backwards from the Rich Daughter, nearly stepping on the foot of the Rich Lady.)
RICH LADY. She's so awkward.
1st MILLINER. They remarked. *(Kate fumbling, trying to tie a hat on the Rich Daughter.)*
RICH DAUGHTER. Her hands are cold.
2nd MILLINER. They said. *(Kate accidentally pushes the hat forward, so it falls over the Rich Daughter's face.)*
RICH LADY. Can she do nothing right? *(The Rich Daughter takes off the hat, Miss Knag takes her coat, the Daughter and the Rich Lady preparing to go, as:)*
3rd MILLINER. And they wondered how Madame Mantalini could have such girls about her—

MADAME MANTALINI. Madame, je regrette infiniment . . .

1st MILLINER. And requested they might see some other young person the next time they came . . .

RICH LADY. Cher Madame, au revoir! (*The Rich Lady and her Rich Daughter sweep out.*)

2nd MILLINER. And so on,

3rd MILLINER. And so forth. (*The Milliners disperse. Kate moves into the workroom area, leaving Madame Mantalini and Miss Knag in the showroom.*)

KATE. And so common an occurrence would hardly be worthy of mention, but for its effect on Kate, who shed many bitter tears when these people were gone, and felt, for the first time, humbled by her occupation. She had, it is true, quailed at the prospect of hard work and drudgery; but she'd felt no degradation in the thought of labour, till she found herself exposed to insolence and pride. (*Kate stays.*)

MISS KNAG. Well, now, Madame Mantalini. That Miss Nickleby is certainly a very creditable young person, indeed.

MADAME MANTALINI. Well, Miss Knag, beyond putting an excellent client out of humour, Miss Nickleby has not done anything very remarkable thus far that I'm aware of.

MISS KNAG. Aware of, no. But, dear Madame, you must make allowances for inexperience. And such.

MADAME MANTALINI. Well, yes, Miss Knag, of course, but in my view she still remains among the awkwardest young girls I ever saw. And not, despite the opinion of her uncle, not that pretty either.

MISS KNAG. Pretty, no. But, Madame Mantalini. That is not her fault, now is it? She should not be blamed for that, and be denied our friendship, should she? (*Slight pause. Madame Mantalini breathes deeply.*)

MADAME MANTALINI. No.

MISS KNAG. No. (*Madame Mantalini goes out. A great beam is spreading across Miss Knag's face, as Kate takes out a letter.*)

KATE. Oh, Nicholas. How happy it makes me to hear from you, in such good spirits. It consoles me so, to think that you at least are comfortable and happy. (*Exit Kate. Miss Knag, quickly.*)

MISS KNAG. I love her. I quite love her. I declare I do.

Scene Twenty-Two

The Dotheboys Hall schoolroom. Bare stage. The boys enter, two of them dragging a pair of steps, the thrashing-horse. They put it centre stage. The boys form two lines either side of it. Nicholas enters, and looks in horror at the thrashing horse. Squeers enters, with a long cane.

SQUEERS. Is every boy here? Every boy keep his place. (*Pause.*) Nickleby, to your place, sir. Coates. Jackson. (*Coates and Jackson go out. Nicholas moves near the thrashing-horse. Mrs. Squeers, Fanny, Young Wackford and Phib enter, and stand to one side. Coates and Jackson re-enter, dragging Smike, who is bound, and filthy, clearly having been caught after spending the night rough. He is brought down to the thrashing-horse.*)

SQUEERS. Untie him, sirs. (*The two boys untie Smike.*) Now, sir, what do you have to say for yourself? (*Pause.*) Nothing, I suppose? (*Pause. Smike glances at Nicholas, who is looking away.*) Well, then. Let's begin.

SMIKE. Oh, spare me, sir.

SQUEERS. What's that?

SMIKE. Oh, spare me, sir.

SQUEERS. Oh, that's all, is it? Well, I'll flog you within an inch of your life, but I will spare you that. (*Pause.*) Coates, Jackson. (*Coates and Jackson help Smike on to a step of the thrashing horse, so that Smike's chin just reaches over the top. Coates and Jackson tie ropes round Smike's hands and the horse, to keep him in place for the flogging.*)

SMIKE. I was driven to it, sir.

SQUEERS. Driven to it? Not your fault, but mine?

MRS. SQUEERS. Hm. That's a good one. (*Squeers goes a little upstage turns, runs, and delivers the first blow. Smike cries out, Squeers grunts. He goes upstage again, runs, and delivers the second blow. He is back upstage again, when Nicholas takes a slight step forward.*)

NICHOLAS. Uh . . . This must stop. (*Squeers looks round.*)

SQUEERS. Who said that? Who said stop?

NICHOLAS. I did. I said that it must stop, and stop it will. (*Pause.*) I have tried to intercede. I have begged forgiveness for the boy. You have not listened. You have brought this on yourself.

SQUEERS. (*Dismissively, preparing for his next stroke.*) Get out, Get out. (*Nicholas walks to stand between Squeers and Smike.*)

NICHOLAS. No sir. I can't.

SQUEERS. Can't? You can't? We'll see. (*Squeers walks to Nicholas and strikes his face. Nicholas doesn't respond.*) Now leave, sir, and let me to my work. (*Nicholas turns, as if to go, then suddenly turns back, grabs Squeers, pulls him round, and hits him.*) What?

NICHOLAS. You have— (*Squeers tries to hit Nicholas, but Nicholas seizes the cane and beats Squeers with it. During the ensuing, the following things happen: Mrs. Squeers, Wackford and eventually Fanny come to Squeers' aid—somewhat ineffectually: The boys crush round to see, and eventually to obscure, the fight. And Smike, let go, slips away. There is much shouting.)*

MRS. SQUEERS. What do you think you're doing, you madman?

FANNY. Get off him! Get off him, you monster!

WACKFORD. Beastly! Beastly, man! You beast! *(And Nicholas, finished, breaks through the boys and runs out.)*

MRS. SQUEERS. After him! After him, you vermin! Move, run after him! *(The boys, who have no intention of doing anything of the sort, nonetheless disperse, revealing Squeers, sitting on the ground, holding himself.)* Oh, Squeery, Squeery. *(She helps Squeers to his feet.)* Oh, my Squeery. *(Mrs. Squeers takes Squeers out. Wackford and Fanny follow.)*

Scene Twenty-Three

In the countryside. Bare stage. Darkness. Nicholas running. John Browdie enters with a lamp. He carries a stout staff.

JOHN. Hey! Hey! Who's that, who's there? Hey! *(John's light reveals Nicholas.)* Eh. It's tha. From school.

NICHOLAS. Yes, I'm afraid so.

JOHN. What's tha mean, afraid?

NICHOLAS. Well, only—

JOHN. Eh, man, what's the matter with thy face?

NICHOLAS. Oh, it's a cut. A blow. But I returned it to the giver, and with interest, too.

JOHN. Nay. Did tha?

NICHOLAS. Yes. For I have been the victim of considerable mistreatment.

JOHN. Eh?

NICHOLAS. At, from the hands of Mr. Squeers. But I have beaten him quite soundly, and am leaving here as a result.

JOHN. Tha what?

NICHOLAS. I said—I've beaten him. *(And John Browdie goes into strange, silent convulsions. It is not immediately clear that he is vastly amused.)* Uh—what . . . ?

JOHN. Tha beat the schoolmaster!

NICHOLAS. Yes, I'm afraid—

JOHN. Who ever heard the like!

NICHOLAS. I'm very sorry, but I was—

JOHN. Give me tha hand.

NICHOLAS. Give you my hand?

JOHN. (*Taking Nicholas's hand and pumping it firmly.*) That's right. Give me tha hand. Tha beat the schoolmaster!

NICHOLAS. Yes, I did, and as a consequence—

JOHN. Eh, man, where is tha going?

NICHOLAS. Well, to London . . .

JOHN. Has tha owt, in way of cash?

NICHOLAS. Well, no, but as I plan to walk—

JOHN. To walk to Lunnon? Look, man, tha needs cash. At least, for food, and suchlike. (*Finds his purse.*) So, here's money.

NICHOLAS. Oh, I couldn't possibly—

JOHN. Tha couldn't possibly? Tha couldn't possibly without. So, come on, man. At least, accept a sovereign.

NICHOLAS. Well, I don't know . . .

JOHN. And, p'raps, tha'll not use all of it, and send the surplus back, eh? Oh, and take this timber. If tha's walking that far, need this too. (*Nicholas takes the staff. Pause.*) Now, go, be off with thee. (*Pause.*)

NICHOLAS. I cannot thank you, sir, enough. I—after what, the words we had—I cannot—

JOHN. Beat the schoolmaster. I've not heard good as that, for twenty year. (*And John gives Nicholas a big, bear-like hug, and goes out. Nicholas follows.*)

Scene Twenty-Four

The parlour at Dotheboys Hall. Bare stage. Enter Fanny, furious, clutching a letter she has written. To the audience:

FANNY. To Mr. Ralph Nickleby. Golden Square. In London. Sir. My pa requests me to write to you, the doctors considering it doubtful whether he will ever recover the use of his legs, which prevents him holding a pen. We are in a state of mind beyond everything, and my pa is one mask of bruises, both blue and green . . . When your nephew, which you recommended for a teacher, had done this to my pa, and jumped upon his body, with his feet, and language I will not pollute my pen with describing, he assaulted my ma with dreadful violence, dashed her to the earth, and drove her back comb several inches into her head. A little more and it must have entered her skull. We have a medical certificate that if it had, the tortoiseshell would have affected the brain. Me and my brother were then the victims of his fury; I am screaming out loud all the time I write and so is my brother which takes off my attention rather, and I hope will excuse mistakes. The monster, having satiated his thirst for blood, ran away, taking with him a boy of desperate character that he had excited to rebellion. I remain yours, and— cetrer, Fanny Squeers. (*Fanny folds the letter. A knock at the door.*) Phib! (*Phib enters.*) Someone at the door. P.S.: I pity his ignorance, and despise him. (*Phib goes to the "door". Brooker enters. He is an old man, dressed in rags, and covered in mud and snow.*)

PHIB. (*Frightened, turning to Fanny.*) Uh . . . (*Fanny looks at Brooker. She looks scared, too.*)

BROOKER. (*Takes a step into the room.*) Boy. I've come about a boy. Lived here. (*Fanny looks at Phib in panic. Phib runs out. Brooker takes another step into the room.*) My name is Brooker. Come about a boy. (*Fanny runs out, Brooker following.*)

Scene Twenty-Five

Nicholas on his own in the countryside. Bare stage.

NICHOLAS. It's morning. (*Nicholas starts to walk out. Something he hears makes him stop. He turns back. Smike stands there.*) Oh, Smike. Oh—Smike. (*Nicholas quickly to Smike, who falls to his knees.*) Why do you, kneel to me?

SMIKE. To go. Go anywhere. Go everywhere. The world's end. To the churchyard grave. (*Pause.*) I can. You'll let me. Come away with you. (*Pause.*) You are my home. (*Nicholas stands there. He doesn't know what to do. Smike turns his face away. He's crying. Nicholas puts his hand out to Smike. Smike looks back. He sees the hand. Nicholas helps Smike to his feet, and the two of them go slowly out together.*)

END OF ACT ONE.

ACT TWO

Scene One

A group of Narrators on the bare stage. During the following, Noggs enters and sits in his old armchair. A hard-featured, thin-faced man, wearing a dirty nightcap and carrying an unlit candle, is behind him. This man is Mr. Crowl.

NARRATION.
In that quarter of London where Golden Square is situated,

There is a bygone, tumbledown old street,

Two rows of blackened, battered houses,

At the top of one of which there is a meagre garret room;

Where, on a wet and dismal winter's evening,

Newman Noggs,

The clerk to that great man of business Ralph Nickleby,

Sat studying a letter,

Written to his master,

Which had arrived that very afternoon.

NOGGS. (*Reading.*) My pa requests—one mask of bruises—language—thirst for blood. Oh, dear. And cetrer, Fanny Squeers. Oh, dear, oh, dear. (*Mr. Crowl knocks.*) What's that?

CROWL. (*Unnecessarily loud.*) It's Mr. Crowl. Your Neighbour. Have you got a light?

NOGGS. Oh, yes, do come in, Mr. Crowl.

(*Narrators withdraw as Crowl to Noggs.*)

CROWL. A nasty night, Mr. Noggs.

NOGGS. Oh, does it rain outside?

CROWL. Oh, does it rain? I'm wet through.

NOGGS. (*Looking at his threadbare sleeve.*) Well, it doesn't take much to wet you and me through, does it, Mr. Crowl.

CROWL. Well, but that only makes it more vexatious, doesn't it? (*Pause.*)

NOGGS. You'll forgive me, Mr. Crowl. I must go downstairs to supper.

CROWL. To the Kenwigses?

NOGGS. That's right. It is their wedding anniversary, and Mrs. Kenwigs' uncle is expected, the collector of the water-rate, and I am invited to make up the punch and the numbers. So, you'll let me—

CROWL. Well, now, think of that.

NOGGS. Yes, what?

CROWL. I was invited too.

NOGGS. You were?

CROWL. Indeed I was, but resolved not to go, thinking you were not invited, and planning to spend the evening in your company.

NOGGS. Well, um . . . I was obliged . . .

CROWL. And now, what's there for me to do? (*Pause. Noggs gestures vaguely.*) I know. I've got it. I'll still spend the evening here. And keep your fire up for you. Hm?

NOGGS. Oh . . . very well. (*Noggs turns to go.*)

CROWL. Um, Mr. Noggs, it being such a night . . . Where do you keep your coals?

NOGGS. They're in the coal scuttle. Where coals ought to be. (*Noggs goes out, Crowl pushes out the armchair.*)

CROWL. (*Out front.*) The following, having the misfortune to treat of none but common people, is necessarily of a mean and vulgar character.

Scene Two

The Kenwigs' living room. A small, cluttered room, full of furniture and people. They are the pregnant Mrs. Kenwigs, her eldest daughter Morleena, two other Little Kenwigses—both girls, Mr. and Mrs. Cutler, Miss Green, Mrs. Kenwigs' Sister, a young man called George, a fierce-looking Stout Lady, in a book-muslin dress, and Miss Petowker, an actress. Noggs sits by a small table on which are glasses, trays and a bowl of punch. Mrs. Kenwigs is just greeting him.

MRS. KENWIGS. Dear Mr. Noggs. Now, Miss Petowker, have you met my husband's old friend, George?

GEORGE. I'm most delighted.

MRS. KENWIGS. Miss Petowker's from the Theatre Royal, Drury Lane, and later on she may recite for us.

MISS PETOWKER. Oh, Mrs. Kenwigs . . . (*Mrs. Kenwigs going to her Sister.*)

GEORGE. Miss Petowker, tell me, how do you fill your days?

SISTER. (*Referring to the Stout Lady.*) My dear, who is that woman?

MRS. KENWIGS. Oh, she's the lady from downstairs.

SISTER. What *does* she think she's wearing?

MRS. KENWIGS. Well, she wouldn't wear it here, but for the fact our supper's cooking on her grate.

SISTER. I see. (*Kenwigs enters, briskly.*)

KENWIGS. Now, Mrs. Kenwigs, if everything's prepared, wouldn't it be best to begin with a round-game?

MRS. KENWIGS. Kenwigs, my dear, I am surprised at you. Would you begin without my uncle?

KENWIGS. Ah. I forgot the collector.

MRS. KENWIGS. (*To Mrs. Cutler.*) He's so particular, that if we begin without him, I shall be out of his will forever.

MRS. CUTLER. Oh, my dear!

MRS. KENWIGS. You have no *notion* how he is. (*To Kenwigs.*) And yet, of course, as good a creature as ever breathed.

KENWIGS. Indeed. The kindest-hearted man that ever was.

GEORGE. It brings the very tears to his eyes, I believe, to be forced to cut the water off when people don't pay.

MRS. KENWIGS. Now, George, if you please.

GEORGE. Oh, I'm sorry. Just my—

MRS. KENWIGS. We'll have none of that.

GEORGE. Was just my little joke.

KENWIGS. Now, George. A joke is a good thing, an excellent thing, but when a joke is made at the expense of Mrs. Kenwigs' feelings I set my face against it. And, even putting Mrs. Kenwigs out of the question—if I *could* put Mrs. Kenwigs out of the question on such an occasion as this—I myself have the honour to be connected with the collector by marriage, and I cannot allow these remarks in my . . . in my apartments. (*Pause.*)

GEORGE. Just my little joke.

KENWIGS. The subject is now closed. (*A ring.*) The bell!

MISS PETOWKER. That's him?

MRS. CUTLER. That's the collector?

STOUT LADY. Who?

MRS. KENWIGS. Yes, yes, it must be, dear Morleena, run straight down and let your uncle in and kiss him most directly when the door is open. Hurry, girl!

MORLEENA. Yes, yes, mama. (*Exit Morleena.*)

MRS. KENWIGS. And, everyone, we must appear to be engaged in light and easy conversation of a general character.

MISS GREEN. Light and easy?

MRS. KENWIGS. Yes, so as to look—

MR. CUTLER. And of a general character?

MRS. KENWIGS. Yes, yes, now Miss Petowker, tell us, if you'd be so kind—

MRS. CUTLER. So as to look—(*Mrs. Kenwigs has turned as sees Mr. Lillyvick, who has been admitted by Morleena.*)

MRS. KENWIGS. Oh, uncle, I'm so pleased to see you.

LILLYVICK. Susan.

MRS. KENWIGS. Oh, so glad.

LILLYVICK. As I, my dear, as I. And may I wish you every happiness. (*Mr. Lillyvick kisses Mrs. Kenwigs.*)

MRS. CUTLER. Well, look at that.

MR. CUTLER. A tax-collector.

MISS GREEN. Kissing.

GEORGE. Actually.

MRS. KENWIGS. And so, uncle, where will you sit?

LILLYVICK. (*Sitting.*) Oh, anywheres, my dear. I'm not particular, at all.

MRS. CUTLER. You hear that?

MR. CUTLER. Anywheres.

MISS GREEN. He's not particular.

GEORGE. At all.

KENWIGS. Um, Mr. Lillyvick, some friends of mine, sir, very anxious for the honour . . .

LILLYVICK. As I am, Kenwigs, just as I am . . .

KENWIGS. Mr. and Mrs. Cutler, Mr. Lillyvick.

MR. CUTLER. I'm proud to know you, sir. As having heard of you so often. In your professional capacity.

KENWIGS. My old friend George you know, I think; of course, Mrs. Kenwigs' sister; Miss Green, who makes up Mrs. Kenwigs' dresses, Mr. Lillyvick; and Mrs. um, downstairs . . . And, Mr. Lillyvick, this here is Miss Petowker of the Theatre Royal Drury Lane, and very glad I am indeed, to make two public characters acquainted.

MISS PETOWKER. I am so pleased to meet you, sir.

LILLYVICK. Yes, yes, most privileged, I'm sure.

KENWIGS. Now, Morleena, where's your sisters, so they can kiss your uncle? (*Morleena pushes forward the two little Kenwigses, and Mr. Lillyvick's attention is reluctantly removed from Miss Petowker so he can kiss them; meanwhile Mrs. Kenwigs is whispered to about Mr. Noggs by her Sister.*)

SISTER. Why doesn't he . . . the threadbare gentleman?

MRS. KENWIGS. Oh, Mr. Noggs, he'd be embarrassed, to be taken notice of. He was a gentleman, you see, before.

LILLYVICK. And where is little Lillyvick?

MRS. KENWIGS. Oh, uncle, in safe hands, in Miss Green's bed, and sleeping like a baby . . .

LILLYVICK. Well, he is a baby.

MRS. KENWIGS. Yes, and minded by a girl, of course,

MISS GREEN. Who's being paid nine pence,

MRS. KENWIGS. And thus will see to it no harm befalls your namesake, uncle.

LILLYVICK. Yes, it should be so. (*Pause.*) Well. Susan. Kenwigs. Anniversary.

KENWIGS. Eight years.

LILLYVICK. Eight years. I still recall my niece . . .

STOUT LADY. Recalls his niece?

LILLYVICK. That very afternoon, she first acknowledged to her mother a partiality for Kenwigs. "Mother," she says, 'I love him.'

MRS. KENWIGS. Actually, 'adore him,' I said, uncle.

LILLYVICK. "Love him," you said, Susan, I remember it, and instantly her mother cries out 'what?' and falls at once into convulsions.

MRS. CUTLER. What?

MISS GREEN. Convulsions?

LILLYVICK. Into strong convulsions. For, I'm sure that Kenwigs will forgive me saying so, there was a great objection to him, on the grounds that he was so beneath the family, and would disgrace it. You remember, Kenwigs?

KENWIGS. Certainly.

LILLYVICK. And I, I must confess, I shared that feeling . . . and perhaps it's natural, and perhaps it's not . . .

MRS. CUTLER. Well, I'd say—

STOUT LADY. *Quite* natural.

LILLYVICK. And after they were married, I was the first to say that Kenwigs must be taken notice of. And he *was* taken notice of, because I said so; and I'm bound to say, and proud to say, that I have always found him a most honest, well-behaved and upright sort of man. Kenwigs, shake hands.

KENWIGS. (*Doing so.*) I am proud to do it, sir.

LILLYVICK. And so am I.

KENWIGS. And a very happy life I have led with your niece, sir.

LILLYVICK. And it would have been your own fault if you hadn't, sir.

MRS. KENWIGS. (*Overcome.*) Oh, dear Morleena, kiss your uncle once again.

LILLYVICK. Oh. Well . . .

MRS. KENWIGS. And all of you, dear children, come and kiss your uncle . . .

LILLYVICK. Well, indeed, and now to see these three young lively girls . . .

MRS. KENWIGS. Oh, yes, oh yes, they are too beautiful.

LILLYVICK. Too beautiful for what, my dear?

MRS. KENWIGS. Too beautiful to live.

MISS GREEN. Oh, Mrs. Kenwigs. . . . (*Mrs. Kenwigs in tears.*)

MRS. KENWIGS. Oh, far, far too . . .

MRS. CUTLER. Oh, dear Mrs. Kenwigs, please . . .

SISTER. Oh, come now, Susan, don't distress yourself.

MISS GREEN. Don't give way, dear . . .

MRS. KENWIGS. I'm sorry, but I cannot help it, it don't signify. They're just . . . they are too beautiful.

KENWIGS. Um, Mrs. Kenwigs, should, perhaps . . . While Mr. Noggs makes up the punch, Morleena do her figure dance for Mr. Lillyvick?

MISS GREEN. Oh, yes. It is a spectacle.

MRS. KENWIGS. Oh, no, my dear, it will only worry my uncle.

MISS PETOWKER. Come, I'm sure it won't, now will it, Mr. Lillyvick?

LILLYVICK. I'm sure, dear lady, it is most—

MRS. KENWIGS. (*Recovered.*) Well, then, I'll tell you what. Morleena does the steps, if uncle can persuade Miss Petowker to recite for us afterwards the Blood Drinker's Burial. (*Much applause and encouragement.*)

GEORGE. Oh, yes, indeed.

MISS GREEN. Oh that would be a treat.

STOUT LADY. Blood Drinker's what?

MISS PETOWKER. Oh, now, you know that I dislike doing anything professional at private parties.

MRS. KENWIGS. Oh, but not here? We're all so very friendly and pleasant, that you might as well be going through it in your own room; besides, the occasion . . .

MISS PETOWKER. Well . . . I can't resist that, Anything in my humble power, I shall be delighted. (*More applause.*)

KENWIGS. Come, then, everyone, form a space here . . .

MRS. KENWIGS. Morleena, dear, have you chalked your shoes?

STOUT LADY. She's going to do a poem?

MRS. CUTLER. No, a dance.

MISS PETOWKER. All ready? (*Morleena nods. Some musical accompaniment—from Miss Petowker, humming or otherwise; or perhaps another member of the party. Morleena does her dance—"a very beautiful figure, comprising a great deal of work for the arms," and it is received with unbounded applause. During this, Noggs hands round punch.*)

GEORGE. Bravo!

MRS. CUTLER. Quite wonderful.

MISS GREEN. Oh, Mr. Kenwigs, you must be so proud . . .

MR. CUTLER. Can say with confidence, have never seen the like.

MRS. CUTLER. I wouldn't like to meet her teacher, that's all I can say.

MR. CUTLER. I say, I'd like to shake her teacher by the hand.

KENWIGS. Ah, Noggs, please, the collector first . . .

MRS. KENWIGS. (*To Lillyvick.*) You see, how beautifully she . . . Oh, dear me . . .

MISS PETOWKER. You know—(*Miss Petowker gains attention.*) If I was ever, blessed . . . And if my child were, such a genius as that . . . I'd have her in the opera at once.

KENWIGS. The opera?

MISS PETOWKER. What's wrong?

MRS. KENWIGS. I think that Kenwigs thinks . . . the younger dukes and marquises . . .

LILLYVICK. Yes, very right.

MISS PETOWKER. Oh, sir, one only needs to keep one's pride. I've kept my pride, and never had a thing of that sort. Not a thing.

KENWIGS. Well, then. Perhaps we should give it serious consideration. (*Miss Petowker graciously prepares herself. She whispers to George, and they put out some of the lights to give a better effect.*)

STOUT LADY. What's she doing now? Another dance?

MRS. CUTLER. She's going to recite.

STOUT LADY. What, in the dark?

KENWIGS. Ladies and gentlemen. Pray silence, please, for Miss Petowker. (*Applause. Miss Petowker strikes an attitude. During this, Crowl enters and goes towards the party.*)

MISS PETOWKER.

'Twas in a back-street tavern that one night it did perchance,
While the wind was howling fiercely, all the bottles were
    a-dance,
The candle gutted fitful as they, fearful, drank their ale,
When a dark-eyed stranger entered, bought a drink, and
    told a tale.
    Oh, he was a—
(*Crowl knocks loudly.*)
What?

MRS. KENWIGS. What's that?

KENWIGS. It sounded like a—

CROWL. It's Mr. Crowl, and Mr. Noggs is wanted.

KENWIGS. (*Admitting Crowl.*) Mr. Noggs?

NOGGS. Who, me?

CROWL. Two people in his room. Both very queer-looking. And covered up with rain and mud.

NOGGS. What, me? By name?

CROWL. By name. (*To Kenwigs.*) The one's a kind of scrawny chap, and not quite right, it seems to me; the other's straighter, darkish, twenty years or so . . . (*Miss Petowker shrugs at George, who relights candles. Noggs, who has been going towards the exit, turns back.*)

NOGGS. Dark? Twenty years?

CROWL. Or so. (*Suddenly, Noggs rushes back into the room, grabs a candle, and takes the cup of punch from Mr. Lillyvick.*) Excuse me. Please. (*Noggs rushes out.*)Well, look at that—

MRS. KENWIGS. Well, suppose it should be an express sent up to say his property has all come back again, and the express accounting for the mud and—

KENWIGS. Well, it's not impossible, perhaps, in that case, we should send a little extra punch up—

LILLYVICK. Kenwigs. I'm surprised at you.

KENWIGS. Why, what's the matter, sir?

LILLYVICK. (*Standing.*) Why, making such a remark as that, sir. He has had punch already, has he not? My punch, in fact. Now, it may well be customary to allow such things here, but it's not the sort of thing I have been used to, when a gentleman is raising up a glass of punch and then another comes and collars it without a 'with your leave' or 'by your leave' . . . This may be called good manners, but it's not by me, and now it's past my hour to go to bed, and I can find my own way home.

MRS. KENWIGS. Oh, uncle!

KENWIGS. Sir, I'm very sorry, sir.

LILLYVICK. Then it should have been prevented, sir, that's all.

KENWIGS. Well, sir, I didn't . . . Just a glass of punch, to put you out of temper . . .

LILLYVICK. Out of temper? Me? Morleena, get my hat.

MISS PETOWKER. (*Bewitchingly.*) Oh, you're not going, sir . . .

LILLYVICK. I am not wanted here. My hat! (*Morleena, terrified, goes to find Lillyvick's hat.*)

MRS. KENWIGS. Oh, do not speak so, uncle, please . . .

LILLYVICK. My hat!

KENWIGS. (*Grabbing the hat from Morleena.*) Sir, I must grovel at your feet, and beg you, for your niece's sake, that you'll forgive me.

LILLYVICK. Hm?

KENWIGS. For, for your niece's sake. And little Lillyvick.

LILLYVICK. Well, then. (*Pause.*) Well, then. You are forgiven. (*Applause.*) But let me tell you, Kenwigs, that even if I'd gone away without another word, it would have made no difference respecting that pound or two which I shall leave among your children when I die.

MRS. KENWIGS. Morleena Kenwigs. Now, go down upon your knees, next to your father, and beg Mr. Lillyvick to love you all his life, for he is more an angel than a man, and I have always said so. (*Lillyvick smiles benignly as Morleena, rather uncomfortably, kneels beside her Father.*)

MORLEENA. Uh. Uncle Lillyvick. Uh . . . (*Suddenly, three high-pitched screams from another room.*)

KENWIGS. What's that?

GEORGE. Where is it?

MRS. KENWIGS. (*To Miss Green.*) Oh, it's your—oh, my baby! (*Mrs. Kenwigs trying to run out, stopped by her sister.*) Oh, my blessed, blessed—

SISTER. Susan, please—

KENWIGS. Now, I will go at once and—

MRS. KENWIGS. Let me go!

KENWIGS. Come, George—

GEORGE. Of course. Where is the—?

MISS GREEN. Up the stairs, just—

MRS. KENWIGS. Oh, my own dear darling, innocent—Oh, let me *go*—

LILLYVICK. What: Little Lillyvick? (*Kenwigs is nearly out of the room, followed by George, when Nicholas bursts into the room, holding little Lillyvick in his arms.*)

KENWIGS. Oh, sir.

LILLYVICK. What's this? Who's this?

NICHOLAS. (*Breathlessly.*) Don't be alarmed. Here is the baby. Safe and sound.

MRS. KENWIGS. (*Rushing to take the baby from Nicholas.*) Oh, oh, my baby . . .

NICHOLAS. It was—a nothing. All that happened was the little girl who watched the baby fell asleep, and the candle set her hair on fire.

MISS GREEN. The wretch! (*Miss Green strides out.*)

NICHOLAS. I heard her cries. And ran down. And the baby was not touched. I promise you.

MISS PETOWKER. Oh, sir, without you, he would certainly have burned to death.

NICHOLAS. Well, no, I'm sure you would have heard it too, and rushed to her assistance. (*Enter Miss Green, pushing a little girl with singed hair.*)

MISS GREEN. Here is the wretch! Look, here she is. Her head all singed.

MRS. CUTLER. And costing ninepence.

MISS GREEN. Which she *won't* receive. Be off with you!

MRS. CUTLER. Yes, off, off, now! (*The poor little girl is pushed out, the little Kenwigses running to catch a glimpse of her singed head before she's gone.*)

LILLYVICK. Now, sir. You have done service, and we must all drink your health.

NICHOLAS. Well, in my absence, I'm afraid, sir. I have had a very tiring journey, and would be most indifferent company. So please forgive me if I go back up to Mr. Noggs. Good night. (*Nicholas goes out.*)

MRS. KENWIGS. That is—the man.

SISTER. And quite delightful.

KENWIGS. Quite uncommonly. Now, don't you think so, Mr. Lillyvick?

LILLYVICK. Well, yes, he is—he seems to be a gentleman.

MISS PETOWKER. Oh, yes . . . There's something in him, looks, now what's the word?

MISS GREEN. What word?

MISS PETOWKER. You know, when lords and dukes and things go breaking knockers, and playing at coaches, and all that sort of thing?

LILLYVICK. Aristocratic.

MISS PETOWKER. Yes, that's right. That's what he is.

MISS GREEN. Indeed.

KENWIGS. Well, now, perhaps . . . There is still supper to be had . . .

STOUT LADY. Downstairs.

KENWIGS. Downstairs. (*Everyone, going out, as:*)

LILLYVICK. I shall . . . I should esteem it a great honour, Miss Petowker, soon to hear the ending of your recitation.

MISS PETOWKER. Oh, dear Mr. Lillyvick, you shall. I swear you shall. (*And Mr. Lillyvick takes the arm of Miss Petowker, and leads her into supper.*)

Scene Three

Noggs' garret room. Nicholas and Smike, and Noggs, who has a bottle and two glasses. Nicholas sits in Noggs' chair, reading Fanny Squeers' letter.

NICHOLAS. Monster . . . boy of desperate character . . . So, has my uncle yet received this outrageous letter?

NOGGS. Yes, he has—

NICHOLAS. Then, I must go to him at once—

NOGGS. No, no, you mustn't—

NICHOLAS. Mustn't? Why.

NOGGS. Because he hasn't read it yet. And he's, gone away from town. Three days.

NICHOLAS. My mother and sister do not know of this?

NOGGS. They don't.

NICHOLAS. Well, then. At once, I must go to them. Tell me, quick, where are they living? I must go there now.

NOGGS. No, no, you mustn't.

NICHOLAS. Mustn't? Why?

NOGGS. (*Handing glasses to Nicholas and Smike.*) Because . . . please, be advised by me. Your uncle—Do not be seen to be tampering with anyone. You do not know this man. And also—(*He pours a drink for each of them. They don't yet drink it.*)

NICHOLAS. Yes? And also?

NOGGS. You come home, after just three weeks. No money, no position. What—what will your mother—

NICHOLAS. Mr. Noggs, I tell you, that three weeks or three hours, if I had stood by—

NOGGS. I know, I know, but still, my dear young man . . . you can't, you mustn't give way to—this sort of thing will never do, you know, and if you want to get on in the world, if you take the part of everybody that's ill-treated. . . . (*Suddenly, clapping Nicholas on the arm.*) Damn it, I'm proud of you. I would have done the same myself!

NICHOLAS. Oh, Newman, Newman, thank you. But you're right, at least. . . . I must find something. Something to keep myself in shoe-leather. Before I see them. (*Cheerfully.*) Well, tomorrow, I will set about it. (*Depressed again.*) We haven't even got a place to stay.

NOGGS. Well, tonight you stay with me. Tomorrow, there's a room downstairs to let. It's hardly less a mean one than my own, but. . . .

NICHOLAS. Mr. Noggs. Your kindness. Unsurpassable. (*Pause.*) I have three friends. Three friends, in all the world. That bluff young fellow up in Yorkshire; Smike, yourself; and Mr. Noggs, our benefactor. (*Slight pause.*) And it is enough. It is enough, indeed. (*Nicholas drinks his drink. Smike, in imitation drinks his. After a second, the effect hits Smike. His eyes pop. He bangs his chest. Nicholas and Noggs look alarmed. Firmly, Smike puts his glass out to Mr. Noggs for more.*)

Scene Four

Westminster. At once, sounds of many busy people. Set up, on one side of the stage, the office of Sir Matthew Pupker, consisting of a desk, an impressive map of the world, and Sir Matthew himself, sitting on a chair, his feet up on desk, his head covered by The Times, asleep. This happens during the following: a sturdy Deputation, consisting of many firm-faced Gentlemen, enters, as Nicholas appears and speaks out front:

NICHOLAS. And the next morning, Nicholas proceeded to the General Employment Office, in search of a position; where, much to his surprise, he was informed that the great member of Parliament, the renowned Sir Matthew Pupker, was seeking a young man of conscientiousness and character, to fill the position of his secretary, at the Palace of Westminster. (*He turns to the passing Deputation.*) Excuse me . . . I have business with Sir Matthew Pupker—

A DELEGATE. What, you as well? Come, follow me. (*The Deputation is at Sir Matthew's door. It knocks.*)

SIR MATTHEW. Wait! (*Sir Matthew removes the Times from his face, adjusts the map, as Nicholas catches up with the rest of the Deputation.*) Come! (*The Deputation, and Nicholas, enter the room.*) Gentlemen, I am rejoiced to see you. Please, come in. (*Sir Matthew returns to his desk as the leader of the Deputation, a Mr. Pugstyles, pushes himself to the front.*) Now, gentlemen. I see by the newspapers that you are dissatisfied with my conduct as your member.

PUGSTYLES. Yes, we are.

SIR MATTHEW. Well, now, do my eyes deceive me? Or is that my old friend, Pugstyles?

PUGSTYLES. I am that man.

SIR MATTHEW. Give me your hand, my worthy friend. Pugstyles, I am so sorry you are here.

PUGSTYLES. I am sorry too, but your conduct has rendered this deputation quite imperative.

SIR MATTHEW. My conduct, Pugstyles? You speak of my conduct?

PUGSTYLES. Yes.

SIR MATTHEW. Well, then . . . (*Rhetorically.*) My conduct, gentlemen, has been, and ever will be, regulated by a sincere regard for the true interests of this great and happy country. Whenever I behold the peaceful, industrious communities of our island home, I clasp my hands, and turning my eyes to the broad expanse above my head, exclaim, 'Thank heaven, that I am a Briton!' (*Long pause.*)

A DELEGATE. Gammon.

SIR MATTHEW. The meaning of that term, I must confess, is quite unknown to me. But if it means you think I'm too benign, too sanguine, too complacent, sir, you would be right. (*He goes to the map and gestures.*) For e'en as we sit here, and lightly chatter, Russia's surly armies, fixed on vile conquest, surge across her borders, threatening the very jugular . . . Sir, do you know Kabul?

THIRD DELEGATE. No, sir.

SIR MATTHEW. Or have you met the Amir of the Afghans, he whose name is perfidy?

THIRD DELEGATE. I have not, sir.

SIR MATTHEW. Or heard the hideous war-cry of the Slavic hordes, intent on rape and pillage?

THIRD DELEGATE. No, I have not heard the Slavic hordes, sir, or their hideous war-cry.

SIR MATTHEW. Well . . . well then. What is the little matter you would speak of? Fishing rights, or water-rates, or timber duty? (*Pugstyles puts on his spectacles and takes out a list of questions. The rest of the Deputation also take out lists of questions, to check Pugstyles' reading.*)

PUGSTYLES. Question number one. Whether, sir, you did not give a voluntary pledge, that in the event of your being returned you would immediately put down the practice of coughing and groaning in the House of Commons. And whether you did not submit to being coughed and groaned down in the very first debate of the session? (*Pause.*)

SIR MATTHEW. Go on to the next one, my dear Pugstyles.

PUGSTYLES. Have you any explanation to offer with reference to that question, sir?

SIR MATTHEW. Certainly not. (*The Deputation looks at each other. Pugstyles breathes deeply, and continues.*)

PUGSTYLES. Question number two. Whether, sir, you did not likewise give a voluntary pledge that you would support your colleagues on every occasion; and whether you did not, the night before last, desert them and vote upon the other side, because the wife of a leader on that other side had invited Lady Pupker to an evening party? (*Pause.*)

SIR MATTHEW. Go on.

PUGSTYLES. Nothing to say on that either, sir?

SIR MATTHEW. Nothing whatever. (*Pause.*)

PUGSTYLES. So, Question number three. If, sir, you did not state upon the hustings, that it was your firm and determined intention, if elected, to vote at once for universal suffrage and triennial parliaments?

SIR MATTHEW. Oh, no!

THE DEPUTATION. Oh! Oh!

SIR MATTHEW. No, not at all. What happened was, that an illiterate voter in the crowd inquired if I would vote for universal suffering and triangular parliaments. To which I replied, in jest of course, "why, certainly." (*A groan from the Deputation.*) So, is that all?

PUGSTYLES. No. Question four. Will you resign?

SIR MATTHEW. No.

PUGSTYLES. Sorry?

SIR MATTHEW. I said, no.

PUGSTYLES. You won't resign, under any circumstances?

SIR MATTHEW. Absolutely not.

PUGSTYLES. Then . . . Then, good morning, sir. (*The Deputation turns to go.*)

SIR MATTHEW. Good morning to you all. (*As the Deputation leaves.*) God bless you! Every one! (*Left alone, as he thinks, Sir Matthew notices Nicholas.*) What? Who's this?

NICHOLAS. It's me, sir.

SIR MATTHEW. Ha! A secret voter! Out, sir, out, you've heard my answer. Follow out your deputation.

NICHOLAS. I should have done so if I had belonged to it.

SIR MATTHEW. (*Tossing down the map.*) You don't? Then what the devil are you in here for?

NICHOLAS. I wish to offer myself as your secretary.

SIR MATTHEW. That's all you came for, is it?

NICHOLAS. Yes.

SIR MATTHEW. You've no connection with the papers?

NICHOLAS. No.

SIR MATTHEW. And what's your name?

NICHOLAS. My name is Nickleby. (*Slight pause. Sir Matthew eyes Nicholas beadily.*)

SIR MATTHEW. Related to Ralph Nickleby?

NICHOLAS. I am.

SIR MATTHEW. Well, then, sit down.

SIR MATTHEW. So, you want to be my secretary, do you?

NICHOLAS. Yes.

SIR MATTHEW. Well, what can you do?

NICHOLAS. Well, I suppose that I can do what usually falls to the lot of other secretaries.

SIR MATTHEW. What's that?

NICHOLAS. Well, I presume, correspondence . . .

SIR MATTHEW. Good.

NICHOLAS. The arrangement of papers and documents—

SIR MATTHEW. Very good, what else?

NICHOLAS. Well, um—the general one, of making myself as agreeable and useful as I can.

SIR MATTHEW. Well, now, that's all very well, young Mr. Nickleby, as far as it goes, but it don't go far enough. I should require, for example, to be crammed, sir.

NICHOLAS. Crammed?

SIR MATTHEW. Yes, crammed. My secretary would need to make himself acquainted with all domestic and all international affairs, to scan the newspapers for paragraphs of lasting or of passing interest, for revolutions, wars, disturbances in Birmingham, "the mysterious disappearance of a potboy," on which I might found a speech or question; he would be required, as well, to study all the printed tables, and to work up arguments about the dire consequences of a raise in tax, or else the terrible result of lowering it, on why we need to increase government expenditure, on the national defence, or else decrease it, to encourage thrift among the lower classes; of gold bullion, and the supply of money, all those things it's only necessary to talk fluently about, as no-one understands 'em; and that's just a hasty, basic outline of your duties, except of course for waiting in the lobby every night, and sitting in the gallery, and pointing me out to the populace, and noting that that sleeping gentleman's none other than the celebrated and renowned Sir Matthew Pupker, and for salary, I'll say at once, although it's much more than I'm used to give, it's fifteen shillings every week and find yourself. So. Any questions? (*Pause.*)

NICHOLAS. One. While I'm performing all your duties, sir, may I inquire what you'll be doing?

SIR MATTHEW. Eh?

NICHOLAS. I said, while I'm performing all your duties, sir, may I inquire what you'll be doing? (*Pause.*)

SIR MATTHEW. Out! Get out! Out, now!

NICHOLAS. (*Turns to go.*) I'm sorry to have troubled you.

SIR MATTHEW. Well, so am I. Out, upstart! Troublemaker! (*Nicholas has been going, but he turns back.*)

NICHOLAS. Humbug.

SIR MATTHEW. Chartist!

NICHOLAS. Charlatan!

SIR MATTHEW. Potboy!

NICHOLAS. Politician! (*This is too much. Sir Matthew goes, and Nicholas does too.*)

Scene Five

The Mantalinis' workroom and showroom. In the workroom, the Milliners, Miss Knag entering, and Kate. In the showroom, an Old Lord, his Young Fiancee and Madame Mantalini.

MISS KNAG. Well, bless you, dear, how very clumsy you were yesterday, again.

KATE. I know, Miss Knag.

MISS KNAG. But don't you worry, I can do all that needs doing, and all you have to do is stay quiet before company and your awkwardness will not be noticed.

KATE. No, indeed.

MISS KNAG. Oh, I do take the liveliest of interests in you, dear, upon my word. It's a sister's interest, actually. It's the most singular circumstance I ever knew. (*Madame Mantalini pulls a bell pull. A bell rings.*) Ah, that's the showroom. Now, perhaps it's best dear, after yesterday, if you do not come up. (*Unlikely.*) Unless, of course, you're called for. (*Miss Knag to the showroom.*)

1st MILLINER. Well.

2nd MILLINER. *Well.*

3rd MILLINER. Has herself took a shine to you. (*The focus shifts to the showroom, as the Milliners narrate.*)

MILLINERS.

And it so happened that an old lord of great family,

Who was going to marry a young lady of no family in particular,

Came with the young lady to witness the ceremony of trying on two nuptial bonnets,

80

Which were presented to her by Miss Knag,

In a charming if not breathless state of palpitation.

(*Miss Knag now in the showroom. The Old Lord is very upper class, very lecherous, and a bit gaga. The Young Financee is not very upper class at all.*)

YOUNG FIANCEE. Well, now. How d'I look?

MADAME MANTALINI. Oh, mademoiselle, tres elegante.

MISS KNAG. Mais oui. C'est entierement exquise, n'est ce pas?

YOUNG FIANCEE. Exsqueeze?

MISS KNAG. Exquisite.

YOUNG FIANCEE. Oh, yes? Is that so? (*A slight hiatus.*)

MADAME MANTALINI. So what do you think, my lord?

YOUNG FIANCEE. Yur, do you think that I'll look fitting, darling?

OLD LORD. Fitting?

YOUNG FIANCEE. For our wedding day.

OLD LORD. Oh, yes. Oh, very fitting. For our wedding day. (*The Young Fiancee blushes, grins, and pokes the Old Lord.*)

YOUNG FIANCEE. Oh, you are, really.

OLD LORD. Am I? Am I, really?

YOUNG FIANCEE. Yur, you are. (*Miss Knag a clucking, disapproving look at Madame Mantalini. The Young Fiancee notices it.*) Mm? Can I help you?

MISS KNAG. Peut-etre—

YOUNG FIANCEE. Pardon?

MISS KNAG. Would madam care to try—?

YOUNG FIANCEE. Yur, why not. (*The Young Fiancee, trying on another bonnet.*) Oh, by the way, dear Madame Mantalini?

MADAME MANTALINI. Mademoiselle?

YOUNG FIANCEE. Tell me, where is that pretty creature we saw yesterday? The young one.

MADAME MANTALINI. Pretty . . . young . . .

MISS KNAG. (*Helpfully.*) Miss Nickleby.

YOUNG FIANCEE. That's right. 'Cos if there's one thing that I can't abide, it's being waited on by frights.

MISS KNAG. Frights, no.

MADAME MANTALINI. By—what? (*Miss Knag has got there.*)

YOUNG FIANCEE. By frights. By old frights, in particular. Well, elderly. (*Pause.*)

MADAME MANTALINI. Mais oui. Certainement. Miss Knag, send up Miss Nickleby.

MISS KNAG. Bring up?

MADAME MANTALINI. Send up. You need not return. (*Pause. Miss Knag goes out as the Young Fiancee looks at her new bonnet in the mirror.*)

YOUNG FIANCEE. Oh, yur. Mais oui. C'est entirement exquise. (*Focus shifts back to the workroom as Miss Knag enters.*)

MISS KNAG. (*To Kate.*) You're wanted in the showroom.

KATE. Me?

MISS KNAG. Yes, you. You have been Asked For.

KATE. Oh, I . . . very well. (*She goes to the door. Miss Knag rather obviously not following.*) Are you not coming?

MISS KNAG. I? Why should I come? A fright like me? (*Pause.*)

1st MILLINER. What's that?

2nd MILLINER. A fright?

MISS KNAG. Why should I come? You chit, you child, you upstart!

KATE. Please, Miss Knag, what have I done?

MISS KNAG. What have you done? She asks me, what she's done?

3rd MILLINER. (*Whispers to 2nd Milliner.*) What has she done?

MISS KNAG. I'll tell you what I've done, my dear Miss Nickleby, what I've done is to be, for fifteen years, the ornament of this room and the one upstairs. And what have you done? Nothing.

KATE. Well, I would not—

MISS KNAG. And never, fifteen years, have I been victim of the vile arts, a creature who disgraces us with her proceedings, and makes proper people blush to see her machinations.

KATE. Miss Knag, what have I—

MISS KNAG. Yes, here she is, look carefully . . . the one who everyone is talking of, the belle, the beauty . . . Oh, you boldfaced thing!

KATE. Miss Knag, please tell me—

MISS KNAG. I will tell you. Go! You're asked for in the showroom. Go! (*Kate stands a moment, shrugs desperately and goes out. Pause. Miss Knag throws herself into a chair. She is surrounded by Milliners.*) Oh, have I worked here, fifteen years. And to be called a fright. (*Pause.*)

1st MILLINER. Oh, no.

3rd MILLINER. Oh, absolutely not.

MISS KNAG. And have I laboured, all these years, to be called elderly.

2nd MILLINER. What, elderly?

1st MILLINER. Well, what a thing to say.

MISS KNAG. (*Stands.*) I hate her. I detest and hate her. Never let her speak to me again. And never let anyone who is a friend of mine have words with her. The slut. The hussy. Impudent and artful, hussy!

Scene Six

Downstage, Noggs' garret, represented by his chair. Noggs and Smike. Upstage, the Kenwigs' room, with Mrs. Kenwigs, Morleena, the two Little Kenwigses, Mr. Lillyvick and Miss Petowker. We will discover that Mr. Lillyvick has a glass of brandy and a jug of water. Enter Nicholas.

NICHOLAS. And so, with a sad and pensive air, Nicholas retraced his steps homewards.

NOGGS. Come back?

NICHOLAS. Yes, and tired to death, and might have stayed at home for all the good I've done.

NOGGS. Couldn't expect too much, one morning.

NICHOLAS. Well, I did. And so am disappointed. I see little to choose between assisting a brutal pedagogue and being a toadeater to a mean and ignorant upstart, member or no member. Oh, Newman, show me in all this wide waste of London, any honest means by which I could at least defray the hire of our poor room; I would not shrink from it, I will do anything, except that which offends my common pride.

NOGGS. Well, then . . . I hardly know . . .

NICHOLAS. Yes? What?

NOGGS. There is a prospect I could offer. . . .

NICHOLAS. Please, dear Newman, tell me.

NOGGS. It concerns the Kenwigses, downstairs. I told them you were Mr. Johnson, thinking perhaps, your circumstances being, as it were . . .

NICHOLAS. Yes, yes.

NOGGS. And said you were a teacher, and she said, well, having talked to Mr. Kenwigs, as is only right, she said that she had long been searching for a tutor for her little ones, to teach them French as spoken by the natives, at the weekly stipend of four shillings current coin, being at the rate of a one a week per each Miss Kenwigs, with a shilling over for the baby. That's all, and I know it's beneath you, but—

NICHOLAS. Dear Newman. I accept at once. Please tell the worthy mother, now, without delay.

NOGGS. (*Delighted.*) Right, then.

(*Narration into the Kenwigs' room, in which will be Mr. Lillyvick, Miss Petowker, Mrs. Kenwigs, Morleena, the Little Kenwigses and Nicholas. Noggs and Smike will have gone.*)

NOGGS. And Newman hastened with joyful steps to inform Mrs. Kenwigs of his friend's acquiescence,

NICHOLAS. And soon returning, brought back word that they would be happy to see Mr. Johnson in the first floor as soon as convenient,

NOGGS. And that Mrs. Kenwigs had upon the instant sent out to secure a second-hand French grammar and dialogues,

MISS PETOWKER. Which had long been fluttering in the sixpenny box at the bookstall round the corner,

MRS. KENWIGS. And that the family,

LILLYVICK. Highly excited at the prospect of this addition to their gentility,

MRS. KENWIGS. Wished the initiatory lesson to come off

MORLEENA. Immediately!

MRS. KENWIGS. Now, uncle, this is Mr. Johnson.

LILLYVICK. How d'ye do, sir?

NICHOLAS. Splendid, thank you sir.

MRS. KENWIGS. Mr. Johnson, this is Mr. Lillyvick, my uncle, The Collector Of The Water Rate.

NICHOLAS. (*Uncertain of how he is supposed to react to this intelligence.*) The Water Rate? Indeed.

MRS. KENWIGS. And this is Miss Petowker, of the Theatre Royal Drury Lane.

NICHOLAS. Oh, I am highly honoured. (*Wrong.*) To make, both of your acquaintances.

MRS. KENWIGS. Now, Mr. Johnson is engaged as a private master to the children, uncle.

LILLYVICK. Yes, Susan, so you said.

MRS. KENWIGS. But I hope, Mr. Johnson, that they don't boast about it to the other children, and that if they must say anything about it, they don't say no more than: "We've got a private master come to teach us at home, but we ain't proud, because ma says it's sinful." Do you hear, Morleena?

MORLEENA. Yes, ma.

MRS. KENWIGS. Then mind you recollect, and do as I tell you. Shall Mr. Johnson begin, then, uncle?

LILLYVICK. In a moment, Susan, in a moment. First, I'd like to ask a question. Sir, how do you think of French?

NICHOLAS. What do you mean, sir?

LILLYVICK. Do you view it as a good language, sir? A pretty language? Sensible?

NICHOLAS. A pretty language, certainly. And as it has a name for everything, and admits of elegant conversation on all topics, I assume it's sensible as well.

LILLYVICK. I see. (*Gesturing with his glass.*) So, what's the French for this, then, sir?

NICHOLAS. For brandy?

LILLYVICK. No, for water. As in, "water rate."

NICHOLAS. Oh, water, sir, is "l'eau."

LILLYVICK. I thought as much. You hear that, Miss Petowker? Water. Low. I don't think anything of that. I don't think anything of French at all.

MRS. KENWIGS. But, still, the children may—

LILLYVICK. Oh, yes. Oh, let them learn it. I have no wish to prevent them. (*Pause. Miss Petowker a slight smile. Mrs. Kenwigs nervously.*)

MRS. KENWIGS. Well, then . . . Mr. Johnson?

NICHOLAS. Well, then . . . Lesson One. (*Enter Noggs, breathless.*)

NOGGS. Oh—oh, Mr. Johnson, this is terrible—

LILLYVICK. What's this?

MRS. KENWIGS. Why, Mr. Noggs!

NOGGS. He's back again—he's gone off to your mother's—

NICHOLAS. What?

NOGGS. —your uncle, and I got the wrong day and I'm terribly—

LILLYVICK. (*To Miss Petowker.*) It's him again.

NICHOLAS. Oh, I must go there now.

NOGGS. Yes. Yes, I s'pose you must.

MRS. KENWIGS. But Mr. Johnson—

NICHOLAS. Oh—uh—mes enfants . . . on doit continuer la lecon demain. Pardon. (*To Lillyvick, taking his drink and giving it to Noggs.*) Pardon. (*Nicholas rushes out.*)

Scene Seven

The Nicklebys' house in Thames St. All that is needed is one chair for Mrs. Nickleby. Miss La Creevy, Kate and Ralph are also there. Ralph is folding up Fanny Squeers' letter.

KATE. No, I won't believe it. Never. It's a lie, that they've invented.

RALPH. No, my dear, you wrong the worthy man. These aren't inventions. Mr. Squeers has been assaulted, Nicholas is gone, the boy goes with him. It's all true.

KATE. It can't be true. Mama, how can you stand there, listening to this?

RALPH. She's no choice, my dear. Her son's committed conduct for which he might well hold up his head at the Old Bailey. (*Pause.*) And it would be my duty, if he came my way, to give him up to justice. As a man of honour and of business, I would have no other course. Though I would wish to spare the feelings of his mother, and his sister.

MISS LA CREEVY. Perhaps I'd better . . .

KATE. No, please, Miss La Creevy, stay.

RALPH. (*Suddenly, forcefully, waving the letter.*) Madam, everything combines to prove the truth of this. He steals away at night, he skulks off with an outlaw boy? Assault, and riot? Is this innocent? (*Unnoticed by anyone, Nicholas stands there.*)

MRS. NICKLEBY. Well, I don't know, I'm sure.

KATE. Oh, mother!

MRS. NICKLEBY. And I never would have thought it of him, certainly.

KATE. You never *would have* thought?

MRS. NICKLEBY. Your uncle—is your uncle, dear.

NICHOLAS. But what he says is still untrue.

RALPH. Oh. You.

MRS. NICKLEBY. Oh, Nicholas! (*Nicholas marching towards Ralph, Kate getting in the way.*)

KATE. Oh, Nicholas, be calm, consider.

NICHOLAS. What?

KATE. Please, please, consider . . . and refute these accusations.

NICHOLAS. What are they? Tell me what he's said to you.

RALPH. I've said, sir, what is true. That you attacked your master, and you nearly killed him, and you ran away. (*Pause. Nicholas is calmer now.*)

NICHOLAS. I see. (*Nicholas speaks to Kate and Mrs. Nickleby, not to Ralph.*) I interfered to save a miserable creature from the vilest cruelty. In doing so, I did inflict punishment upon the wretch who was abusing him. And if the same scene was repeated now, I'd take exactly the same part. Except, that I would strike him heavier and harder.

RALPH. Hm. The penitent.

KATE. Please, Nicholas, where is this boy?

NICHOLAS. He's with me now.

RALPH. Will you restore him?

NICHOLAS. No. Not to that man. Not ever.

MRS. NICKLEBY. Oh, I don't know what to think . . .

RALPH. Now, sir, you'll listen to a word or two?

NICHOLAS. Say what you like. I shan't take heed of it.

RALPH. Then I won't speak to you, but to your mother. She may find it worth her while to listen, because what I have to say is, that he, Nicholas, shall not have access to one penny of my money, or one crust of my bread, or one grasp of my hand that might save him from the gallows. I will not meet him, and I will not hear his name. I will not help him, nor help anyone who helps him. So now he knows what he has brought on you, by coming back, and as I will not ask you to renounce him, I must renounce you. (*Pause.*)

MRS. NICKLEBY. Oh, I can't help it—

RALPH. What?

MRS. NICKLEBY. I know you have been good to us. But still, I—even if he has done everything you say—

KATE. You heard what he said, mother—

MRS. NICKLEBY. Still. I can't renounce my son. I really can't. (*Pause. Mrs. Nickleby weeping.*) And all that, thinking that he'd be headmaster. . . .

RALPH. Then I'll go.

NICHOLAS. You needn't.

RALPH. Needn't I?

NICHOLAS. Because I will. (*Kate runs to Nicholas and embraces him.*)

KATE. Nicholas, oh Nicholas, don't say so, or you'll break my heart . . . Mama, please speak to him. Mama, don't let him go. Don't leave us here, with no-one to protect us. Please.

NICHOLAS. I can't protect you. How can I protect you?

RALPH. My dear, there is your answer.

MRS. NICKLEBY. Oh, Kate. We'll go to rack and ruin. To the workhouse, or the Refuge for the Destitute. Or Magdalen Hospital. One or the other. Or the third. (*Nicholas takes Kate's arms from him.*)

NICHOLAS. No, mother. I'm the one that's going.

KATE. (*Horrified.*) Where? Where, Nicholas?

NICHOLAS. Don't know. (*Pause.*) It is hard. To have done nothing, but to be proscribed, just like a criminal. And to be forced to leave the ones I love. It is quite hard to bear. But still, I must, or else . . . you're destitute.

KATE. It might be—years.

NICHOLAS. Don't know. (*Nicholas turns to go. Kate runs after him, embraces him.*)
KATE. Please, you won't—
NICHOLAS. I must—
KATE. You won't forget us. Everything we had. The days, the years we spent together.
NICHOLAS. (*Taking her arms from him.*) And I don't need to entreat your sympathy. I know you won't forget them.
MISS LA CREEVY. No.
NICHOLAS. (*To Ralph.*) This isn't over. You will hear from me. (*To Kate.*) Oh, my darling girl. (*Nicholas goes out, leaving Mrs. Nickleby, Miss La Creevy, and Kate.*)

Scene Eight

The street. Early morning. Bare stage. Nicholas, Smike and Noggs appear during the narration, which is delivered by members of the company who stand round, watching the scene. Nicholas ana Smike have bundles. Noggs has a can.

NARRATORS.
It was a cold, foggy morning in early Spring . . .

And a few meagre shadows flitted to and fro in the misty streets.

At intervals were heard the tread of slipshod feet,

And the chilly cry of the sweep as he crept shivering to his early toil;

The sluggish darkness thickened as the day came on,

And those who had the courage to rise and peep at the gloomy street from their curtained windows,

Crept back to bed again,

And coiled themselves up to sleep.

NICHOLAS. But Nicholas and Smike were up,

NOGGS. And Newman too, who had expended a day's income on a can of rum and milk to prepare them for their journey. (*Smike shoulders the bundles.*) Which way are you going?

NICHOLAS. Kingston first.

NOGGS. And afterwards? (*Slight pause.*) Why won't you tell me?

NICHOLAS. Because I scarcely know myself.

NOGGS. I am afraid you have some deep scheme in your head.

NICHOLAS. So deep that even I can't fathom it. Don't worry, I'll write soon.

NOGGS. You won't forget?

NICHOLAS. Oh, I'm not likely to. I've not so many friends that I can grow confused about the number, and forget the very best.

NOGGS. And, despite Newman's insistence that he be allowed to walk an hour or two with them,

NICHOLAS. Nicholas and Smike eventually made their farewells and turned, and left, and turned again,

NOGGS. To see their friend still waving to them,

NICHOLAS. Till they turned the corner, and could see old Newman Noggs no more. (*Noggs has gone. Smike and Nicholas trudging on.*)

NICHOLAS. Now, listen to me, Smike. We're bound for Portsmouth.

SMIKE. Ports—mouth.

NICHOLAS. Yes, because it is a seaport town, and I am thinking we might board some ship. I'm young and active, so are you.

SMIKE. And I am very willing.

NICHOLAS. Yes, you are. Too willing, for example, with that bundle. Let me carry it a while.

SMIKE. (*Stops.*) No. No.

NICHOLAS. (*Stops.*) Why not?

SMIKE. Because I thought of carrying it. For you. (*They walk on. Narration:*)

NARRATORS.

It was by this time within an hour of noon, and although dense vapour still enclosed the city they had left,

As if to clothe its schemes of gain and profit,

In the open country it was clear and fair.

SMIKE. Hey. I—

NICHOLAS. Yes, Smike?

SMIKE. The ship. On ship. I, when I was at—that place—(*He doesn't want to name Dotheboys Hall.*)

NICHOLAS. Yes?

SMIKE. I used to milk the cows and groom the horses.

NICHOLAS. Um—it is a ship, Smike. Not that many cows and horses on board ship. Well, I don't believe . . . (*Smike looks at Nicholas. He gets the joke. It's infectious. Nicholas laughs too. Music plays and the Narrators sing. As they sing, Smike jumps on Nicholas' back, and the two of them career round the stage, blissfully happy.*)

NARRATORS. (*Sing.*)*

A broad fine honest sun
Lighted up the green pasture
And dimpled water with the semblance of summer,
Leaving the travellers with the freshness of spring.

The ground seemed to quicken their feet,
The sheep bells were music to their ears,
And hoping made them strong
And strength awakened hope
And they pushed onward with the courage of lions.

And so the day wore on
And so the day wore on
And so the day wore on.

(*Nicholas and Smike stop, put down the bundles, and sit.*)

NICHOLAS. Smike. Do you have a good memory?

SMIKE. I don't know. I had once, I think. But now all gone.

NICHOLAS. Why do you think you had one once?

SMIKE. Because I could remember, when I was a child.

NICHOLAS. Do you remember, when you went to Yorkshire? What the day was like. The weather, hot or cold?

SMIKE. Wet. Very wet. And afterwards. When it was raining. I could see myself. The day I came.

NICHOLAS. Did you come there alone?

SMIKE. No. No. A man—a dark and withered man, they used to say. And I think I remember, too. Remember—being frightened of him. Glad he went away. But frightened at the place he left me, too.

NICHOLAS. Now look at me. Don't turn away. Do you remember, any-

* See special note on copyright page.

thing or anyone or anywhere, before that house in Yorkshire? Think, Smike, think. (*Pause.*)

SMIKE. A room. (*Slight pause.*) I slept once in a room, a large and lonesome room, beneath the attic, there was a hook in the ceiling above me. I was frightened of it, covered up my head. (*Pause.*) Used to dream. Dream terribly about the room. And people in it. Things, that changed. But that room—never changes. (*Pause.*) Till now, I have not known two days together, when I haven't been afraid. (*A Narrator—the actor who will play the Landlord, enters, as a table and a bench are brought in behind him.*)

LANDLORD. And the sun went down, and in the morning it rose up again, and they rose with it, and walked onwards, until Smike could go no further. And they found a little inn, yet twelve miles short of Portsmouth.

Scene Nine

The courtyard of a roadside inn. The Landlord, sitting on the bench beside the table. Nicholas and Smike standing there, looking bedraggled and tired.

NICHOLAS. Ah. How far to Portsmouth, sir?

LANDLORD. Twelve miles. Long miles.

NICHOLAS. A good road?

LANDLORD. No. A bad one.

NICHOLAS. We must get to Portsmouth by tonight.

LANDLORD. Well, don't let me influence you, in any way . . . But if I were you, I wouldn't go.

NICHOLAS. You wouldn't?

LANDLORD. No.

NICHOLAS. Look, I . . . Look here, it's obvious enough. We are both, very humble, and we can't afford to stay the night. But if you had a little food . . . ?

LANDLORD. What would you like?

NICHOLAS. Cold meat?

LANDLORD. No, sorry.

NICHOLAS. Mutton chops?

LANDLORD. Clean out.

NICHOLAS. An egg?

LANDLORD. No, yesterday, had more than we could cope with. And tomorrow, mountains of 'em coming in.

NICHOLAS. Today?

LANDLORD. No eggs today. (*Enter Mr. Vincent Crummles and his sons, Master Crummles and Master P. Crummles. Mr. Crummles is a theatrical manager. His sons are dressed in sailor suits, and are presently practising a stage fight with wooden swords. The fight finishes spectacularly, with the defeat of the taller Master Crummles by the shorter Master P. Crummles. Crummles himself applauds.*)

CRUMMLES. That's capital! You'll get a double encore if you take care, boys. You'd better go and get your travelling clothes on now. (*The boys go out, one of them leaving his sword where it fell. Nicholas to the Landlord.*)

NICHOLAS. Well, then, we'll have to walk on hungry. Portsmouth, twelve bad miles. (*Nicholas and Smike turn to go.*)

CRUMMLES. Portsmouth?

NICHOLAS. Sir?

CRUMMLES. You're set for Portsmouth?

NICHOLAS. Yes, we—

CRUMMLES. So am I.

NICHOLAS. I'm pleased to hear it, sir. (*Crummles comes over.*)

CRUMMLES. And may I venture, short of money for the stage?

NICHOLAS. You've guessed it, sir.

CRUMMLES. Why, then, you'll ride with me, upon my phaeton.

NICHOLAS. Um—

CRUMMLES. That's settled. Landlord, see my pony's fetched. (*The Landlord goes out. Crummles sees the dropped sword, picks it up, and waves it.*) So, what d'you think of that, sir?

NICHOLAS. What? Oh, very good indeed. Quite—capital.

CRUMMLES. You won't see such as that too often.

NICHOLAS. No. And if they'd been, perhaps, a little better matched—

CRUMMLES. What, matched? Why sir, it's the very essence of the combat that there should be a foot or two between 'em. Otherwise, how are you to get up the sympathies of the audience in a legitimate manner?

NICHOLAS. Oh, I see. They are—you are—theatricals?

CRUMMLES. Why yes, of course. And playing Portsmouth from tonight. Yes, I am Vincent Crummles, and I am in the theatrical profession, my wife is in the theatrical profession, and my children are in the theatrical profession. I had a dog that lived and died in it from a puppy, and my chaise-pony goes on in Timour the Tartar. (*The Master Crummleses re-enter with baggage. Re-enter, too, the Landlord, and a stable-boy. During the following, they move the table, place the bench in front of it, and pile baggage on the table, so that the table is converted into the small carriage that Crummles calls his "phaeton." The final additions are two washing tubs and a water-pump, piled on top, and two reins, running out from the front of the table, which, when Crummles picks them up, will suggest the presence of the imaginary pony in front of the carriage.*) Ah, now it's just my baggage, and we're set to go.

NICHOLAS. This is—this is most generous.

CRUMMLES. Oh, not at all. It's my self-interest. I have an eye for talent, Mr. . . . .

NICHOLAS. Oh, uh, Johnson.

CRUMMLES. Johnson? And yours struck me immediately.

NICHOLAS. Talent for what?

CRUMMLES. Why, for the stage! There's genteel comedy, your walk and manner, juvenile tragedy, your eye, and touch-and-go farce in your laugh.

NICHOLAS. But, sir—

CRUMMLES. (*Dropping his voice.*) And as for your, associate, I've never seen a better for the starving business. Only let him be quite tolerably well-dressed for the Apothecary—Romeo and Juliet—the slightest red dab on his nose, and he'll be guaranteed three rounds the moment he pops his head round the practicable door.

NICHOLAS. The practicable—

CRUMMLES. In the front grooves, O.P. Sir, can you write?

NICHOLAS. Well, I am not illiterate.

CRUMMLES. Well, that could not be better. You will write our new piece, for a week on Monday, if you'd be so kind. Now, boys—

NICHOLAS. But, sir—I can't—I've never written anything.

CRUMMLES. What stuff! Do you speak French?

NICHOLAS. Yes, like a native. (*Crummles takes a script from a bag and tosses it to Nicholas.*)

CRUMMLES. Then turn that into English, put your name on it, and there's the play. Oh, but for one more thing . . . I've just bought a real pump and two fine washing tubs—I got 'em cheap—and you must work them in. You know, the bills, we'll advertise 'em: "Splendid Tubs," "A Real Pump," that kind of thing, you'll probably be writing out the bills yourself, now are we set and can we go?

NICHOLAS. Sir, I must ask one more question. (*Crummles turns back.*)

CRUMMLES. Ask away.

NICHOLAS. Will I be paid for this?

CRUMMLES. Will you be paid? Will you be paid? Dear sir, with your own salary, your friend's, and royalties, you'll make a pound a week!

NICHOLAS. A pound a week.

CRUMMLES. At least. Now come, sirs, come. (*Nicholas turns to Smike who is looking rapt.*)

NICHOLAS. Well, Smike, what times we've fallen on, who could have . . . Smike?

SMIKE. The stage! (*Everyone now on the phaeton. Music, a light change, and horse-shoe effect from off. Crummles has picked up the reins, and everyone mimes being on a moving vehicle. The Landlord and Stable-boy have gone.*)

CRUMMLES. (*With a nod at the pony.*) He's a good pony at bottom.

NICHOLAS. I am sure of it.

CRUMMLES. And quite one of us. His mother was on the stage, of course.

NICHOLAS. She was?

CRUMMLES. Yes, yes, ate apple-pie at a circus for upwards of fourteen years, fired pistols, went to bed in a nightcap, and in short, took the low comedy entirely. (*Crummles, confidentially, to Nicholas.*) His father was a dancer.

NICHOLAS. Oh? Distinguished?

CRUMMLES. No, not very. The fact is, that he'd been jobbed out in the days originally, and never lost his bad habits. He was cleverish in melodrama, but too broad, too broad. And when the mother died, he took the port-wine business.

NICHOLAS. Port-wine business.

CRUMMLES. Yes, you know, the drinking of the port-wine with the clown. But he was greedy, and one night he bit the bowl right off, and choked himself to death. Vulgarity—the end of him at last. (*And they have arrived. Everyone gets off the phaeton, and the boys strike the props, bench and table, as:*) Well, here we are boys, Portsmouth, for three weeks. All men have their trials, and this is ours. Come on, boys, bustle, bustle.

NICHOLAS. And Nicholas jumped out, and, giving Smike his arm, accompanied the manager up the High Street towards the theatre, feeling nervous and uncomfortable at the prospect of an introduction to a scene so new to him. (*Nicholas follows Crummles out. Smike and the Master Crummleses follow, too.*)

Scene Ten

The stage of the Portsmouth Theatre. It is bare, and looks very dusty and dour. Enter most of the Crummles Theatre Company. They are Mr. Bane, Mr. Wagstaff, Mr. Pailey, Mr. Fluggers, Mr. Hethering-

ton, Mr. Blightey, Miss Bravassa, Miss Belvawney, Miss Gazingi, Mrs. Lenville, and, at the centre of it all, Mrs. Crummles. A moment as they survey the scene. Then Mrs. Grudden, the Stage Manager, pulls a clothes rail across the stage. A certain amount of animation follows: Mr. Bane and Mr. Hetherington fetch a chair and table for Mrs. Crummles, others open luggage, practise attitudes, look round. The bustle continues throughout the scene. Enter Crummles, Nicholas, Smike and the Master Crummleses.

CRUMMLES. Well, here we are. Good afternoon to one and all. And welcome to Portsmouth! (*The Performers look back, not very enthusiastically. Mrs. Crummles calls to her husband.*)

MRS. CRUMMLES. Vincent.

CRUMMLES. (*Going to her.*) Ah—Mrs. Crummles.

MRS. CRUMMLES. Vincent. (*They embrace. Mrs. Crummles notices Nicholas and Smike.*) Who are those men, so withered and so wild in their attire? (*Crummles whispers to Mrs. Crummles.*)

SMIKE. Is this a theatre? I thought it would be a blaze of light and finery.

NICHOLAS. Why, so it is. But not by day, Smike, not by day.

CRUMMLES. Uh, Mr. Johnson. Please, meet Mrs. Crummles. (*Nicholas and Smike come over.*)

MRS. CRUMMLES. I am so glad to see you see, so glad. And overcome to welcome you, (*To Crummles.*) provisionally, (*To Nicholas.*) as a promising new member of our corps. (*She looks at Smike.*) And this—yet more? An undernourished friend. You too are welcome, sir. (*Smike is brought forward to shake the hand of Mrs. Crummles as the Infant Phenomenon dances on. She is of doubtful age, though dressed in a little girl's ballet costume. She pirouettes and falls in an attitude of terror. She is followed on by Mr. Folair, a pantomimist, not in the first flush of youth, who wears buff slippers and is brandishing a walking stick. Mrs. Grudden appears with a list and tries to attract Mr. Crummles' attention as it becomes clear that Folair and the Phenomenon are practising a dance.*)

FOLAIR. And one and two and three—

CRUMMLES. What's this?

MRS. CRUMMLES. It's the Indian Savage and the Maiden.

FOLAIR. Pose and one and two and growl and threaten—

CRUMMLES. (*Explaining to Nicholas.*) Oh, yes, the little ballet interlude. Capital, capital.

FOLAIR. And attitude . . . and he loves her, and she loves him, and spin . . . (*The Phenomenon executes a little spin, aided by Folair. A trailing hand hits Folair in the mouth.*) . . . Thank you, and climax . . . (*A complicated and uncertain climax, culminating with Folair kneeling, and the Phenomenon standing with one foot on his knee, her hand over his face. Crummles applauds.*)

CRUMMLES. Bravo, bravo! (*Crummles takes the Phenomenon to introduce her to Nicholas. During the following, two latecomers, Miss Snevellicci and Miss Ledrook, appear. The former is the leading young actress of the company, and knows it. She whispers to Miss Bravassa, asking her about Nicholas.*) And this, sir, is Miss Ninetta Crummles, better known to half the nobility of England, as the Infant Phenomenon.

NICHOLAS. Your daughter?

CRUMMLES. Our daughter, sir, and the idol of every place we go into. The talent of this child is not to be imagined. She must be seen, sir, seen—to be even faintly appreciated. Now, kiss your mother, dear. (*The Infant Phenomenon kisses Mrs. Crummles. Something unpleasant transfers itself from daughter to mother.*)

MRS. CRUMMLES. What has the child been eating. Mrs. Grudden? Where are you? (*Mrs. Crummles drags the Phenomenon off.*)

NICHOLAS. May I ask how old she is?

CRUMMLES. You may, sir. She is ten years of age, sir.

NICHOLAS. Not more!

CRUMMLES. Not a day.

NICHOLAS. Dear me, it's quite—extraordinary! (*Folair joins the conversation. Smike has wandered off, and soon he will be collared by Mrs. Grudden, who tries costumes on him.*)

FOLAIR. Oh, great talent, there, sir. Great talent.

NICHOLAS. Well, yes, ind—

FOLAIR. Oh, yes, she shouldn't be in the provinces, she really shouldn't.

CRUMMLES. (*Suspiciously.*) What do you mean?

FOLAIR. I mean that she is too good for country boards, and that she ought to be in one of the large houses in London, or nowhere; and I tell you more, that if it wasn't for envy and jealousy in some quarters, she would be. Perhaps you'll introduce me here, Mr. Crummles.

CRUMMLES. Mr. Folair. This is Mr. Johnson, who's to write our new piece for Monday, and when he's done that he's to study Romeo—oh, don't forget the tubs and pumps, sir, by-the-by . . . (*Crummles is presenting Nicholas with bits of script from his pockets.*) and Rover, too, of course, you might as well while you're about it, and Cassio and Jeremy Diddler. You can easily knock them off; one part helps all the others so much. Here they are, cues and all.

NICHOLAS. But—

CRUMMLES. Ah, there's Miss Belvawney. (*Crummles goes off after Miss Belvawney.*)

FOLAIR. Happy to know you, sir. (*He shakes Nicholas's hand.*) Well, did you ever see such a set-out as *that*. (*He tosses his head in the general direction of the Phenomenon and pulls a face.*)

NICHOLAS. Do you mean the Infant Phenomenon?

FOLAIR. Infant humbug, sir. With half a pint of gin a morning, every day since infancy, you could look ten for life, I'd venture.

NICHOLAS. I see. You seem to take it to heart.

FOLAIR. Yes, by Jove, and well I may. Isn't it enough to make a man crusty to see that sprawler put up in the best business every night, and actually keeping money out of the house? Why, I know of fifteen and sixpence that came to Southampton to see me dance the Highland Fling, and what's the consequence? I've never been put up in it since—never once—while the Infant Phenomenon has been grinning through artificial flowers at five people and a baby on the pit, and two boys in the gallery, every night. Oh, halloa, fellow, how are you? (*For some moments, Nicholas has been aware of Mr. Lenville, the Tragedian, fencing towards him.*)

LENVILLE. Well, Tommy, do the honours, do the honours.

FOLAIR. Ah, yes. This is Mr. Johnson, joined us suddenly, this afternoon. Mr. Lenville, who does our first tragedy.

NICHOLAS. First tragedy?

FOLAIR. Oh, yes, the major tragic roles, and—

LENVILLE. What's he joined to play, then, Tommy?

NICHOLAS. Well, I've been asked to—

FOLAIR. (*Interrupts.*) Bits and pieces, bits and pieces. Cassio, and other things, and such.

LENVILLE. What other things?

FOLAIR. And writing a new piece as well.

LENVILLE. A new piece, eh? What's in it?

NICHOLAS. Well, the play is based on a fascinating French fable—

LENVILLE. I meant for me. Something, you know, in the tragic and declamatory line—(*Luckily, Mr. Lenville has said this while looking round at other activity, so Folair can whisper to Nicholas.*)

FOLAIR. But Not Too Young.

NICHOLAS. Oh, yes. Well, sir, there is a character who turns his wife and child out of doors, and in a fit of jealousy stabs his eldest son in the library.

LENVILLE. Ah yes, that's very good.

NICHOLAS. After which, he is troubled by remorse till the last act, and then he makes up his mind to destroy himself. But just as he—or, you —are raising the pistol to your head, a clock strikes ten.

LENVILLE. I see. Yes, excellent.

NICHOLAS. You pause. You recollect to have heard a clock strike ten in your infancy. The pistol falls from your hand, you burst into tears, and become a virtuous and exemplary character for ever afterwards.

LENVILLE. Capital. Yes, sir, that will definitely serve. Ha.

FOLAIR. (*Anxiously.*) Anything for me?

NICHOLAS. (*Enjoying himself.*) Well, let me see . . . I imagine you would play the faithful and attached servant who is turned out of doors with the wife and child—

FOLAIR. Always coupled with that infernal phenomenon! (*He strides off. Smike, who has been dressed in a vaguely renaissance costume—a long grey gown and velvet hat—rushes forward to Nicholas, waving in delight, and rushes back again to Mrs. Grudden. Miss Snevellicci glides over to Nicholas.*)

MISS SNEVELLICCI. I beg your pardon, sir. But did you ever play at Canterbury?

NICHOLAS. Uh . . . No, never.

MISS SNEVELLICCI. It's just—I recollect meeting a gentleman at Canterbury, only for a few moments, for I was leaving the company as he joined it, so like you that I felt almost certain it was the same.

NICHOLAS. Well, I do assure you that you are mistaken, for I'm certain, if we had met, I'd remember it.

MISS SNEVELLICCI. Oh, I'm sure that's very flattering of you to say so. But now, as I look at you again, I see that gentleman had not your eyes. You'll think me foolish, doubtless, that I take notice of such things.

NICHOLAS. Why, not at all. How can I feel otherwise than flattered by your notice in any way?

MISS SNEVELLICCI. Oh, Mr. Johnson. All you men are such vain creatures, aren't you? Mm? (*Snevellicci has been gesturing with a hand to Miss Ledrook, who refuses to come over, so Snevellicci turns and calls.*) Led, my dear.

MISS LEDROOK. Yes, what is it?

MISS SNEVELLICCI. It's not the same.

MISS LEDROOK. The same what?

MISS SNEVELLICCI. He never was at Canterbury, come here, I want to speak to you. (*Crummles appears. Miss Ledrook doesn't move, so Miss Snevellicci has to go to her, and they have a little argument, as:*)

CRUMMLES. A genius, sir, a genius. I'm thinking, that we will bring out your new piece for her bespeak.

NICHOLAS. Bewhat?

CRUMMLES. Her benefit, when her friends and patrons bespeak the play. In fact, sir, you might do us some other little assistance. There is a little—what shall I call it—a little Canvassing on these occasions—

NICHOLAS. Among the friends and patrons? (*Miss Snevellicci aware of this conversation.*)

CRUMMLES. Yes, just half an hour tomorrow morning, calling on the house, drumming up support . . . You know, new author, all the way from London, book now to avoid a disappointment, all that kind of thing . . .

NICHOLAS. Now, sir, I am afraid that I should not like to do that.

CRUMMLES. Not even with the infant?

NICHOLAS. No. (*Miss Snevellicci rushes to Crummles and Nicholas.*)

MISS SNEVELLICCI. Oh, Mr. Johnson. Sir, you surely aren't so cruel, so heartless . . . and after I have been so looking forward to it, too.

NICHOLAS. Well, I'm very sorry, but—(*Mrs. Crummles sails in.*)

MRS. CRUMMLES. What's this? A problem, with the canvass?

CRUMMLES. Yes, dear. Mr. Johnson seems to have objections.

MRS. CRUMMLES. What? Object? Can this be possible?

NICHOLAS. Well, it's—

MRS. CRUMMLES. This Mr. Johnson, is it, with objections? This one, plucked, as 'twere, from dank obscurity, took off the streets—the highway—and presented with a chance that half of London would donate a vital limb for? Vincent, this is inconceivable. I am convinced his sense of what is proper, nay is chivalrous, nay once again is gallant, all will sweep him to enlistment in this noble cause. (*Looking at Nicholas. Slightly coquettishly.*) Is this not so?

NICHOLAS. Well . . . It is not in my nature to resist any entreaty, unless it is to do something positively wrong. I know nobody here, and nobody knows me. So be it, then. I yield.

MRS. CRUMMLES. (*With a look at Crummles, as if to say, "must I cope with everything?"*) Well. There. (*And Mrs. Crummles, Crummles and Miss Snevellicci leave Nicholas, and join the company. Nicholas now sees the full Company ranged before him.*)

MRS. GRUDDEN. Quiet. Quiet, everybody!

CRUMMLES. Ladies and gentleman! May I introduce to you Mr. Johnson and Mr.—

NICHOLAS. (*Giving a new name to Smike.*) Digby.

CRUMMLES. Thank you. Mr. Johnson, you have met Mr. Folair and

Mr. Lenville, Miss Snevellicci and my wife and family. This is Mr.
Bane, who does the tenor lovers; (*Mr. Bane waves weakly.*) Mr. Wagstaff, who's our virtuous old gentleman; (*Mr. Wagstaff is holding a
suitcase, and as he stands to nod at Nicholas, we hear the clink of
many bottles inside it. This confirms the impression that his red nose
and uncertain gait has already given us.*) And Mr. Fluggers, who does
the cloth, and can do everything from country parsons to the Pope.
(*Mr. Fluggers looks up from his newspaper.*) Now, that is Mr.
Blightey, who's irascible—
BLIGHTEY. (*Benignly.*) Hallo.
CRUMMLES. Mr. Hetherington, who swaggers, and Mr. Pailey who is
country comical; (*Mr. Pailey grins.*) There's Miss Ledrook, who's our
secondary romance, Miss Belvawney, who does the pages in white
hose; Mrs. Lenville, who's the wife to Mr. Lenville; Miss Bravassa,
Miss Gazingi, and Mrs. Grudden. Now, tomorrow morning, ten
o'clock, we'll call The Mortal Struggle and then it's all the Chorus for
the Raising of the Siege of Ghent. Good evening, everyone! (*As all the
Company except for the Crummles Family itself disperse:*)
MRS. GRUDDEN. Ten o'clock, call, ten o'clock, The Mortal Struggle.
Half past Siege of Ghent. All those lodgings, go to 'em. All those without, see me. Good evening, everyone. (*Mrs. Crummles leads her Fam-
ily to Nicholas and Smike. Nicholas a little shrug, which Mrs. Crummles interprets as a request that he should be put out of his agony.*)
MRS. CRUMMLES. Yes, sir, I think you'll do. (*Crummles relieved. The
Family sweep out. Nicholas and Smike follow.*)

Scene Eleven

*The Mantalinis' showroom. The mirror, a clothes rail, clothes stands,
and tailors' dummies. Miss Knag crossly fiddling about. Enter Kate.*

KATE. Um, Miss—
MISS KNAG. Oh, well. If it isn't that young and pretty creature, Miss
Kate Nickle—
KATE. Please, Miss Knag. You're wanted in the workroom.
MISS KNAG. Workroom. Thank you. (*As she goes.*) Well, one might
have thought, some people would have had the sensitivity, to seek al-
ternative employment. Yes, one might have thought, but it's a queer
world. (*Miss Knag goes out. Enter Madame Mantalini.*)

MADAME MANTALINI. (*Adjusting a dress on a stand.*) Well, Miss Nickleby, and how are you?

KATE. I'm quite well, thank you, Madame Mantalini. (*Kate starting to help.*)

MADAME MANTALINI. Hm. I wish that I could say the same.

KATE. Why, Madame Mantalini, what's the matter?

MADAME MANTALINI. Nothing, nothing. Now, get these things in order, do. (*Mantalini's head pops into the room.*)

MANTALINI. Now, is my life-and-soul here present?

MADAME MANTALINI. No.

MANTALINI. But how can that be so, when I see it blooming in the room before me like a little rose in a demd flowerpot? So, may its poppet enter?

MADAME MANTALINI. No, he may not. For he knows he's not allowed in here. So, go along. (*Mantalini enters the room and embraces Madame Mantalini.*)

MANTALINI. Oh, will it vex itself?

MADAME MANTALINI. I said that—

MANTALINI. Will it twist and crunch its little face?

MADAME MANTALINI. Oh, I can't bear you—

MANTALINI. What, can't bear me? I, whose only joy is gaining such a lovely creature, such a Venus, such a demd enchanting, and bewitching, and engrossing, captivating little Venus?

MADAME MANTALINI. (*Breaking away.*) Mantalini, you, your debts, extravagances, they will ruin me.

MANTALINI. (*Airily.*) Oh, that. Oh, it's a nothing, money will be made, and if it don't get made, enough, old Nickleby can stump up once again, or else I'll cut his jugular from ear to—

MADAME MANTALINI. Hush. Hush, don't you see?

MANTALINI. Oh. Dear Miss Nickleby. Well, I'll be demd. (*Pause.*) Well, then, as I am commanded, and quite demnibly admonished, by my little rapture . . . I'll withdraw. (*He goes to the door. Then turns back.*) Unless . . . My little joy and bliss . . . Would care to join her slave for breakfast? (*Pause. Then, after a look to Kate, Madame Mantalini follows Mantalini to the door. He holds it open for her to go through. Pause. Kate carries on, working alone, for a moment. Then a new head pops round the door. It belongs to Mr. Scaley, a rather rough-and-ready, though completely professional, gentleman.*)

SCALEY. Psst.

KATE. Oh! What?

SCALEY. (*Coming into the room.*) Please don't alarm yourself, Miss. Is this the millinery concern, proprietor one Mister Muntlehiney?

KATE. Yes, what do you want?

SCALEY. (*Calling out of the door.*) Yes, Mr. Tix, we have the right establishment. (*Enter Mr. Tix, another professional gentleman. Kate, fearing that these men are thieves, backing away.*) Oh, please don't go yet, Miss. I haven't yet presented you my card. (*He hands a square, white card to Kate.*) My name is Scaley. This is Mr. Tix. Perhaps you'd be so kind as to acquaint your guv'nor with our presence. (*Kate backs to the wall and pulls the bell pull. Bell rings.*) Thank you ever so. (*Pause. Kate stands there, by the bell pull. Mr. Tix is looking up at the ceiling.*)

TIX. I like the ceiling. Nice high ceiling.

SCALEY. Isn't it.

TIX. A boy could grow up here, grow up to be a man, a tall 'un too, and never bump his head on that.

SCALEY. Now, that is very true. (*Tapping a mirror.*) Good plate here, Tix.

TIX. Oh, yur. (*Fingering a dress.*) And this here article weren't put together without outlay of considerable expense, nor, neither. (*Pause as they continue looking round the room. Then Tix, to lighten the atmosphere, to Kate.*) And a very pretty colour. (*Enter Madame Mantalini.*)

MADAME MANTALINI. Kate, what's the—oh? Oh!

SCALEY. Ah. Mrs. Muntlehinney?

KATE. Madame.

SCALEY. Scaley. (*He waves at Tix.*) Mr. Tix. (*He waves a document.*) This is a writ of execution, and if it's not immediately convenient to settle, we'll set to work at once, please, taking the inventory. (*Madame Mantalini stumbles in horror, grabs the bell, pulls it, and falls into a chair. Kate to her.*) Oh, dear. I do suspect, Tix, that we'd better make a brisk commencement. (*Tix has already taken out his inventory book. He stands behind a dress on a stand, to note its features, so that, to us, he appears to be wearing it.*)

TIX. Dress. One. Fetching shade of blue. (*Enter Mantalini.*)

SCALEY. Ah. Um, monsieur? (*Mantalini stands there a moment. He is not unused to this situation, or to men like Scaley and Tix.*)

MANTALINI. So, what's the total, demn you?

TIX. Fifteen hundred, twenty-seven pound, and four and ninepence ha'penny.

MANTALINI. The ha'penny be demd.

SCALEY. By all means. And the ninepence, too. But with regard to the outstanding . . . ? (*Mantalini shrugs, and waves his hand. Madame Mantalini is in tears.*)

SCALEY. Oh, well. I fear that Mrs. Tix and all the little Tixes'll be minus their papa a day or two.

TIX. (*Looks around.*) Or even three.

SCALEY. (*To comfort Madame Mantalini.*) Now, come on, madam, take a little consolation, for I'll warrant half of this stuff in't been paid for, eh? (*Scaley and Tix set about their business as Mantalini goes to his wife.*)

TIX. Two cheval-glasses. One with damaged frame.

MANTALINI. Now, dear, my cup of happiness's sweetener, will you listen to me for two minutes?

MADAME MANTALINI. (*Suddenly, in great passion.*) Oh, don't you speak to me. You've ruined me, and that's enough.

TIX. Three bonnets. Styling, various.

MANTALINI. (*Recoiling, as if from a blow.*) What? Do not speak to you? All this, and I, your drudge and potboy, I am not to speak to you? (*Kate looking at Mantalini with some cynicism, as are Messrs. Scaley and Tix.*)

TIX. One bust. A Roman gentleman.

MANTALINI. Oh, it's too much. Too much! (*Mantalini rushes from the room. Madame Mantalini stands, quickly.*)

MADAME MANTALINI. Quick! Quick, Miss Nickleby! Make haste, for heaven's sake, he will destroy himself. (*She runs to the exit.*) I spoke unkindly to him, and he cannot bear it. Alfred, Alfred! (*She runs out. Suddenly, chase music. Mantalini, who has found a pair of scissors, runs on, pursued by Milliners and Madame Mantalini. The chase goes all round the stage, and even, if possible, into the auditorium, before arriving back in the showroom.*)

MANTALINI. No, I'm going to do it. Right now. No question. Going to do it. Yes, I'm going to do it. I will do it now! (*Everyone is back in the showroom. Miss Knag appears on the sidelines. Mr. Scaley and Mr. Tix carry on their work calmly.*)

1st MILLINER. Eh, what's he doing?

2nd MILLINER. Got my scissors.

1st MILLINER. Lor.

MADAME MANTALINI. (*Flinging her arms round her husband.*) Oh, Alfred, stop, I didn't mean to say it, promise you, I didn't mean to say . . .

2nd MILLINER. That's highly dangerous.

MANTALINI. I have brought ruin on the best and purest creature ever threw herself away on some demned vagabond. I'll do it! Demmit, let me go! (*He pulls himself away from her.*)

MADAME MANTALINI. Compose yourself, my angel, please, someone, disarm him! (*Mantalini raises the scissors, to plunge them in his breast. The two Milliners, without much difficulty, grab him and disarm him.*)

2nd MILLINER. Now, come on. Mr. Mantalini—

1st MILLINER. Drop the scissors, like a nice man.

2nd MILLINER. There!

MANTALINI. No! No! You, fetch me poison!

2nd MILLINER. Poison?

MADAME MANTALINI. It was no-one's fault.

MANTALINI. (*Banging his head against an absent wall.*) Fetch me a pistol. You, ma'am, blow my brains out.

1st MILLINER. Me?

MADAME MANTALINI. It was my fault as much as yours—(*Mantalini grabs the scissors back from the 2nd Milliner.*)

2nd MILLINER. Hey—

MANTALINI. Rope! A rope to hang myself—(*He tries to hang himself by the bell pull. The bell rings. He looks at Madame Mantalini.*) What did you say?

MADAME MANTALINI. I said—that it was no-one's fault. Or, if it was, then mine as much as yours. My love. (*Pause. Mantalini raises the hand, in which he holds the scissors.*)

MANTALINI. Oh, my little pepperpot. Demnation, gravy-boat. (*He drops the scissors.*)

SCALEY. One pair, scissors . . .

MANTALINI. My—little—apfel strudel. (*Madame Mantalini aware for the first time of the open-mouthed Milliners and the faintly smiling Miss Knag.*)

MADAME MANTALINI. Please, now, Alfred. Come. (*Madame Mantalini puts out her hand to Mantalini. He walks to her, and they go out together. Miss Knag picks up the scissors.*)

1st MILLINER. Well, hark at that.

2nd MILLINER. Well, hark at *her.*

MISS KNAG. Well, now, young ladies. After all this, wild excitement, shall we return, and recommence our labours? Hm? (*The Milliners turn out front to narrate.*)

MILLINERS.
And return they did, but after half an hour they were informed their services would be immediately dispensed with;

And on the next day Mr. Mantalini's name appeared among the list of bankrupts;

And on the third day, the young ladies were all re-engaged,

Except for Miss Kate Nickleby.

MISS KNAG. (*Maliciously, to Kate.*) Miss Nickleby. I think *you* needn't recommence your labours. I think that *you* Need Not Return. (*She goes out, the Milliners go out too, and finally Kate.*)

Scene Twelve

Portsmouth, various locations. Bare stage. Enter Nicholas.

NICHOLAS. And at the hour next morning stipulated for the canvassing of Miss Snevellicci's friends and patrons, Nicholas repaired to the lodgings of that lady, which were at the house of a tailor in Smollet St. And having been admitted to her apartments by the tailor's daughter, he was told to wait. (*Enter Miss Snevellicci, carrying a pile of sheets and towels, and, on top of them, a scrapbook. She is followed by the Infant Phenomenon.*)
MISS SNEVELLICCI. Oh, Mr. Johnson. Please forgive me. We're all at sixes and sevens this morning.
NICHOLAS. Oh, I'm sorry to—
MISS SNEVELLICCI. My darling Led—Miss Ledrook, from the company . . .
NICHOLAS. Oh, yes.
MISS SNEVELLICCI. —was taken so ill in the night, we had to all move rooms. I thought she would expire, there, in my arms!
NICHOLAS. Well, such a fate is almost to be envied. But—
MISS SNEVELLICCI. Oh, Mr. Johnson, what a flatterer you are. (*Miss Snevellicci, moving towards the exit, artfully drops the scrapbook.*) Oh, dear, look—
NICHOLAS. (*Picking up the scrapbook.*) Allow me, please.

MISS SNEVELLICCI. Oh, thank you, sir. Forgive me for a moment. (*Miss Snevellicci goes out. Nicholas reads the scrapbook.*)

NICHOLAS.

"Sing, God of Love, and tell me in what dearth,
Thrice-gifted Snevellicci came on earth,
To thrill us with her smile, her tear, her eye,
Sing, God of Love, and tell me quickly why."

(*Miss Snevellicci has reappeared, without the sheets and towels.*)

MISS SNEVELLICCI. Mr. Johnson!

NICHOLAS. Oh, I'm—

MISS SNEVELLICCI. Mr. Johnson, I'm surprised at you.

NICHOLAS. I'm sorry, I—

MISS SNEVELLICCI. You are a cruel creature, I'm ashamed to look you in the face.

NICHOLAS. I thought, perhaps . . . You'd dropped it here on purpose?

MISS SNEVELLICCI. Mr. Johnson. I would not have had you see it For The World. Now, shall we go? (*Nicholas out front, as Miss Snevellicci and the Phenomenon move to the area which will represent the home of the Curdles.*)

NICHOLAS. And go at once they did, and the first house to which they bent their steps was situated in a terrace of respectable appearance, where lodged the Curdles, to whose apartments they were instantly directed. (*Nicholas joins the Phenomenon and Miss Snevellicci.*)

MISS SNEVELLICCI. Now, Mrs. Curdle is well-known to have quite the London taste in matters relating to the drama; and as to Mr. Curdle, he has written a pamphlet of sixty-four pages,

NICHOLAS. (*Out front.*) Proving that by altering the reccived mode of punctuation, any one of Shakespeare's plays could be made quite different, and the sense completely changed. (*Enter Mr. and Mrs. Curdle. Mr. Curdle has a chair for his wife, who sits.*)

CURDLE. To be or not? To be that, is the question! Hm?

NICHOLAS. Oh, yes, indeed.

MRS. CURDLE. Dear Miss Snevellicci, and how do you do?

MISS SNEVELLICCI. Oh, I'm alarming well, dear Mrs. Curdle, and ventured to call for the purpose of asking whether you would put your name to my bespeak.

MRS. CURDLE. Oh, I really don't know what to say. . . . It's not as if, now is it, that the theatre was in high and palmy days—the drama's gone, perfectly gone.

MISS SNEVELLICCI. Well, p'raps, but surely—

CURDLE. As an exquisite embodiment of the poet's visions, and laying upon a new and magic world before the mental eye, the drama is gone, perfectly gone.

MRS. CURDLE. What man is there now living who can present before us all those changing and prismatic colours with which the character of Hamlet is invested?

CURDLE. What man indeed—upon the stage; why, Hamlet! Pooh! He's gone, perfectly gone. (*Pause.*)

MISS SNEVELLICCI. The play is new.

MRS. CURDLE. Oh, yes, what is the play?

MISS SNEVELLICCI. A new one, written by this gentleman, and in which he will make his first appearance on the stage.

CURDLE. I trust he has preserved the unities.

NICHOLAS. The piece is in French—originally—there is an abundance of incident, sprightly dialogue, well-fleshed, three-dimensional characters, two tubs, a pump—

CURDLE. All unavailing—pump and all—without the unities.

NICHOLAS. May I inquire, sir, as to what are the unities?

CURDLE. The unities, sir, are a completeness—a kind of universal dove-tailedness, and oneness, and general warmth, and harmony, and tone . . .

MISS SNEVELLICCI. And I am sure that Mr. Johnson will preserve the unities—all three of them—most closely. May I put your names . . . ?

CURDLE. (*Taking a sheet of paper from Miss Snevellicci.*) Well, I suppose . . . We must accept it as our duty to the drama, even if—Four Shillings?

MISS SNEVELLICCI. Yes, that's right.

MRS. CURDLE. Four shillings for *one box?*

MISS SNEVELLICCI. Yes, that's correct.

CURDLE. Four shillings for *one play?* (*Miss Snevellicci looks desperately at Nicholas.*)

NICHOLAS. Well. With a lot of people in it. (*Slight pause.*) And it is very long.

CURDLE. Well, it had better be.

NICHOLAS. (*Out front.*) And Miss Snevellicci took the money with many smiles and bends, and Mr. Curdle rang the bell as a signal for breaking up the conference. (*The Curdles going.*)

CURDLE. Oh, what? A rogue and peasant slave, am I? (*Exit the Curdles.*)

NICHOLAS. What odd people.

MISS SNEVELLICCI. Oh, I assure you, Mr. Johnson, they get even odder. (*Miss Snevellicci and the Phenomenon leaving during:*)

NICHOLAS. As indeed they did, and three hours later, with two pounds and nine shillings taken—

MISS SNEVELLICCI. (*Calls.*) And a further ten and sixpence definitely promised—

NICHOLAS. Nicholas repaired, as he had been instructed, to the lodgings of the Vincent Crummleses. (*Enter Crummles in a dressing gown.*)

CRUMMLES. Ah, Johnson, there you are. Come in, come in. How goes it, Johnson?

NICHOLAS. Uh—the canvass?

CRUMMLES. No, the play.

NICHOLAS. It's not quite finished yet.

CRUMMLES. Thank heavens.

NICHOLAS. Oh?

CRUMMLES. I have another novelty, that must at all costs be included, in a prominent position.

NICHOLAS. Uh . . . I'm sorry, I can't guess.

CRUMMLES. What would you say to a young lady up from London? Say, Miss Someone, of the Theatre Royal, Drury Lane?

NICHOLAS. Well, that would look excellently, on the bills.

CRUMMLES. Exactly. (*Crummles produces a poster, unrolls it, on which is prominently displayed the name of Miss Petowker, of the Theatre Royal, Drury Lane.*) So, what d'you think of that?

NICHOLAS. Dear me, Miss Petowker, I know that lady.

CRUMMLES. Then you are acquainted, sir, with as much talent as was ever compressed into one young person's body. The Blood Drinker, sir, the Blood Drinker will die with that girl; and she's the only sylph *I* ever saw who could stand upon one leg, and play the tambourine on her other knee, *like* a sylph.

NICHOLAS. When is she expected?

CRUMMLES. Why, today. She is an old friend of Mrs. Crummles's, who taught her, as it happens, everything she knows. And here she comes. (*Mrs. Crummles entering.*) You're probably aware that Mrs. Crummles was the original Blood Drinker.

NICHOLAS. I didn't know that, no.

MRS. CRUMMLES. Why, yes indeed, sir. I was obliged to give it up, however.

NICHOLAS. Oh, I'm sorry, why?

MRS. CRUMMLES. Oh, the audiences, sir. They couldn't stand it. It was too tremendous. Vincent, there's a letter here—from Miss Petowker.

CRUMMLES. Ah. (*Crummles reads the letter. Nicholas feels it necessary to converse with Mrs. Crummles.*)

NICHOLAS. You teach, I gather, ma'am.

MRS. CRUMMLES. Oh, yes, I do. In fact, I did receive some pupils here in Portsmouth, on a previous occasion. I imparted some tuition in the art of acting to the daughter of a dealer in marine provisions. Sadly, it emerged that all the time she was coming to me she'd been totally insane.

NICHOLAS. Insane! How—most extraordinary.

MRS. CRUMMLES. Well, I thought so too, until I learnt she was of the strong opinion she was living on the moon, which sad delusion went a long way to explain the style of her performances, which were distinctly lunar. So, then, Vincent, it *is* true! (*For Mr. Crummles has finished the letter.*)

CRUMMLES. Well, so it must appear. Who would have thought it?

MRS. CRUMMLES. I would, Vincent. Any woman would. It is—demonstrably—her mission.

MISS PETOWKER. (*Off.*) Mrs. Crummles! Mr. Crummles!

MRS. CRUMMLES. Ah, and here she is. Boys, boys! (*The Master Crummleses run on, and help Miss Petowker and her luggage into the room.*)

MISS PETOWKER. Oh, Mrs. Crummles, Mr. Crummles . . . Oh, why, Mr. Johnson!

MRS. CRUMMLES. You two are acquainted?

NICHOLAS. Yes, we . . .

MISS PETOWKER. Mr. *Johnson.* We met—oh, I don't recall, on two or three occasions, Lady—Thing, and Mrs. Whatsit's salon, at the opera . . . Well, Mr. Johnson, what a pleasure. (*Nicholas is embraced by Miss Petowker. Miss Petowker to Mrs. Crummles.*) Why, Mrs. Crummles, I had no *idea.* . . .

MRS. CRUMMLES. We are all quite delighted, Henrietta, with The News.

MISS PETOWKER. (*Confidentially.*) Oh, but now, Mrs. Crummles, there must be no *word,* no *hint,* of anything. . . .

MRS. CRUMMLES. My lips, my dear, are glued. Now, at this instant, dinner. (*Mrs. Crummles has been escorting Miss Petowker into another room. She changes her mind, however, and turns back to Nicholas, who is moving towards the door.*) Mr. Johnson?

NICHOLAS. Mrs. Crummles?

MRS. CRUMMLES. We have but a shoulder of mutton with onion sauce but such as our dinner is, we beg you to partake of it.

NICHOLAS. Oh, Mrs. Crummles, I should be delighted.

MRS. CRUMMLES. (*As she escorts Miss Petowker out.*) Then let the mutton and onion sauce appear! (*Exit the two women as the Master Crummles and the Phenomenon run on and drag Nicholas into dinner.*)

Scene Thirteen

Ralph Nickleby's office. To one side, Ralph's desk and chairs either side, in one of which Ralph sits, working. To the other side, a high stool and ledger table, on which are account books and a bell. This is Noggs' room, and we imagine the two rooms are divided. Noggs is in Ralph's part of the office. Mr. Mantalini is banging the bell on Noggs' desk. Noggs goes out of the "door" and round into his own area.

MANTALINI. What a demnation long time you have kept me ringing at this confounded old cracked tea-kettle of a bell, every tinkle of which is enough to throw a strong man into blue convulsions.

NOGGS. Didn't hear it more than once, myself.

MANTALINI. Then you are most demnibly and outrageously deaf. Now, where's Ralph Nickleby?

NOGGS. Might not be home. What purpose?

MANTALINI. (*Striding past Noggs to Ralph's office.*) Purpose? It's to melt some dirty scraps of paper into bright and shining, clinking, trinkling demd mint sauce. (*Ralph Nickleby looks at Mr. Mantalini.*) Ah. Nickleby. You are at home. (*Ralph a look at Noggs, who has followed.*)

NOGGS. (*Shrugs.*) He wouldn't wait. (*Ralph tosses his head at Noggs. Noggs returns to his desk.*)

MANTALINI. Well, Nickleby, you're looking well today. You look quite juvenile and jolly, demmit!

RALPH. What do you want with me?

MANTALINI. Demnation discount.

RALPH. Money's scarce.

MANTALINI. Demnd scarce, or else I wouldn't want it.

RALPH. But—as you're a friend . . . Bills of exchange?

MANTALINI. Yes, two. One for £40, and one for thirty-five.

RALPH. So, seventy-five in all. When are they due for payment?

MANTALINI. Two months one, the other four.

RALPH. Names of the guarantors? (*Mantalini hands over the bills. The front doorbell rings again. Noggs goes to answer it.*) Well, they are not cast-iron . . . But they're safe enough. I'll give you fifty for 'em.

MANTALINI. Only fifty.

RALPH. Yes.

MANTALINI. Not even, just a little more, as we are friends . . .

RALPH. But this is business, Mr. Mantalini. You'll not get a better rate. (*Noggs admits Madame Mantalini and Miss Knag.*) And so? Do you accept?

MANTALINI. I must.

RALPH. (*Opening a cash box.*) Well, then . . . (*Madame Mantalini, followed by Miss Knag, has strode in past Noggs and into Ralph's office.*)

MADAME MANTALINI. Oh, here you are.

MANTALINI. Oh. You.

MADAME MANTALINI. Yes. Me. Forgive us, Mr. Nickleby, for this intrusion. Which is attributable to the gross and most improper misbehaviour of, of Mr. Mantalini. (*Mantalini stands and tries to embrace Madame Mantalini.*)

MANTALINI. What's this you're saying, juice of pine-apple?

MADAME MANTALINI. No, none of that. I won't allow it. I will not be ruined by your profligacy any more. (*Mantalini sits.*) Mr. Nickleby, I call on you to witness what I'm going to say.

RALPH. Pray, do not ask me, madam. Settle it among yourselves.

MADAME MANTALINI. Well, settle it is what I plan to do. (*To Mantalini.*) This morning, you appropriated, from my desk, some bills belonging to the company, without permission. Is that not the case?

MANTALINI. It is, my precious, it is true, my tulip. I'm the demdest villain ever lived.

MADAME MANTALINI. And, knowing of my debts and obligations, caused by your extravagance, you have come here to change those bills of mine to cash. Do you deny it?

MANTALINI. No, I cannot. Oh, I'll fill my pockets up with ha'pennies, and drown myself.

MADAME MANTALINI. Well then, I tell you, Mr. Nickleby, Miss Knag, once and for all, that I never will supply this man's extravagance again. (*Pause. Mantalini looks up at his wife. He says nothing.*) I have been his dupe and his fool for long enough, and in future, he shall support himself if he can, and he may spend all that he pleases, and on whom he likes, but it shall not be mine.

MANTALINI. What are you saying, seraphim?

MADAME MANTALINI. I am insisting on a separation.

RALPH. Madam, you are not in earnest.

MADAME MANTALINI. Oh, I am.

RALPH. Madam, consider. A married woman has no property. The company belongs to Mr. Mantalini.

MADAME MANTALINI. Oh, no, sir. It does not. That company is bankrupt. But, to save what little has been left, of the furnishings and stock, I was obliged to call upon another party, who had, I'm pleased to say, sufficient capital to meet outstanding bills, to re-employ the staff, and to engage me as the manager of her new company.

MISS KNAG. New company. (*Slight pause. Mantalini looks at Miss Knag in horror.*) Yes, it's quite true, Mr. Nickleby. It's very true indeed. And I never was more glad in all my life, that I had the strength of mind to resist all offers of marriage, however advantageous, than I am when I think of my present position as compared with your most unfortunate and most undeserved one, Madame Mantalini. (*To Ralph.*) Otherwise, where would I be today?

MANTALINI. Oh, demmit, demmit, will it not slap and pinch the envious dowager, that dares so to reflect upon its own delicious?

MADAME MANTALINI. No, of course not. For Miss Knag is now, perforce, my very greatest friend.

MANTALINI. This is a dream, a demned, demned horrid dream.

MADAME MANTALINI. You have brought it on yourself.

MANTALINI. Oh, has it come to this? Oh, have I cut my heart into a demned extraordinary number of little pieces, and given them away one after another to the same little engrossing captivator, and it's come to this?

MADAME MANTALINI. It has. You know it has. (*Slight pause. Madame Mantalini goes to Ralph and puts out her hand. Ralph hands over the Bills of Exchange. Miss Knag trots over, and puts out her hand. Madame Mantalini gives the Bills to Miss Knag. To Ralph.*) I did . . . A long time. I did love that creature, Mr. Nickleby. (*Madame Mantalini and Miss Knag go out. Mantalini runs, and cries after them.*)

MANTALINI. Oh, I will drown myself! (*But they have gone. Back to Ralph.*) Oh, Nickleby, how can you sit there, watching such a cruel, brazen chick-a-biddy savaging the very heart of one who—

RALPH. Come, sir, you must put away these fooleries, now.

MANTALINI. You—what?

RALPH. And live by your own wits again. (*Pause.*)

MANTALINI. But, demmit, you'll help me, won't you, Nickleby?

RALPH. No, I will not. Good day.

MANTALINI. You can't be serious.

RALPH. I seldom joke. Good day.

MANTALINI. Now, look here, Nickleby, you know, without me, you'd've not got one brass farthing out of—

RALPH. Without you, sir, my credit would not have been needed. As you well know. And now, good day to you. (*Pause.*)

MANTALINI. Well. Well, demnation—cruelty. (*He makes to go, turns back. He can't believe it.*) It's over. (*Mantalini goes out.*)

RALPH. Hm. Love him. Love that. All love, is cant and vanity. (*Noggs has appeared. He coughs.*) Yes, what?

NOGGS. (*Presenting a card to Ralph.*) Two gentlemen. Are out the back. Their card. (*Enter Mr. Scaley and Mr. Tix.*)

SCALEY. Well, good day, Mr. Nickleby. Here is the tally. Thirteen hundred pounds. That's plus or minus the odd bonnet, or an underskirt or two.

RALPH. I thank you.

SCALEY. And dare I venture, you'll be kindly helping out the business once again? Another loan? And in a threemonth, when the interest falls due . . .

RALPH. No, I think not, Mr. Scaley. There has been a change of ownership. The business is now in more able hands.

TIX. Oh, dear.

SCALEY. Oh, very sorry, sir.

RALPH. So, then, your task's complete. How much? (*Scaley hands Ralph a bill, which Ralph signs and hands back to Scaley.*)

SCALEY. It's always such a pleasure doing business with you, Mr. Nickleby.

TIX. It's such a joy.

Scene Fourteen

Portsmouth. In the wings of the theatre. The Crummles Company runs on from their curtain call. We hear applause. They have been performing Nicholas's play for Miss Snevellicci's benefit. The women are mostly clustering round Nicholas, the Men round Miss Petowker. Smike looks on.

MISS GAZINGI. Oh, Mr. Johnson, what a triumph.

NICHOLAS. Well, I—Was it?

MISS BRAVASSA. Oh, my dear, you quite divided the applause, despite it being for Miss Snevellicci—

NICHOLAS. Well, I'm sure I—(*Crummles comes to Nicholas, as Mrs. Crummles sweeps back on to the stage.*)

CRUMMLES. Johnson. Sir. This has been magnificent. Why, quite magnificent. I have not, sir, seen such a debut since the Phenomenon herself first danced the Fairy Porcupine. (*The Infant Phenomenon curtseys and does a twirl.*) And everyone, well done. (*The Phenomenon bumps into Miss Bravassa and there is a little altercation. Lenville and Folair step forward.*)

LENVILLE. Hm. In my view, grossly over-rated.

FOLAIR. (*Leading him aside.*) Oh, come on, now, old man . . .

CRUMMLES. (*Taking Nicholas's arm.*) So what did you think of Miss Petowker, sir?

NICHOLAS. Oh, quite extraordinary. (*Crummles looks at Nicholas quizzically. During this a knock at the outer door and the Page-clad Miss Belvawney, out of force of habit, goes out to answer it.*) Good, is not the word. But what I did observe, additional to all her talents, was that every time she spoke, or even entered, there was quite a fearful opening and closing, in the upper boxes, of a green umbrella.

CRUMMLES. Was there? I can't say I noticed.

NICHOLAS. Yes, it was most striking. Every time she—(*Miss Snevellicci approaches bearing vast numbers of flowers, followed by Miss Ledrook, carrying the rest.*)

MISS SNEVELLICCI. Mr. Johnson.

NICHOLAS. Oh, Miss Snevellicci.

MISS SNEVELLICCI. Mr. Johnson, I—(*But even Miss Snevellicci is interrupted by the entrance of Mrs. Crummles.*)

MRS. CRUMMLES. So, are you *all* deaf?

CRUMMLES. Why, Mrs. Crummles, what's the matter?

MRS. CRUMMLES. What's the matter? The audience is what's the matter, the great Portsmouth public is the matter, they are calling for an encore from the shepherdesses, they're insisting Miss Petowker does another dance, they're shrieking out for anything from Mr. Johnson, there is a concerted move to rip the cupids and the muses from the lower boxes if Miss Snevellicci doesn't—

CRUMMLES. Then, come, let's return! Come, come, at once!

MRS. CRUMMLES. If you'd all be so kind. (*The Company running back on, as Miss Belvawney appears.*)

MISS BELVAWNEY. Psst, Mr. Johnson.

NICHOLAS. Yes?

MISS BELVAWNEY. There's someone here to see you.

NICHOLAS. But—

MISS BELVAWNEY. He says it's very urgent.

NICHOLAS. But I—(*Nicholas sees that Mr. Lillyvick has come in.*) Why, in the name of wonder, Mr. Lillyvick! (*Miss Belvawney scuttles across and out.*)

LILLYVICK. (*A little bow.*) Sir, I am your servant. (*He puts down a large, green umbrella.*)

NICHOLAS. And I yours. Why, there's the green umbrella!

LILLYVICK. Ah, yes, that it is. What did you think of that performance?

NICHOLAS. Your performance with the—?

LILLYVICK. What? No, I refer to Miss Petowker's.

NICHOLAS. Well, as far as I could judge, I found it most agreeable.

LILLYVICK. Agreeable? I would say, sir, it was much more than agreeable. I'd say, in fact, it was delicious.

NICHOLAS. Well, she is a clever girl.

LILLYVICK. She's a divinity. I have known divine actresses before now, sir; I used to collect the water rate at the house of a divine actress, but never in all my experience did I see a diviner creature than Miss Henrietta Petowker.

NICHOLAS. Well, yes—

LILLYVICK. (*Grasping Nicholas's arm.*) *A bachelor's a miserable* wretch, sir.

NICHOLAS. Is he?

LILLYVICK. I have been one nigh on sixty years. I ought to know.

NICHOLAS. That's certain.

LILLYVICK. But you know that the reason, the great reason, against marriage, is expense. That's what has kept me off it, or else, lord! I might have married fifty women.

NICHOLAS. Fifty.

LILLYVICK. But, you see: the wondrous Miss Petowker earns a salary herself. (*Pause. Lillyvick leaves Nicholas's arm. He moves a step or two away and eyes Nicholas inquiringly.*)

NICHOLAS. Uh, Mr. Lillyvick, d'you mean you're going to marry Miss Petowker?

LILLYVICK. Day after tomorrow, sir.

NICHOLAS. Well . . . Mr. Lillyvick. Congratulations.

LILLYVICK. The only problem is, the family.

NICHOLAS. What family?

LILLYVICK. The Kenwigses, of course. If my niece and her husband had known a word of it before I came away, they'd have gone into fits at my feet, and never have come off 'em till I took an oath not to marry anybody, or they'd have got out a commission of lunacy, or some such dreadful thing.

NICHOLAS. Yes, they would certainly have been quite jealous.

LILLYVICK. To prevent which, we resolved to marry here, in fact, to be married from the Crummleses, old friends of Miss Petowker, and we should be most pleased if you were there for breakfast, nothing fancy, muffins, coffee, p'raps a shrimp or something for a relish. . . .

NICHOLAS. Mr. Lillyvick, I'd be delighted. And I am most happy for you both.

LILLYVICK. Most happy? Yes. Yes—I should think it *is* a pleasant life, the married one—eh?

NICHOLAS. There is no doubt about it.

LILLYVICK. Um. No doubt. Oh, yes. Yes, certainly. (*Enter Mrs. Crummles.*)

MRS. CRUMMLES. Ah, Mr. Johnson. *Here* you are.

NICHOLAS. Oh, Mrs. Crummles. (*Lillyvick slips out, as:*)

MRS. CRUMMLES. Mr. Johnson, you are called for, in the lower circle. You're demanded in the gallery, which is, in fact, quite near collapse from all the stamping. Your appearance was entrated by dear Mrs. Curdle, till she had a palpitation and was rushed off horizontal in a fly . . . Without, of course, the wish in any way to interrupt your evening —would you be so kind, sir, as to come?

NICHOLAS. Of course I will. (*Mrs. Crummles sweeps out. Nicholas turns out front to introduce the next scene.*)

Scene Fifteen

Portsmouth. Miss Snevellicci's apartments, and the Crummles' lodgings. Bare stage, but as Nicholas speaks, Miss Snevellicci, Miss Petowker and Miss Ledrook enter with a chair on one side; and Folair, Lenville, Lillyvick and the rest of the Crummles' Company Men enter the other side.

NICHOLAS. And on the morning designated for the nupital coupling of Mr. Lillyvick and Miss Petowker, the parties were assembling; with the bridegroom and his best man Tom Folair already at the Crummleses; and Miss Petowker being finally prepared at the apartments of Miss Snevellicci. (*Miss Petowker is sitting, having a sustaining glass of something.*)

MISS PETOWKER. Oh, Lillyvick! If you only knew what I am under-taking . . . Leaving all my friends, the friends of youthful days, for you!

MISS LEDROOK. Of course he knows it, love, and never will forget it.

MISS PETOWKER. Are you sure? You're sure that he'll remember?

MISS SNEVELLICCI. Oh, yes, I'm absolutely sure that he'll remember. (*Focus shifts to Lillyvick.*)

FOLAIR. Come, sir, cheer up, it is soon done.

LILLYVICK. What is?

FOLAIR. The tying up, the fixing of one with a wife. It is quickly o'er. Just like a hanging, what?

LILLYVICK. Like hanging?

LENVILLE. Come on, now, Tommy none of that.

FOLAIR. Yes, yes, you know, to hang oneself takes but a moment—

LILLYVICK. Do you compare, sir, do you draw a parallel—(*Folair miming a hanging.*) Between my matrimony and a hanging?

FOLAIR. (*Still miming.*) Yes, yes, the—

LILLYVICK. You say this in the house of Mr. not to mention Mrs. Crummles, who have brought up such a family, chock full of blessings and phenomena, you call their state a noose?

FOLAIR. Well, just a little joke—(*The Bridal Party has arrived.*)

MISS PETOWKER. Oh, Lillyvick.

LILLYVICK. (*Turning to Miss Petowker.*) My dear, d'you know what this, your actor friend—

MISS PETOWKER. Oh, Lillyvick . . . (*Lillyvick stops, realising his Bride has arrived in her full finery on her wedding morning. He embraces Miss Petowker.*)

MISS PETOWKER. Oh, Lillyvick . . . You will remember, won't you? Always, always, always?

LILLYVICK. Uh, remember what, my dear? (*Enter Crummles in 18th Century costume, clearly dressed as the Heavy Father, followed by the Infant Phenomenon, covered in artificial flowers, and Mrs. Crummles, as the Distraught Mother. Some "oohs" and "ahs" from the rest. Mrs. Crummles kisses Miss Petowker, and is overcome.*)

CRUMMLES. Come, stir, stir, stir! The second cock hath crow'd, the curfew bell has rung, 'tis—(*He looks at an enormous fob watch.*) Nine o'clock.

MISS PETOWKER. (*Dramatically.*) 'Tis nine o'clock, dear Lillyvick. Come, stir. (*A wedding anthem plays. Mr. Crummles takes the arm of the bride, and walks upstage with a feeble gait. The Company form into a procession, two by two: the Bridesmaids, Mrs. Crummles with*

*the Phenomenon, the other Actresses; then Lillyvick and Folair, the
other Actors, Nicholas and Smike, and, at the rear, the drunken Mr.
Wagstaff. Mr. Lillyvick is having difficulty trying to imitate the dra-
matic gait of the Company, and in particular of Mrs. Crummles. The
Company arrives at the back of the stage, forms up in two lines—the
Bride and Groom now together in the middle—and they all walk forward.)*

THE ANTHEM.

How blest are they that fear the Lord
And walk in His way
For thou shalt eat the labour of thine hands
Well, well is thee and happy shalt thou be.
Thy wife shall be
The fruitful vine on the walls of thy house
Thy children like the olive branches
Growing, growing round about thy table.
Lo, thus shall the man be blest
That feareth the Lord.
Lo, thus shall the man be blest
That feareth the Lord.

*(And there is Narration as the Bride and Groom run out, the former
throwing her bouquet, which is caught by Miss Snevellicci.)*

NARRATORS.

And Mr. Lillyvick and his bride departed to take the steamboat to
Ryde, where they were to spend the next two days in profound re-
tirement. (*The Company beginning to disperse, leaving only Nicholas and Smike.*)

And Mr. Crummles declared his intention of keeping the celebra-
tions going till everything to drink was disposed of;

But Nicholas, having to play Romeo for the first time on the ensuing evening, and anxious on account of Smike—who would have
to sustain the character of the apothecary—contrived to slip away.
(*And only Nicholas and Smike are left.*)

Scene Sixteen

*Portsmouth and London. Bare stage. This is a double scene, counter-
pointing Nicholas's rehearsal of Smike as the Apothecary with Ralph's
dealings in London. There is an overlap between each scene, so*

Smike and Nicholas don't go out until the next little sequence is underway, and visa versa. First, Nicholas and Smike; and, during it, Ralph and Noggs enter. Nicholas has a copy of Romeo and Juliet *with him.*

NICHOLAS. (*Prompting.*) Who calls so loud?

SMIKE. Who calls so loud.

NICHOLAS.
Come hither, man. I see that thou art poor.
Hold, there is forty ducats. Let me have
A dram of poison. Such soon-speeding gear
As will disperse itself through all the veins
That the life-weary taker may fall dead,
And that the trunk may be discharged of breath
As violently as hasty powder fired
Doth hurry from the fatal cannon's womb.
(*Pause. Prompting.*)
Such mortal drugs I have—

SMIKE.
Such mortal drugs I have . . .

NICHOLAS.
But Mantua's law—

SMIKE.
But Mantua's law. . . .
Is death to any—one who utters them.

NOGGS. Are you at home?

RALPH. I'm not.

NOGGS. You're sure?

RALPH. Of course I'm sure.

NOGGS. Well, they're downstairs.

RALPH. Who are?

NOGGS. Two gentlemen.

RALPH. You didn't tell me.

NOGGS. Didn't ask. Ah, here they are. (*Enter Sir Matthew Pupker and Mr. Bonney. Noggs remains in the background.*)

RALPH. Sir Matthew Bonney. What can I—

BONNEY. Look, Nickleby. This matter, your investment in our company—

RALPH. Yes, yes. I have resolved to realise my capital.

BONNEY. But, Nickleby—withdrawal of a sum of that proportion, now —nine thousand?

RALPH. Ten.

BONNEY. At this stage, when the stock's still going up—

RALPH. Will make the price fall. Yes, I know.

BONNEY. The bubble—bursts!

RALPH. Yes, certainly. But I have need of it.

SIR MATTHEW. Now, Nickleby. . . .

RALPH. Sir Matthew?

SIR MATTHEW. Have you not considered this, this matter, who's involved? The highest level? Have you no thought for your country?

RALPH. I have thought of it, my country, to the same extent as you have, sir. Good day. (*Sir Matthew looks at Bonney, who shrugs apologetically. Sir Matthew, with a huge gesture of rage and frustration, storms out followed by Bonney. Ralph to Noggs.*) My hat and stick.

NOGGS. Your hat and stick.

RALPH. Well, then? Don't stand, repeating what I've said. You're not a parrot.

NOGGS. Wish I was.

RALPH. Well, so do I. Then I could wring your neck. And then I would be done with you. (*Ralph strides out. Noggs stands there for a few moments, as Smike and Nicholas re-enter.*)

NICHOLAS.

Art thou so bare and full of wretchedness,
And fearest to die? Famine is in thy cheeks,
Need and oppression starveth in thy eyes,
Contempt and beggary hangs upon thy back:
The world is not thy friend, nor the world's law;
The world affords no law to make thee rich;
Then be not poor, but break it, and take this.
(*Pause. Prompting.*)
My poverty—

SMIKE.

My poverty. . . .

MRS. NICKLEBY. (*Off.*) Kate. Kate, my dear.

NICHOLAS.

But not my will—

KATE. (*Off*) Mama?

SMIKE.

But not my will—consents.

(*Smike and Nicholas go as Mrs. Nickleby, with Ralph, enters to Kate.*)

MRS. NICKLEBY. You are to dine, dine with your uncle, half-past six tomorrow.

KATE. Uncle, what is this?

RALPH. I have a party of—of gentlemen, to whom I am connected in some business, at my house tomorrow and your mother's promised that you shall keep house for me. I'm not much used to parties; but such fooleries are often part of business—and I hope that you won't mind obliging me.

MRS. NICKLEBY. Mind? Mind? My dear Kate, tell—

KATE. I shall be very glad, of course—but I'm afraid you'll find me very awkward and embarrassed.

RALPH. No, oh no . . . Come when you like, and take a hackney coach. I'll pay for it. Good night and, um, God bless you. (*Exit Ralph.*)

MRS. NICKLEBY. Well, Kate. Your uncle's taken quite a fancy to you, that is clear, and if good fortune doesn't come to you from this, I shall be most surprised. (*Kate and Mrs. Nickleby go out during Smike and Nicholas.*)

SMIKE.

My poverty and not—

NICHOLAS.

My will—

SMIKE.

Consents.

My poverty and not my will consents.

NICHOLAS.

I pay thy poverty and not thy will.

SMIKE.

My poverty and not my will consents.

NICHOLAS. Uh—no—(*Nicholas takes Smike out, as a Man enters one side, and on the other, Ralph and Noggs. Noggs has a plate of muffins, which he gives to Ralph.*)

NOGGS. He's here. I got him tea. But he's not eating it. (*Ralph gestures to Noggs, who goes. Ralph to the Man.*)

RALPH. Sir Mulberry. (*Sir Mulberry Hawk is an elegant, though dissipated, rake. He holds a bottle and a glass.*)

HAWK. (*Pouring a drink.*) Hm. Nickleby. Is everything arranged.

RALPH. It is. Um—have you taken tea? (*Sir Mulberry Hawk raises his glass, in answer.*) The gull will come?

HAWK. Lord Frederick? Of course. I told him that the evening would be both—an entertainment, and of profit. Will it be?

RALPH. Oh, yes. For us, at least. And, for the first, I think . . . there will be an attraction, for his lordship, present. For the second, I am able to advance. . . . as much as he, and you, will need.

HAWK. You're sure of that?

RALPH. Oh, yes. I am prepared. (*Offering the plate.*) Look, please, Sir Mulberry, at least . . . Do have a muffin. Hm? (*Enter Smike and Nicholas. They are in costume for the performance: Nicholas as Romeo and Smike in a grey gown as the Apothecary.*)

NICHOLAS.

There is thy gold—worse poison to men's souls,
Doing more murder in this loathsome world,
Than these poor compounds that thou mayst not sell.
I sell thee poison; thou hast sold me none.
Farewell.

(*Ralph goes. Mrs. Grudden, dressed as Juliet's Nurse, marches across the stage.*)

MRS. GRUDDEN. Act Three! Act Three! Beginners, orchestra! (*Nicholas and Smike smile at each other.*)

SMIKE. Who calls so loud?

NICHOLAS. Who calls so loud. (*They go out.*)

Scene Seventeen

Ralph's drawing room, in London. A chaise longue, surrounded by Men in evening dress, including Sir Mulberry Hawk, his young friend Lord Frederick Verisopht, and his acolytes Mr. Pluck and Mr. Pyke. On another chair sits the elderly Colonel Chowser, near to him stand the Honourable Mr. Snobb and a Makeweight. A Flunkey is in attendance. Ralph enters with Kate.

RALPH. Gentlemen. My niece, Miss Nickleby. (*Kate notices they're all men.*)

VERISOPHT. Eh. What the devil.

PYKE. (*To Pluck.*) Hm . . . Hm.

RALPH. My niece, my lord. Kate, Lord Frederick Verisopht.

VERISOPHT. (*Coming forward.*) Well, then me ears did not deceive me, and it's not a waxwork. How d'ye do, Miss Nickleby. (*Kate curtseys.*)

PYKE. (*Coming forward.*) Now, don't you leave me out, now, Nickleby.

RALPH. And this is Mr. Pyke.

PLUCK. Nor me.

RALPH. And Mr. Pluck, my dear. (*Kate curtseys again. Snobb stands.*) And the Honourable Mr. Snobb, and (*Chowser getting to his feet, not without difficulty.*) this is Colonel Chowser. (*The Makeweight obviously isn't going to be introduced, but takes advantage of the situation to go and get another drink from the Flunkey.*)

CHOWSER. Pleased. So very. Pleased. (*A slight hiatus, broken as Sir Mulberry Hawk, in one assured movement, takes the Makeweight's glass of wine, Kate's arm, and everyone's attention.*)

HAWK. Miss Nickleby, forgive us. Let me sit you down.

KATE. Why, sir I—

HAWK. (*Gliding Kate to the chaise.*) And, as I'm left out, damn you, Nickleby, I'll do the offices myself. (*Kate sits.*) Hawk, Miss Nickleby, and at your service. (*Hawk gives Kate the glass of wine.*)

KATE. Why, thank you, sir.

RALPH. (*To explain to Kate.*) Sir Mulberry. (*Verisopht to Ralph.*)

VERISOPHT. An unexpected pleasure, Nickleby. Indeed, one might say, it'd almost warrant the addition of an extra two and a half percent.

HAWK. (*Turns to Pluck.*) Eh, Nickleby should take the hint, and tack it on to the other five-and-twenty, and give me half for the advice. (*Pluck and Pyke laugh uproariously as Verisopht comes to stand on the other side of Kate's chair from Hawk.*)

VERISOPHT. Well, certainly, if he'll see to it you're not monopolising dear Miss Nickleby all night, Sir Mulberry.

RALPH. (*Lightly, as he goes to the Flunkey.*) Well, my lord, he does have a tolerable share of everything you lay claim to.

VERISOPHT. Gad, so he has. Devil take me, sometimes, if I know who's master in me own house. But I swear . . . I'll cut him off with but a shilling, if he—

HAWK. Sir, when you're at your last shilling, I'll be cutting you. While here is poor Miss Nickleby who's doubtless bored to tears with all this talk of discount, and hoping that some gallant fellow'll make love to her. Now, ain't that so, Miss Nickleby?

KATE. No, sir, indeed. . . .

HAWK. In fact, I'll hold you, any of you, fifty pounds, that Miss Nickleby can't look me in the face, and then deny that she was hoping so. (*To Lord Frederick Verisopht.*) My Lord?

KATE. Oh, sir. . . .

VERISOPHT. Well, why not? Done! Within a minute.

HAWK. Done. Now, Mr. Snobb, you'll take the stakes, and keep the time?

SNOBB. (*Coming to them.*) Of course. (*The Gentlemen produce money. Kate standing and going to Ralph.*)

PYKE. That's fifty pounds. . . .

CHOWSER. (*Unable to get up, pulling at Pluck.*) Hey, you, sir, pass me bet. . . .

KATE. Uncle, please. . . . please, stop them making me the subject of a bet.

RALPH. Oh, my dear . . . It's done in a moment, and there's nothing in it. . . . If the gentlemen insist—

SNOBB. One—minute! (*Hawk comes and takes Kate's hand, and leads her back to the chaise.*)

HAWK. I don't insist on it. That is, I don't insist that she denies, for even if I lose, it's worth it just to see her eyes, which seem to love the carpeting so much.

VERISOPHT. That's true. It's just too bad of you, Miss Nickleby.

PYKE. Too cruel.

PLUCK. Quite horrid cruel.

SNOBB. The lady can't deny that she was hoping for a gentleman to— um—within a minute . . . (*45 second pause.*)

HAWK. How goes it, Snobb?

SNOBB. Fifteen seconds left.

VERISOPHT. Won't you, for me, Miss Nickleby, just make one effort. . . .

HAWK. Oh, not a chance, my lord. Miss Nickleby and I understand each other very well.

SNOBB. Six, five, four, three. . . . (*Kate, outraged, looks Sir Mulberry straight in the eye. Pause. Then she breaks, stands, and runs to the side of the room.*)

HAWK. Capital. That's a girl of spirit, and we'll drink to her health. (*Hawk nods to the Flunkey, who passes round drinks as Hawk collects his winnings.*)

PYKE. Oh, yes, we will.

PLUCK. Most definitely.

PYKE. Many times.

RALPH. But, perhaps, sirs, now the sport is over, you would care to drink it over dinner.

HAWK. Well, certainly. (*Pyke and Pluck dislodge Chowser from his chair. Lord Verisopht to Kate.*)

VERISOPHT. (*Offering his arm.*) Miss Nickleby. . . .

KATE. No, no. . . .

RALPH. (*Gesturing the Company out.*) I'm sure Miss Nickleby will join us in a moment. When she has, composed herself.

VERISOPHT. But, Nickleby—

RALPH. I'm sure she will be down directly. Please, please, gentlemen. (*The Company leaves. Ralph is the last to go and Kate goes to him.*)

KATE. Please, uncle, don't—

RALPH. My dear. We are connected. And I can't afford . . . What is it, after all? We all have challenges. And this is one of yours. (*Ralph goes out. Kate is left there. Enter a heavily edited section of Act Three, Scene Five of* Romeo and Juliet, *Crummles as Capulet, Mrs. Crummles as Lady Capulet, Miss Snevellicci as Juliet and Mrs. Grudden as the Nurse. This scene is played around Kate.*)

CAPULET.

How? Will she none? Does she not give us thanks?
Is she not proud? Doth she not count her blest,
Unworthy as she is, that we have wrought
So worthy a gentleman to be her bride?

JULIET.

Proud I can never be of what I hate.

CAPULET.

God's bread! It makes me mad.
Day, night; hour, tide, time; work, play;
To have her matched; and having now provided
A gentleman of noble percentage,
To answer "I'll not wed. I cannot love;
I am too young, I pray you pardon me."!
Graze where you will, you shall not house with me.
Nor what is mine shall never do thee good.

(*Exit Capulet.*)

JULIET.

Is there no pity sitting in the clouds
That sees into the bottom of my grief?
Oh, sweet mother, cast me not away!

LADY CAPULET.

Talk not to me, for I'll not speak a word.

(*Exit Lady Capulet, Juliet and the Nurse. Re-enter Hawk.*)

HAWK. Yes, capital.

KATE. Oh, sir. . . .

HAWK. What a delightful studiousness. Was it real, now, or only to display the eyelashes? Why did I speak and destroy such a pretty picture?

KATE. Then please, be silent, sir. (*Hawk goes and sits next to Kate.*)

HAWK. No, don't. Upon my life, you mustn't treat me like this, dear Miss Nickleby. I'm such a slave of yours.

KATE. I wish, sir . . . You must understand, that your behaviour. . . .

HAWK. Come on, now, be more natural, Miss Nickleby, more natural, please. . . . (*Kate looks at him. Then she stands quickly. Hawk catches her skirt.*) A bit more natural, eh?

KATE. Oh, sir. Please. Instantly! Please let me go at once.

HAWK. Not for the world, Miss Nickleby. . . . (*Ralph has entered.*)

RALPH. What's this? (*Hawk looks round. He sees Ralph, lets Kate go, sits down and crosses his legs. Kate gestures vaguely.*) (*To Hawk, gesturing towards the door.*) Your way lies there, sir. (*Pause. Ralph shaking.*)

HAWK. (*Furious.*) Do you *know* me, you madman?

RALPH. Well. (*Pause.*)

KATE. (*In tears.*) Please, uncle. Let me go.

RALPH. Yes. Yes, of course. I'll take you to your carriage presently. (*Ralph takes Kate's arm.*) But just one word. I didn't know it would be so; it was impossible for me to foresee it. (*Kate looking at Ralph. Ralph looking over her shoulder at Hawk.*) You have done no wrong. (*Kate goes out.*)

HAWK. Hm. You want the lord. Your pretty niece an "entertainment" for that drunken boy downstairs. (*He turns to Ralph.*) And if *he'd* come up here instead of me, you would have been a bit more blind, and deaf, and a deal less flourishing than you have been? (*Pause.*) Who brought him to you first? Without me, could you wind him in your net?

RALPH. That net's a large one, and it's rather full. Take care that it chokes no-one in its meshes.

HAWK. Oh—

RALPH. I tell you this. That if I brought her here, as a matter of business—

HAWK. Oh, yes, well, that's the word—

RALPH. (*Interrupts.*) Because I thought she might make some impression on the silly youth that you are leading into ruin, I knew, knowing him, that he'd respect her sex, and conduct. But I did not envisage I'd subject the girl to the licentiousness of a hand like you. And now we understand each other. Hm?

HAWK. Especially, of course, as there was nothing you could gain by it.

RALPH. Exactly so. (*Enter Lord Frederick Verisopht.*)

VERISOPHT. So, there you are, the both of you. Now, are we not to dine? And do some business too?

RALPH. (*Deliberately.*) Of course, my lord. We'll dine. But business first. Two months to pay. At interest of twenty-five percent. Those are the terms, what sum had you in mind?

VERISOPHT. Oh, five—or ten?

HAWK. Say, ten.

RALPH. Ten thousand pounds. Now, gentlemen, I'll join you very soon. (*Hawk and Verisopht go out one way, Ralph another. Two Crummles stage-hands run in with flats, which they set up as if the prompt side wing of our theatre was the audience of the Portsmouth theatre. Nicholas, as Romeo, walks on to "stage"—facing off our stage. In the Portsmouth wings, downstage in our theatre, are Master Crummles, waiting to enter as Balthazar, and Smike, waiting to go on as the Apothecary. Smike is concentrating very hard, mumbling through his lines.*)

ROMEO.
If I may trust the flattering truth of sleep,
My dreams presage some joyful news at hand.
(*"Enter" Balthazar.*)
News from Verona! How fares Juliet?
For nothing can be ill if she be well.

BALTHAZAR.
Then she is well, and nothing can be ill.
Her body sleeps in Capel's monument,
And her immortal part with angels lives.

ROMEO.
Is it e'en so? Then I defy you, stars!
Thou knowest my lodgings. Get me ink and paper
And hire post-horses. I'll be with you straight.
(*Exit Balthazar.*)
Well, Juliet, I will lie with thee tonight.
Let's see for means. O mischief, thou art swift
To enter in the thoughts of desperate men!
I do remember an apothecary,
And hereabouts 'a dwells, which late I noted
In tatt'red weeds, with overwhelming brows,
Culling of simples. This should be the house.
What, ho! Apothecary!
(*Pause. Smike has been concentrating so hard, he's missed his cue. Nicholas repeats.*)
What, ho! Apothecary!
(*Smike rushes on, and bellows out.*)

APOTHECARY.
WHO CALLS SO LOUD?
(*And Nicholas leads him away, as Ralph brings Kate downstage.*)
KATE. And as the door of her carriage was closed, a comb fell from
Kate's hair, close to uncle's feet; and as he picked it up and returned it
into her hand, the light from a neighbouring lamp shone upon her face.
(*Ralph is lit.*)
RALPH. The lock of hair that had escaped and curled loosely over her
brow, the traces of tears yet scarcely dry, the flushed cheek, the look of
sorrow, all fired some dormant train of recollection in the old man's
breast; and the face of his dead brother seemed present before him, with
the very look it wore on some occasion of boyish grief, of which every
minute circumstance flashed upon his mind, with the distinctness of a
scene of yesterday. (*And Newman Noggs appears.*)
NOGGS. And Ralph Nicklcby, who was proof against all appeals of
blood and kindred—who was steeled against every tale of sorrow and
distress—staggered while he looked, and reeled back into the house, as
a man who had seen a spirit from a world beyond the grave. (*Darkness.*)

Scene Eighteen

*The stage of the Portsmouth Theatre. A tatty, Crummlesian set for
the last scene of* Romeo and Juliet. *Downstage, Miss Snevellicci—as
Juliet—and Mr. Lenville—as Tybalt—lie on couches, as if dead.
Upstage, a badly painted cut-out of two arches, and behind that, a
backcloth of Verona.*
*A note on this scene: There is much opportunity here, in addition to
the written jokes, for merriment. In the original production, one of
the best visual jokes was an increasing pile of mattocks, irons,
torches and swords that were dumped, during the first half of the
scene, downstage, between the two couches, and over which people
had to walk. There are many other opportunities for making the
point that the Crummles Company are a troupe of not-very-good actors and actresses who have to rehearse plays very quickly, and
therefore do not always get everything sorted out beforehand. Enter
Mr. Bane as Paris and Miss Belvawney as his Page.*

PARIS.
Give me thy torch. Do as I bid thee, go.

PAGE. (*Aside.*)

    I am almost afraid to stand alone
    Here in the churchyard; yet I will adventure.

PARIS.

    Sweet flower, with flowers thy bridal bed I strew
    Which with sweet water nightly I will dew;
    (*The Page whistles.*)
    The boy gives warning something doth approach.
    (*Paris retires. Enter Nicholas as Romeo, and Master Crummles as
    Balthazar, with a mattock and a crow of iron.*)

ROMEO.

    Give me that mattock and the wrenching iron.
    Give me the light. Therefore hence, be gone.
    Live, and be prosperous, and farewell, good fellow.

BALTHAZAR.

    (*Aside.*) For all this same, I'll hide me hereabout.
    His looks I fear, and his intents I doubt.
    (*Balthazar retires. Romeo, opening the tomb.*)

ROMEO.

    Thou detestable maw, thou womb of death,
    Gorged with the dearest morsel of the earth.
    (*Paris strides forward.*)

PARIS.

    Stop thy unhallowed toil, vile Montague!
    Condemned villain, I do apprehend thee.

ROMEO.

    Good gentle youth, tempt not a desperate man,
    By urging me to fury. O, be gone!

PARIS.

    I apprehend thee for a felon here.

ROMEO.

    Wilt thou provoke me! Then, have at thee, boy!

PARIS' PAGE.

    O, lord, they fight! I will go call the watch.
    (*Paris falls.*)

PARIS.

    Oh, I am slain! If thou be merciful,
    Open the tomb, and lay me with Juliet.
    (*He shuts his eyes.*)

ROMEO.

    In faith I will. Let me peruse thy face.

Mercutio's kinsman, noble County Paris!
(*Pulling Paris' body into the tomb.*)
I'll bury thee in a triumphant grave.
A grave? Oh, no, a lanthorn, slaughtered youth,
(*Dropping Paris' body and running to Juliet.*)
For here lies Juliet, and her beauty makes
This vault a feasting presence full of light.
Tybalt, liest thou there in thy bloody sheet?
Why art thou yet so fair? Shall I believe
That unsubstantial death is amorous.
For fear of that I still will stay with thee
With worms that are thy chambermaids. O, here
Will I set up my ever lasting rest.
Here's to my love! Thus with a kiss I die.
(*He drinks the poison and kisses Juliet. Outside the tomb, enter
Mr. Fluggers as Friar Lawrence. He carries a crow and spade.*)

FRIAR.

St. Francis be my speed! How now! Who's there!

BALTHAZAR.

Here's one, a friend, and one that knows you well.

FRIAR.

Alack, alack, what blood is this which stains
The stony entrance of this sepulchre?

BALTHAZAR.

Then what I took to be a dream is true,
And—further horror—I did hear him speak
Of some fell liquor that with venomous speed
Would him to death's black bosom swift despatch.

FRIAR.

Then all is lost! Juliet still sleeps—
What unkind hour is guilty of this chance!
The watch approaches, we must fast away;
Come, come, good friend, we dare no longer stay.
(*The Friar and Balthazar run out. In the tomb, Juliet wakes.*)

JULIET.

What's here? A cup, closed in my true love's hand?
Poison, I see, hath been his timeless end.
Oh, churl! Drunk all, and left no friendly drop
To help me after? What, and Paris too?
(*Juliet goes to Paris's body.*)

Oh, County, that would take my maidenhead:
Lie here, thy dagger rests in Juliet's bed.
(*Juliet about to stab herself with Paris's dagger. Romeo sits up.*)

ROMEO.

Hold, hold! I live!

JULIET.

What, Romeo, not dead?

ROMEO.

The pothac's poison coursed throughout my veins
A dizzy drowsiness which I mistook
For that numb torpor which doth presage death,
But in an instant it has passed. What, Juliet?

JULIET.

Oh, Romeo, thou starts. I am not dead
For I too drank a draught of fluid that
Had longer but the same benign effect!
(*The Watchman, played by Mr. Pailey, the comic countryman, appears.*)

WATCHMAN.

What's there? Who's that within! What's there! What ho!
Come, lights! Come, malting hooks! Look! Here! Look ho!

ROMEO.

We are approached.
(*Enter the Prince, played by Mr. Wagstaff, the drunken, virtuous old man. Falling to his knee.*)

WATCHMAN.

Good morrow, noble Prince.

PRINCE.

What calls our person from our morning rest?
(*He goes into the tomb. The Watchman stands. Enter Crummles as Capulet.*)

CAPULET.

What should it be, that is so shrieked abroad?
(*He goes into the tomb. Enter Mrs. Crummles as Lady Capulet, and Juliet's Little Brother, played by Master P. Crummles, and Peter, played by Mr. Folair.*)

LADY CAPULET.

What fear is this which startles in our ears?
(*They go into the tomb.*)

PRINCE.

Ah, Romeo!

JULIET'S BROTHER.
     Oh, sister!
LADY CAPULET.
       Paris!
PETER.
         Slain!
CAPULET.
  What strange reversal hath this morning brought,
With Romeo returned—
LADY CAPULET.
       He having fled,
Dead Juliet alive,
CAPULET.
       Quick Paris dead.
  (*Paris sits up.*)
PARIS.
  Not dead so much as stunned, for Romeo's blow
Deflected from my heart, did but a moment give
The appearance and accoutrements of death.
JULIET.
  As with my potion!
ROMEO.
      And the pothac's draught!
  (*Enter the irascible Mr. Blightey as Montague, Mrs. Lenville as Lady Montague, Miss Gazingi as an Attendant, and the Phenomenon as Romeo's Little Sister.*)
MONTAGUE.
  What's this? The people cry of blackest death,
LADY MONTAGUE.
  Some others of deliverance divine,
MONTAGUE.
  Talk both of grief and joy's on every breath:
  (*Enter Miss Ledrook as Rosaline.*)
ROSALINE.
  Oh Romeo!
ROMEO.
     Good heavens.
  (*To Juliet.*)
       Rosaline.
  (*Pause. Mr. Wagstaff's attention has wandered. Mrs. Grudden's head appears from the prompt corner.*)

MRS. GRUDDEN. But mourning—

PRINCE.

> But mourning flowers now adorn a festival,
> And merry peals o'ertake the tolls of funeral.

ROMEO.

> 'Tis true, our joy demands a cheerful bell:
> Oh, Mother, Father, Sister mine as well!
> (*Romeo embraces his Little Sister. Pause. Someone nudges Mr. Wagstaff.*)

PRINCE.

> Who's there?
> (*Enter the Friar, who throws himself to the ground before the Prince.*)

FRIAR.

> Dread sovereign, in guilty flight
> I did attempt to 'scape your wrathful judgement.
> But conscience stayed my steps, and turned them round,
> And, penitent, I here abase myself.

PRINCE.

> What, penitent? There is no crime, stand, see!
> All those in chains of death are unbound, free.

FRIAR.

> What joy! Then further tidings I must tell,
> For on my hurried passage, I did meet
> Another whom the jaws of death let go:
> See, here, Prince, is your kin, Mercutio!
> (*Enter Mr. Hetherington, the swaggerer, as Mercutio, and Miss Bravassa, dressed as a man, as Benvolio.*)

CAPULET.

> Mercutio! Recover'd!

MERCUTIO.

> Ay, sirs, ay,
> For though thought dead, and bourn for balming up
> My friend Benvolio observed a breath
> Of slight proportion on my countenance
> And I was taken to a nearby town,
> Where I was cured by surgeons of renown.

FRIAR.

> And further news comes with him. Speak, Benvolio!
> (*Pause. Folair gestures to Miss Bravassa, who shrugs, and points at Mr. Wagstaff.*)

MRS. GRUDDEN. (*Appearing again.*) Yes, yes—
PRINCE.
    Yes, yes, Benvolio, speak.
BENVOLIO.
               I shall, my lord,
But 'tis a tale I fear will try thy patience,
But I swear 'tis true. My friends know, oft
In their society have I been told
In jest, I am too gentle for our revels,
And almost feminine in countenance,
With not a hair of manhood on my chin.
Oft has it been so said; and I have laughed,
And spoken gruff, and slapped my thigh, to counter it.
But now deception's o'er, and I confess
That from this same near town I once did flee,
Pursuant of a love that fate denied,
And so t'effect my passage, took myself
The form and outward clothing of that sex
To which my love but not myself belongs.
(*Benvolio reaches up, takes off his cap, and lets fall her long hair.*)
From nature let deceit no more disbar:
Benvolio become Benvolia!
PARIS.
    Ah me.
CAPULET.
        Ah?
LADY CAPULET.
          You?
BENVOLIA.
             Ay, sirs, 'tis he,
Who thus from fell disguise releases me.
PRINCE.
    So everything is done—
    (*Enter Paris' Page, followed by Balthazar and the Apothecary.*)
PAGE.
            What Paris? Oh!
Hath sweet concord o'ertaken—
BALTHAZAR.
           Romeo!
Upon the road, in flight, I did perchance

To come upon this wizened, withered man,
Who hobbling was along the way from Mantua,
And asked where he might find a desperate man
Who might have bought a deathly liquid from him.
From your description I resolved it was
That self-same wretch from whom you bought the dram
Of poison in that self-same town. I asked
What was his purpose, and he told me straight,
The darkness, and his age, and dread infirmity,
Had caused him to prepare not poison, but
An harmless cordial, of sharp effect
But of no lasting peril.
(*Balthazar notices everything else.*)
Oh. What's this?

ROMEO.

Good Balthazar, all matters are resolved,
And good apothecary, thy mischance
Has proved the most enduring, happy circumstance.

PRINCE.

And now at last may tocsin loudly ring?
And tabor sound? And minstrels sweetly sing?

ROMEO.

Yes, yes. All's concluded. Everything is done.
(*The Company is leaving the tomb, when Lady Capulet runs to the corpse of Tybalt, and cradles it in her arms.*)

LADY CAPULET.

But what of Tybalt? Tybalt, still lies locked
Within the dread embrace of dreader death.

CAPULET.

Why, come, dear wife, a half an hour ago,
We'd thought a half-a-dozen kin were slain.
Let grievance cease, let Tybalt's bones remain.

LADY CAPULET.

Yes, let it be.
(*She drops Tybalt back on the slab. This gesture hurts Mr. Lenville's head.*)
                Let Tybalt lie still there.
And to a merry dance let us repair.

PRINCE.

A blooming peace this morning with it brings,
The sun for happiness shines forth his head,

Go hence, to have more talk of happy things,
All shall be pardoned, and none punished.
For never was a story better set
Than this of Romeo and his Juliet.

(Blackout. The Crummles Company form up for their curtain call, except for Mrs. Crummles, and the doubles—if they are in the Company—of Squeers, Young Wackford and Brooker, who have a quick change. The lights come up, for the Company's curtain call. Then they go down again, and Mrs. Crummles enters as Britannia, with helmet and union flag. The lights come up, and with them, the music of the Crummles' closing song.)

MRS. CRUMMLES.

England, arise:*
Join in the chorus!
It is a new-made song you should be singing.
See in the skies,
Fluttering before us,
What the bright bird of peace is bringing.

CRUMMLES COMPANY.

See upon our smiling land,
Where the wealths of nations stand,
Where Prosperity and Industry walk ever hand in hand.
Where so many blessings crowd,
'Tis our duty to be proud:
Up and answer, English yeomen, sing it joyfully aloud!
Evermore upon our country,
God will pour his rich increase:
And victorious in war shall be made glorious in peace.

(And now the Crummles' closing song becomes our closing song, and the rest of our Company enter: Kate, Mrs. Nickleby, Mr. and Mrs. Lillyvick; Squeers, Young Wackford and one or more Dotheboys Hall Boys; The Mantalinis; available Kenwigs; Sir Matthew Pupker, Hawk, Verisopht and Ralph, representing High Society; Mr. Crowl, Noggs and the ragged beggar Brooker representing the low. And in the middle, Nicholas and Smike, triumphant; as the Song moves to its climax.)

WHOLE COMPANY.

See each one do what he can
To further God's almighty plan:
The benificence of heaven help the skilfulness of man.

* See special note on copyright page.

Every garner filled with grain,
Every meadow blest with rain,
Rich and fertile is the golden corn that bears and bears again.

Where so many blessings crowd,
Tis our duty to be proud:
Up and answer, English yeomen, sing it joyfully aloud!

Evermore upon our country
God will pour his rich increase:
And victorious in war shall be made glorious in peace.

(*And the lights fade finally on the tableau.*)

END OF PART ONE.

Part Two

ACT ONE

Scene One

As the audience come in, the Company mingles with them, welcoming them to the show. Eventually, the whole company assembles on stage. A Narrator steps forward, to start the re-cap of the story of Part One. During this Narration, the Company makes small tableaux that remind us of incidents in Part One. It does not matter at all if actors or actresses who double appear, now, in the "wrong" costume.

NARRATOR. The story so far. There once lived, in a sequestered part of the county of Devonshire,

MRS. NICKLEBY. A mother,

KATE. And a daughter,

NICHOLAS. And a son,

NARRATORS.

Who, recently bereaved, were forced to journey up to London,

And to throw themselves upon the mercy of their only living relative, Ralph Nickleby.

RALPH. All three of 'em in London, damn 'em,

NOGGS. He'd growled to his clerk,

RALPH. And you, sir? You're prepared to work?

NARRATORS.
    He'd demanded of his nephew,

    And receiving the firm answer

NICHOLAS. Yes!
NARRATORS. Ralph took Young Nicholas and found him a position in a school in Yorkshire run by
SQUEERS. Mr. Wackford Squeers.
NICHOLAS. Well, thank you, uncle. I will not forget this kindness.
NARRATOR. And arriving at the school, he met with
MRS. SQUEERS. Mrs. Squeers,
FANNY. Their daughter Fanny,
YOUNG WACKFORD. Their son young Wackford,
NARRATOR. And their poor drudge:
MRS. SQUEERS. Smike!
NARRATORS.
    And forty boys,

    With pale and haggard faces,

    Lank and bony figures,

    Children with the countenances of old men,

    All darkened with the scowl of sullen, dogged suffering.

SQUEERS. So—what d'you say?
BOYS. For what we have received, may the Lord make us truly thankful.
NARRATORS.
    Meanwhile, in London,

    Nicholas' sister Kate

    Was found employment by her uncle
MISS KNAG. At the millinery establishment,
MADAME MANTALINI. Of Mr. Mantalini,
MANTALINI. And his demned, engaging, captivating little Venus
MILLINER. Of a wife.
NARRATOR. She and her mother were taken from their lodgings in the Strand

MISS LA CREEVY. And from their friend and landlady, the portrait painter Miss La Creevy

NARRATOR. To a grim and meagre house nearby the Thames.

NOGGS. I'm sure, although it looks a little gloomy, that it can be made, quite—

KATE. Yes.

NARRATOR. While up in Yorkshire, Nicholas took tea with Fanny Squeers

TILDA. Her best friend Tilda Price

JOHN. And her bluff beau John Browdie

NARRATOR. And tried to make it absolutely plain to everyone that his supposed affection for Miss Squeers

NICHOLAS. Is the grossest and most wild delusion that a human being ever laboured under or committed.

NARRATOR. A statement which did not improve his status at the school—

FANNY. Oh, sir, I pity you—

NARRATOR. Any more than did his firm resolve to stop the thrashing of the poor drudge Smike—

NICHOLAS. Uh—this must stop.

NARRATOR. His beating of the schoolmaster himself—

MRS. SQUEERS. Get off him! Off him, monster!

NARRATOR. Or his and poor Smike's escape with the assistance of John Browdie.

JOHN. Eh? What? Beat the schoolmaster?

NARRATORS.

To London.

Where their new friend Newman Noggs

NOGGS. Was making up the number and the punch

NARRATOR. At a party given by the Kenwigses downstairs.

KENWIGS. That's Mr.—

MRS. KENWIGS. Mrs.—

MR. LILLYVICK. And the latter's uncle, Mr. Lillyvick, the collector of the water-rate—

NARRATOR. And the latter's uncle's fancy—

MISS PETOWKER. Miss Petowker of the Theatre Royal, Drury Lane.

NICHOLAS. Three friends.

NARRATOR. Said Nicholas,

NICHOLAS. Three friends, in all the world. That bluff young fellow up in Yorkshire, Smike; yourself; and Mrs. Noggs our benefactor. And it is enough. It is indeed.

KATE. I won't believe it,

NARRATOR. Kate cried to her uncle, who had heard of everything from Fanny Squeers.

NICHOLAS. It is untrue,

NARRATOR. Insisted Nicholas.

MRS. NICKLEBY. I don't know what to think,

NARRATOR. Said Mrs. Nickleby.

RALPH. Then I'll renounce you all—

NARRATORS.

Announced their uncle.

And Nicholas was forced to leave his family once again . . .

NICHOLAS. Or else . . . you're destitute.

NARRATOR. And he and Smike then journeyed south to Portsmouth, with the thought perhaps, of going on board ship, and little knowing what in fact did lie in store for them.

CRUMMLES. Yes, I am Vincent Crummles, and I am in the theatrical profession, my wife is in the theatrical profession, and my children are in the theatrical profession.

NICHOLAS. What?

CRUMMLES. (*Handing scripts to Nicholas*): And you can study Romeo, and Rover too, of course, you might as well, while you're about it, Cassio . . .

NARRATORS.

And also an array of histrionic talent

That has never been assembled in one place

And on one stage before!

OTHER NARRATORS. Or since.

SMIKE. The stage!

MRS. Grudden. Stand by! (*We are now beginning to transform into the next scene.*)

KATE. And Kate,

NARRATOR. In London,

MISS KNAG. Lost her situation with the millinery establishment.

NARRATORS.
   While Nicholas,

   In Portsmouth,
MISS SNEVELLICCI. Found *his* increasingly congenial.
KATE. And Kate was invited by her uncle to a private party
RALPH. For some gentlemen with whom he was connected in a business matter.
NICHOLAS. While Nicholas was witness to the secret nuptials of Mr. Lillyvick and Miss Petowker,
MISS PETOWKER. Lately—of the Theatre Royal, Drury Lane. (*Nicholas and Smike slip out.*)
NARRATOR. And at her uncle's, poor Kate was subjected to attentions that were neither honourable nor welcome—
VERISOPHT. How d'ye do, Miss Nickleby.
HAWK. Oh, come on, now, be more natural, Miss Nickleby, more natural, please . . .
NARRATORS.
   While, back in Portsmouth,

   Nicholas and Smike

   Went on from strength to strength,

   And it seemed

   For at least that moment

   That their troubles and misfortunes were at last, behind them.
(*Smike enters in his apothecary costume, with Nicholas, carrying his Romeo costume.*)
SMIKE. (*Raptly.*) Who calls so loud?
NICHOLAS. Who calls so loud. (*And we are in the next scene.*)

Scene Two

Portsmouth Theatre. Backstage. A couple of skips, a flat or two. It is immediately after the Crummles' triumphant performance of Romeo and Juliet. Mrs. Grudden drags a clothes rail across the stage. The rest of the Company are around, packing their costumes and props, preparing to go.

MRS. GRUDDEN. All called at ten. Theatre now closing. Have you no homes to go to? (*Smike happily lopes off to give his costume to Mrs. Grudden. Lenville, who is clearly in some passion, is haranguing a doubtful-looking Folair, as Miss Snevellicci glides over to Nicholas.*)

MISS SNEVELLICCI. Well, Mr. Johnson.

NICHOLAS. Ah. Miss Snevellicci.

MISS SNEVELLICCI. Mr. Johnson, I have asked some members of the company, to come to supper, Sunday. My father, and my dear mama, are to visit me in Portsmouth, and I am sure will be dying to behold you.

NICHOLAS. Well, I'm sure I—

MISS SNEVELLICCI. And the Lillyvicks have now returned from honeymoon, and are so keen to see you once again.

NICHOLAS. Dear Miss Snevellicci, I can require no possible inducement, beyond your invitation.

MISS SNEVELLICCI. Oh, Mr. Johnson. How you—how you talk. (*The Misses Bravassa and Gazingi cross the stage, as Miss Snevellicci graciously withdraws and Folair, leaving Lenville drifts over to Nicholas.*)

MISS BRAVASSA. So I said to Mr. Crummles, that it's him or me—

MISS GAZINGI. Well, I said, if he does that trip again, once more, I'll kill him.

FOLAIR. Well, Johnson. Yet another great performance.

NICHOLAS. (*Thinking he was referring to Miss Snevellicci.*) Was it? (*Realising he isn't.*) Oh. You think so?

FOLAIR. Yes. Oh, yes. And Mr. Digby. After all the pains you took, with his rehearsal. (*Smike U., is having a whale of a time, in conversation with Mr. Blightey and Miss Ledrook.*)

NICHOLAS. Well, he deserves all the help and kindness I can give him.

FOLAIR. He is a little—odd, though, isn't he?

NICHOLAS. He is, God help him.

FOLAIR. And devilish close. Nobody can get anything out of him.

NICHOLAS. What *should* they get?

FOLAIR. Zooks, Johnson! I'm only talking of natural curiosity. Of who you are, and who he is, and if indeed your name is really Mr. Johnson, and if Digby's Digby, and if not—

NICHOLAS. Whose—natural curiosity?

FOLAIR. Oh, Johnson, it's just jealousy, you know, theatricals, I tell them, after all, what if you had, escaped from gaol or something of that sort, or—(*Lenville is now standing watching Folair and Nicholas, surrounded by other men.*)

LENVILLE. Well, Tommy, have you told him?

FOLAIR. Oh. (*Slight pause.*)

NICHOLAS. Um—told me what?

FOLAIR. (*Whispering.*) Oh, it's just that, since you joined, you see, old Lenville never gets the rounds he used to, and you get a couple every scene . . .

LENVILLE. Well, Tommy?

FOLAIR. (*Still whispering.*) And then the final insult, Tybalt, after all . . .

NICHOLAS. Go on.

FOLAIR. Go on. (*Breathes deeply.*) Now, Mr. Johnson, I'm to tell you, Mr. Lenville's ire will not be brooked.

NICHOLAS. That's Mr. Lenville's what?

FOLAIR. He naturally, presents his compliments, via me, and informs you that it's his intention—(*To Lenville.*) Now? (*Mr. Lenville nods.*) Intention, now, to pull your nose in front of all the company.

NICHOLAS. To pull my nose?

FOLAIR. That's right.

NICHOLAS. Folair, I've half a mind to pull your nose for saying so.

FOLAIR. (*Whispering.*) Now, come on, Johnson—(*Lenville strides forward.*)

LENVILLE. Right. (*He takes a step or two towards Nicholas, and then strikes a pose.*) Object of my scorn and hatred. I hold you in the most rank contempt. (*Lenville adjusts his cuff, walks over, and is promptly knocked down by Nicholas, Mrs. Lenville utters a scream and runs to the prone Mr. Lenville, and falls on him.*)

MRS. LENVILLE. Lenville! Dear, my Lenville.

LENVILLE. (*Raising his head.*) Do you see this, monster? Do you see this?

NICHOLAS. (*Walking over.*) What? Oh, yes. Well, now, why don't you apologise for all this nonsense, and we'll say no more about it.

LENVILLE. Never!

MRS. LENVILLE. Yes, yes, for my sake, Lenville, please, unless you'd see your wife a blasted corpse, dead at your feet!

LENVILLE. This is affecting. Yes, the ties of nature. The weak husband, and the father that is yet to be . . . relents.

NICHOLAS. Well, then, very good. And p'raps, sir, you'll be very careful, to what lengths your envy carries you another time, before you've ascertained your rival's temper. (*And Nicholas picks up Lenville's cane and breaks it across his knee, dusts his hands, and walks over to the exit, where he bumps into the entrance of Crummles, Mrs. Crummles, and the Infant Phenomenon.*)

MRS. CRUMMLES. Mr. Johnson. Pray, pray, what is going on?

NICHOLAS. Oh, Mrs. Crummles. Well—

MRS. CRUMMLES. It is past midnight. (*Mrs. Grudden crossing.*)

MRS. GRUDDEN. Everybody out!

MRS. CRUMMLES. (*To everyone.*) We have performances to give. Upon the morrow. We must be prepared. Have slept. And rested. Run through our lines. Mused on our dance steps. And rehearsed our songs. Resolved to act a little better. Sobered up. (*Varied mumblings.*)

BLIGHTEY. Yes, well . . .

MISS BRAVASSA. Certainly. . . .

MRS. CRUMMLES. (*Sweeping all before her.*) So, now, stand not upon the order of your going. Go. Be off. Be absent. Now. Begone. (*The Company disappear, except for Crummles, Smike and Nicholas.*)

CRUMMLES. Ah, Johnson. What a woman.

NICHOLAS. Yes. I'm sorry, Mr. Crummles—

CRUMMLES. No. No, no. (*Pause.*) Sometimes, I think, the strain, the running of a company . . . Sometimes, I think, we're not immortal, Johnson. Even Mrs. Crummles. Sometimes I think, to settle down, a plot of land, we might bequeath to those who follow us . . . (*Pause.*) But, then. We're strolling players, Johnson. Outcasts. Rogues and vagabonds. That is our lot. We carry on. (*Mrs. Crummles reappears.*)

MRS. CRUMMLES. Well, Vincent?

CRUMMLES. (*More cheerfully.*) Yes. We carry on. (*Crummles goes out with Mrs. Crummles.*)

SMIKE. Outcast.

NICHOLAS. No, Smike. Not any more. (*Slight pause.*) Oh, Smike. I wish that this was over.

SMIKE. What's the matter?

NICHOLAS. Smike, I'm worried. And I've written to our dear friend Newman Noggs. To ask him of my mother and my sister.

SMIKE. Worried. Why?

NICHOLAS. Because . . . Because I have an enemy. He's rich and powerful, and he's done me many wrongs.

SMIKE. What is his name?

NICHOLAS. He is my uncle. His name's Ralph Nickleby.

SMIKE. I'll learn that name by heart. Ralph Nickleby. (*Smike notices Lenville's stick and picks it up.*) You beat my enemy.

NICHOLAS. Oh, Smike. The time that we've spent dallying here. (*Miss Snevellicci and Miss Ledrook, in their street clothes, stand there.*)

MISS SNEVELLICCI. Oh, Mr. Johnson.

NICHOLAS. Ah, Miss Snevellicci. (*Slight pause.*) Might I have the privilege . . . escort you home? (*Miss Snevellicci puts out her arm.*)

MISS SNEVELLICCI. With the very greatest pleasure, Mr. Johnson. (*Nicholas takes Miss Snevellicci's arm and leads her out. Smike—in imitation—takes the arm of Miss Ledrook and leads her out too.*)

Scene Three

Regent St., London. A sofa, on which Sir Mulberry Hawk and Lord Frederick Verisopht are asleep. Debris around them. Mr. Pluck and Mr. Pyke explain.

PYKE. The place:

PLUCK. A handsome suite of private apartments in Regent Street. The time:

PYKE. Three o'clock in the afternoon to the dull and plodding—

PLUCK. The first hour of the morning to the gay and spirited. The persons: one: Lord Frederick Verisopht.

PYKE. And, two: his friend, the gay Sir Mulberry Hawk. (*The two men note the debris.*)

PLUCK. Two billiard balls, all mud and dirt.

PYKE. A champagne bottle, with a soiled glove twisted round the neck,

PLUCK. To allow it to be grasped more firmly in its capacity as an offensive weapon. A broken cane—

PYKE. An empty purse—

PLUCK. A handful of silver, mingled with fragments of half-smoked cigars,

PYKE. All hinting at the nature of last night's gentlemanly frolics. (*Pause. Then Lord Verisopht wakes.*)

VERISOPHT. What's that?

HAWK. (*Waking.*) What's what?

VERISOPHT. What's that you said?

HAWK. I didn't.

VERISOPHT. Yes, you did. Last night. You said something. About, eight hours ago. (*Slight pause.*) And then I fell asleep.

HAWK. Perhaps . . . I do recall. Uh—Nickleby.

VERISOPHT. The moneylender or the niece?

HAWK. The niece, of course.

VERISOPHT. Ah, yes. The niece. (*Verisopht sits up. Shortly.*) You promised me you'd find her out.

HAWK. I did. But thinking of it. You should find her out yourself.

VERISOPHT. Who, me? Why. How?

HAWK. (*Sits up.*) Just ask her uncle. Say to Nickleby, you must know where she lives, or else you'll cease to be his customer. That's if you're that concerned.

VERISOPHT. Oh, I am, that concerned. Upon my soul, Hawk she's a perfect beauty, a—a picture. 'Pon my soul, she is.

HAWK. Well, if you think so—

VERISOPHT. You thought so. You were thick enough with her that night at Nickleby's.

HAWK. Oh, just enough for once. But hardly worth the trouble to be agreeable again. (*Pause. He stands.*) So. Shall we go?

VERISOPHT. (*Stands.*) Let's go. (*As they turn to go, the two men notice Mr. Pluck and Mr. Pyke.*)

PLUCK. Good morning.

PYKE. Good morning.

HAWK. Good morning, Pyke.

VERISOPHT. Good morning, Mr. Pluck. (*Verisopht and Hawk walk out uneasily.*)

PYKE. And so Sir Mulberry accompanied his pupil, young Lord Verisopht,

PLUCK. to old Ralph Nickleby's at Golden Square.

Scene Four

A drawing room in Sloane St. A chaise longue, a small table with a bell, and two chairs, are set up during the Narration. Enter Kate and Mrs. Nickleby.

KATE. As, meanwhile, Miss Kate Nickleby herself,

MRS. NICKLEBY. And her mother Mrs. Nickleby,

NARRATORS.

Set off from their mean lodgings in the East End for Cadogan Place, off Sloane St.

Cadogan Place:

With the air and semblances of loftiest rank,

But the realities of middle station;

Cadogan Place: the one great bond that joins two great extremes;

The link between the aristocratic pavements of Belgravia
And the barbarism of Chelsea.

Upon this doubtful ground lived Mrs. Julia Wititterly,

Whose advertisement for a companion had been read that day by
Mrs. Nickleby,

MRS. NICKLEBY. In a newspaper of the very first respectability. (*And
now Mrs. Wititterly herself, a delicate woman in her late 30s, is reclin-
ing on the chaise longue, Mrs. Nickleby and Kate are sitting on the
chairs, and the page, Alphonse, is standing in attendance. Alphonse
wears his wig and livery untidily. He doesn't much like being called
Alphonse, either.*)
MRS. WITITTERLY. Now leave the room, Alphonse.
ALPHONSE. Or right. (*Alphonse goes.*)
KATE. I have ventured to call, ma'am, from having seen your adver-
tisement.
MRS. WITITTERLY. Yes . . . One of my people put it in the paper.
(*Pause.*)
KATE. If you've already—
MRS. WITITTERLY. Oh, dear, no. I am not so easily suited. Dear me,
no. Well, I really don't know what to say. How is your temper?
KATE. Well, I hope it's good.
MRS. WITITTERLY. You have a respectable reference for everything?
KATE. I have. (*As she places a card on Mrs. Wititterly's table, Mrs.
Wititterly glowers at her through her eyeglasses.*) Mr. Ralph Nickleby.
My uncle.
MRS. WITITTERLY. (*Ringing her little bell.*) I like, I do like your ap-
pearance. (*Enter Alphonse.*) Alphonse, request your master to come
here.
ALPHONSE. Please. (*A look from Mrs. Wititterly. Alphonse goes.*)
MRS. WITITTERLY. Now, you have never actually been a companion be-
fore? (*Mrs. Nickleby can stay silent no longer.*)
MRS. NICKLEBY. No, not to any stranger, ma'am, but she has been a
companion to me for some years. I am her mother, ma'am.

MRS. WITITTERLY. Oh, yes. I apprehend you.

MRS. NICKLEBY. I assure you, ma'am, that I very little thought at one time that it would be necessary for my daughter to go out into the world at all, for her poor dear papa was an independent gentleman, and would have been so now if he had listened to my entreaties—

KATE. Please, mama.

MRS. NICKLEBY. My dear Kate, if you will allow me, I shall take the liberty—(*She is interrupted by the entry of Mr. Wititterly, who is 38.*)

MR. WITITTERLY. (*To Mrs. Wititterly.*) Yes? My love?

MRS. WITITTERLY. (*With a vague gesture.*) Companion. And her mother.

MR. WITITTERLY. Oh, yes. Yes, this is a most important matter. For Mrs. Wititterly is of a very excitable nature, very delicate, very fragile: one could describe, a hothouse plant; one could say, an exotic.

MRS. WITITTERLY. Oh, now, Henry, dear.

MR. WITITTERLY. You are, my love, you know you are. One breath and —(*He blows, as if a feather.*) Phoo, you're gone. (*Mrs. Wititterly sighs.*) Your soul is too large for your body. Your intellect wears you out, and all the doctors say so. "My dear doctor", said I to Sir Tumley Snuffim in this very room, "dear doctor, what's my wife's complaint? Please tell me, I can bear it." "My dear fellow", he replied, "be proud of her, that woman. Her complaint is soul."

MRS. WITITTERLY. You make me out worse than I am, now, Henry.

MR. WITITTERLY. I do not, Julia, do not: think, my dear, the night you danced with the baronet's nephew at the election ball at Exeter. It was tremendous!

MRS. WITITTERLY. (*To Kate.*) Yes, I always suffer for these triumphs afterwards.

MR. WITITTERLY. My wife is sought after by glittering crowds and brilliant circles. She's excited by the opera, the drama, the fine arts.

MRS. WITITTERLY. Henry, hush—

MR. WITITTERLY. I'll say no more. I merely mention it to demonstrate that you are not an ordinary person, that there is a constant friction going on between your mind and body, that you must be soothed and tended, and that you must have a companion, in whom there is gentleness, great sweetness, an excess of sympathy, and of course, complete repose.

MRS. WITITTERLY. I am decided, Henry, that Miss Nickleby would be quite suitable. Now, I'm growing weary. Please . . .

MR. WITITTERLY. Yes, of course. (*To Kate.*) So, can you start tomorrow?

KATE. Yes, that would be most convenient.

MR. WITITTERLY. Then that is settled.

MRS. WITITTERLY. And in the evening you will join us to the opera.

MR. WITITTERLY. And Alphonse will appear to show you out. (*Mr. Wititterly leads out Mrs. Wititterly.*)

MRS. NICKLEBY. They are distinguished people, certainly.

KATE. You think so?

MRS. NICKLEBY. She is pale, however, and looks much exhausted. I do hope she isn't . . . wearing herself out.

KATE. What do you mean?

MRS. NICKLEBY. Oh, just . . . if suddenly the gentleman became a widower, and, after some appropriate elapse of time, decided to remarry, and, of course, with you engaged here—

KATE. (*Getting it.*) Oh, mama! You are impossible. (*Alphonse enters to show the ladies out.*)

ALPHONSE. This way.

Scene Five

Ralph's office. On one side, a desk, with chairs either side. On the other side, a high stool in front of a high clerk's desk, on which are ledgers and a bell. Ralph sits at his desk, a watch to his ear. Noggs is on his high stool.

NARRATOR. And at the very moment that they left Cadogan Place, in Golden Square, Kate's uncle Ralph sat in his office, being stared at through the little grubby window by his clerk, (*Ralph rings a little handbell on his desk.*) Who heard the bell, and went to answer it. (*Noggs goes round into Ralph's office.*)

RALPH. How now?

NOGGS. (*Turns to go.*) I thought you rang. I'm sorry.

RALPH. Stop. I did ring.

NOGGS. Yes. What for?

RALPH. I called to say my watch had stopped.

NOGGS. I'm sorry.

RALPH. And to know the time.

NOGGS. It's half past three. Perhaps it isn't wound.

RALPH. It is.

NOGGS. Or overwound, then.

RALPH. That can't be.

NOGGS. Must be. It's stopped.

RALPH. Well, then. Perhaps it is. (*Hawk, Verisopht, Pluck and Pyke appear in Noggs' office. Hawk rings the bell.*) That is the bell.

NOGGS. It is.

RALPH. Then answer it. (*Noggs goes out and is passed by Hawk, Verisopht, Pluck and Pyke. There is some acidity between Ralph and Hawk.*)

RALPH. Gentlemen. Good afternoon.

HAWK. Is it?

RALPH. Ah. A late night. But, I trust, a pleasurable one.

VERISOPHT. (*Joking.*) Well, an expensive one, at any rate. I'm fearful, Nickleby, I shall be drawing on your generosity again. (*A look from Hawk to Ralph.*)

RALPH. Oh, if . . .

VERISOPHT. And now, concerned with that, I'd like a word with you.

RALPH. Um . . . Certainly. (*Hawk, Pyke and Pluck withdraw a little.*) What is it, then, my lord?

VERISOPHT. Your niece, sir.

RALPH. So, what of her?

VERISOPHT. She's a devilish pretty girl. You can't deny it.

RALPH. I believe she is considered so.

VERISOPHT. Look, Nickleby, I want another peek at her. And you must tell me where she lives. (*Slight pause.*)

RALPH. My lord—

VERISOPHT. Now, come on, Nickleby—

RALPH. My lord, she is a virtuous, country girl. She has been, well brought up. It's true, she's poor, and unprotected—

VERISOPHT. Nickleby, I only want to look at her. (*Slight pause. Raising his voice.*) Nickleby, you know you're making a small fortune out of me, and 'pon my soul—

RALPH. (*Interrupting, in case Hawk hears.*) My lord, if I *did* tell you—

VERISOPHT. Yes?

RALPH. (*With a nod towards Hawk.*) You would, you'd have to keep it to yourself.

VERISOPHT. Oh, yes, of course I wouldn't—(*Enter Noggs.*)

NOGGS. Erm—

RALPH. (*Sharply.*) What is it?

NOGGS. Mrs. Nickleby. (*Hawk gestures to Verisopht. They withdraw a little—as do Pyke and Pluck—so Mrs. Nickleby cannot immediately see them on her entrance. Mrs. Nickleby sails in.*)

MRS. NICKLEBY. Dear brother-in-law, I'm sorry to intrude, but I was sure you'd want to be the first to know that Kate is situated as companion with a Mrs. Julia Wititterly— (*Pause. Ralph stops her with a gesture. Mrs. Nickleby notices the gentlemen.*) Oh, I'm so sorry—

HAWK. Mrs. Nickleby! (*Noggs goes out.*)

RALPH. Uh, sister-in-law, these gentlemen were leaving—

HAWK. Leaving? Nonsense. So, this is Mrs. Nickleby, the mother of Miss Nickleby? But no. It can't be. No. This lady, is too young.

MRS. NICKLEBY. I think, dear brother-in-law, you can tell the gentleman, that Kate Nickleby's my daughter.

HAWK. (*To Verisopht.*) Daughter, my lord, did you hear that? Daughter!

MRS. NICKLEBY. Lord?

HAWK. Now, Nickleby, at once, please, you must introduce us.

RALPH. Mrs. Nickleby: Lord Frederick Verisopht. Sir Mulberry Hawk. And, uh, Mr. Pluck and Mr. Pyke.

VERISOPHT. Upon my soul, this is a most delightful thing. Uh—how d'e do?

HAWK. I'm deeply charmed, dear lady.

PYKE. As am I.

PLUCK. And not to mention me.

MRS. NICKLEBY. (*Confused.*) Well, I don't—I'm quite overcome. (*Pause. Hawk nods at Verisopht.*)

VERISOPHT. And, how's your daughter, Mrs. Nickleby?

MRS. NICKLEBY. Oh, she's quite well, I am obliged to you, my lord . . . Quite well. She *wasn't* well for some days after she dined here, and I can't help thinking, that she caught cold in that hackney coach coming home. Hackney coaches, my lord, are such nasty things. I once caught a severe cold, my lord, from riding in one. I think it was in eighteen hundred and seventeen, and I was sure I'd never get rid of it, and I was only cured at last by a remedy that I don't know if you've happened to hear of, my lord. (*Sir Mulberry Hawk nods to Pyke and Pluck, who glide, as if on oiled rails, to either side of Mrs. Nickleby.*) You heat a gallon of water as hot as you can possibly bear it, with a pound of salt and six pen'orth of the finest bran, and sit in it for twenty minutes every night, well, not all in it, obviously, but just your feet, and I tell you I used it on the first day after Christmas Day and by the end of April it had gone, the cold I mean, and I had had it since September. Now isn't that a miracle, my lord? (*Pause. Verisopht doesn't know quite how to react. Mrs. Nickleby becomes aware of the presence of Mr. Pluck and Mr. Pyke.*)

PYKE. What an affecting calamity.

PLUCK. It sounds quite—perfect horrid.

PYKE. But worth the pain of hearing, Pluck, to know that Mrs. Nickleby recovered.

PLUCK. That's the circumstance which gives it such a thrilling interest, there's no doubt, Pyke.

MRS. NICKLEBY. Oh, do you think so?

RALPH. Gentlemen . . .

HAWK. So. Your daughter has secured an attractive situation, ma'am?

MRS. NICKLEBY. That's right, Sir Mulberry, as from tomorrow, when her first task is to escort her new employers to the opera. (*Hawk flashes a look at Pluck and Pyke. Mrs. Nickleby misinterprets.*) And I knew you'd be so pleased, dear brother-in-law, I walked straight here to tell you so. (*Another look from Hawk.*)

PYKE. But surely you don't intend walking home, Mrs. Nickleby?

MRS. NICKLEBY. Oh, no, Mr. Pyke, I intend to go back in an omnibus.

PLUCK. Well, isn't that a strange coincidence.

MRS. NICKLEBY. It is?

PYKE. Seeing as how the omnibus lies quite directly on our route, Pluck, isn't that the case?

PLUCK. It is indeed, and as we were just going—

PYKE. At this very instant.

PLUCK. We can escort dear Mrs. Nickleby.

MRS. NICKLEBY. (*Overcome.*) Well—I would be most grateful.

PLUCK. (*Ushering Mrs. Nickleby out.*) Not half so grateful, Mrs. Nickleby, as we. (*Mrs. Nickleby goes out with Pyke and Pluck. A silence between Ralph and Hawk and Verisopht. The latter two bow and go out. Ralph alone.*)

RALPH. Sometimes—I wish I had not done this. (*Slight pause.*) But still—she must take her chance.

Scene Six

A London street. Bare stage. Enter Mrs. Nickleby, Pluck and Pyke.

MRS. NICKLEBY. Well, Mr. Pyke, and Mr. Pluck, I must express my gratitude, a seventh time.

PYKE. Oh, please don't, Mrs. Nickleby. A friend of Sir Mulberry Hawk, a friend of ours. Is that not so, Pluck?

PLUCK. Pyke, it's automatic. And, particularly, someone whom Sir Mulberry holds in such esteem.

MRS. NICKLEBY. Oh, surely not—

PLUCK. Now, Pyke, is Sir Mulberry's esteem of Mrs. Nickleby the highest?

PYKE. I should say the very highest, Pluck.

PLUCK. She cannot be in ignorance, of the immense impression that her daughter has—

PYKE. Pluck! Pluck, beware. (*Mrs. Nickleby's eyes popping. Pause.*)

PLUCK. Pyke's right. I should not have mentioned it. Thanks, Pyke.

PYKE. Pluck, not at all.

MRS. NICKLEBY. I'm sure that—

PLUCK. Mrs. Nickleby should take no heed of what I said. It was imprudent, rash. And injudicious.

PYKE. *Very* injudicious.

MRS. NICKLEBY. Now, you mustn't—

PLUCK. But, to see such sweetness and such beauty on the one hand, and such ardour and devotion on the other—pardon me, I didn't mean to speak of it again. Please change the subject, Pyke.

PYKE. Consider it, Pluck, changed.

PLUCK. But to think that we may actually see your daughter, at the opera, tomorrow evening!

MRS. NICKLEBY. What's that?

PLUCK. Oh, you didn't know?

PYKE. Of course she didn't, Pluck, how could she? It is just, dear Mrs. Nickleby, as luck would have it, we—that is, Sir Mulberry, Lord Verisopht, myself and Pluck, are going to the opera tomorrow!

MRS. NICKLEBY. You are!

PYKE. We are. (*Pause. Elaborately, Pluck and Pyke snap their fingers, as if to indicate that they have here simultaneously realised the most obvious thing in the world.*)

PLUCK. Pyke, are you thinking what I'm thinking?

PYKE. Pluck, I believe our minds must be as one. Mrs. Nickleby.

MRS. NICKLEBY. Yes?

PYKE. Would you care to join us, in our box, at the opera tomorrow?

PLUCK. When we are sure you would be more than welcome.

MRS. NICKLEBY. But—

PLUCK. There's not a but in it, dear Mrs. Nickleby, we'll send a carriage round, at twenty before seven.

PYKE. And, see, here is the omnibus. (*Enter the Omnibus. It is formed by Performers, jogging in pairs, each pair holding a pair of chairs behind and in front of them. In front jogs a Coachman with a whip. The Omnibus stops, the Chairs are put down. The coachman sits on the back of a chair, his feet on its seat. Mrs. Nickleby sits on one of the back chairs. The Performers left without chairs become standing Passengers. They mime being on a moving vehicle. Pluck and Pyke disappear. The Passengers narrate.)*

PASSENGER. And Mrs. Nickleby leant back in the furthest corner of the conveyance, and, closing her eyes, resigned herself to a host of most pleasing meditations.

MRS. NICKLEBY. Oh, Lady Hawk!

PASSENGER. She thought,

MRS. NICKLEBY. On Tuesday last, at St. George's, Hanover Square! By the most Reverend the Bishop of Llandaff! To Catherine, the only daughter of the late Nicholas Nickleby, Esquire, of Devonshire!

PASSENGERS.

And then her thoughts flew back, to old meditations, and the times she'd said that Kate would marry better with no fortune than some other girls with thousands,

And as she pictured, with all the brightness of a mother's fancy, all the grace and beauty of the girl who struggled cheerfully with her new life of hardship,

Her heart grew too full, and tears began to trickle down her face. *(Fade on Mrs. Nickleby.)*

Scene Seven

A London Opera House. Downstage are two boxes, represented by four chairs on either side of the stage. They face downstage. We imagine a corridor behind them. Behind that is the actual stage of the opera house, on which a genuine, complete, three-minute Opera is presented, in Italian. It tells the story of two lovers, the father of the female one of whom objects strongly to their secret love. Downstage of this, the following things happen in dumbshow: A box-keeper leads on Mr. Pluck and Mr. Pyke, who in turn are escorting Mrs. Nickleby. Much solicitation of the latter by the two gentlemen. They are led into the first box, when the box-keeper realises from the tickets he has made a mistake, and leads them out again. As Pluck leads Mrs. Nickleby into the second box, Mr. Pyke clearly threatens the poor box-keeper with great violence for his error; Pluck seats

*Mrs. Nickleby in the second box with great charm and ceremony.
Pyke joins them.*

*The box-keeper, having gone out, re-enters with Sir Mulberry Hawk
and Lord Frederick Verisopht, both dressed up to the nines, but a
little unsteady. The box-keeper, fearful of meeting up with Pyke
again, points the two men to the second box. Hawk and Verisopht
enter, greet Pluck, Pyke, and, with much bowing and kissing of
hands, Mrs. Nickleby. Mrs. Nickleby looks round, as if expecting
someone else, but as no-one else is there, allows herself to be settled.*

*The box-keeper enters again, this time with Kate Nickleby, Julia Wi-
titterly and Henry Wititterly. They are shown into the first box. Conversation about who should take which chair is overheard by Sir
Mulberry Hawk, who lays his finger on his lips—Mrs. Nickleby is
speaking—and summons Verisopht to the front of the box. Mrs.
Nickleby recognizes her daughter's voice, stands, and greets her.*

*Mrs. Nickleby indicates the other gentlemen in her box to Kate, who
is clearly not best pleased. Mrs. Nickleby gestures that she is coming
round, and she—followed by the entire population of the second
box, ups, goes into the corridor—during which Kate is explaining
who these people are to the Wititterlies, the male half of which
rushes eagerly to welcome all these lords and baronets. Kate stands
there as Mrs. Nickleby, Hawk, Verisopht, Pyke and Pluck—the latter two only just—enter the box.*

*Mrs. Nickleby gestures towards Kate to recognise Sir Mulberry. Kate
turns away but Sir Mulberry Hawk comes forward with extended
hand, and she is forced to shake it. Mrs. Nickleby then gestures Kate
—with some impatience, to recognise the others—Vesrisopht, Pluck
and Pyke—and then Mrs. Nickleby, unable to understand Kate's ret-
icence, waves at her to indicate that she should introduce the party
to the Wititterlies. Kate introduces Verisopht, Pluck, Pyke and Hawk
to Mr. and Mrs. Wititterly.*

*At the end of this ceremony, Pluck suggests to Hawk that they
should, perhaps, adjourn, as this box is very full. "With so much
skill were the preliminaries adjusted, that Kate, despite all she could
do or say to the contrary, had no alternative but to be led away by*

Sir Mulberry Hawk". *Kate and Hawk are joined in the second box by Pluck, who occupies Mrs. Nickleby in conversation. Remaining in the first box are Verisopht, the Wititterlies and Pyke. The young lord is being fawned upon by Julia Wititterly. Mrs. Nickleby is studiously avoiding interfering with the conversation between Hawk and her daughter.*

Finally, Hawk's attentions becomes intolerable, and Kate stands, and makes to run into the corridor. At this point, everyone turns their chairs upstage, to face the opera, and so the corridor that Kate runs into is downstage of the chairs. Hawk follows and tries to kiss her. Kate pushes him away. Verisopht emerges, with Pyke, from the Wititterlies' box. Kate runs back into the Wititterlies' box, and Hawk and Pyke escort Verisopht back into their box, so we are now back where we started, as the Opera finishes, and everyone except Kate stands and applauds the Performers. Flowers are thrown as the chairs are whisked away.

Scene Eight

Ralph's office. Ralph at his desk. Noggs admits Kate to her uncle.

RALPH. Well, well, my dear. What now? (*Ralph a sharp gesture. Noggs withdraws, but we see he waits outside the room and listens. Kate too upset to say anything.*) Sit down, sit down. And tell me what's the matter. (*Kate sits. Ralph sits near her. "He was rather taken aback by the sudden firmness with which Kate looked up and answered him."*)

KATE. Uncle, I've been wronged. My feelings have been hurt, insulted, wounded, and by men who are your friends.

RALPH. What friends? I have no friends, girl.

KATE. By the men I saw here, then. And have been persecuting me. And if they're not your friends, and you know what they are—more shame on you for bringing me among them.

RALPH. There's something of your brother, in you, I can see.

KATE. I hope there is. I should be proud to know it. I will not bear these insults any longer.

RALPH. Insults? What d'you mean?

KATE. What do I mean? You ask me that? Remember, uncle, what took place in this house. (*Pause. She stands, goes to Ralph, puts her hand on his shoulder.*) I'm sorry, I don't mean to shout, be angry, violent. But you don't know what I have suffered. Oh, of course, you cannot tell what being a young woman feels like—how could I expect it? —but still, when I tell you that my heart is breaking, I am wretched, all I can ask is that you believe me. (*Ralph looking away.*) Uncle. I have had no counsellor, no-one to help or to protect me. Mother thinks they're honourable men, distinguished, and that, sad delusion, is the only thing she has to make her happy, and how could I undeceive her? You're the only person left. My only friend at hand. Almost my only friend at all. I need your help.

RALPH. Help? How can I help you, girl?

KATE. By telling them to stop. To leave me be. (*Ralph looks up at Kate. Pause.*) So will you tell them, uncle? (*Pause.*)

RALPH. No. They are my friends, in business. I cannot afford for them to be my enemies. Please understand. (*He turns to her. A slight smile.*) Some girls, would be quite proud, to have such, gallants at their feet. (*Pause.*) And even if, they are . . . it won't last long. Oh, soon enough, they'll find another entertainment. (*Pause.*) Surely, it is not too much to bear, just for a time?

KATE. Just for a time? I am to be wretched and degraded, and debased? Just for a time? (*Pause.*) Oh, uncle. You've been selling me. (*She turns and runs out. Ralph motionless. Outside, Kate stops, and breaks. Noggs steps towards her, puts his arm round her. She is too far gone to resist.*)

NOGGS. Oh, yes. Oh, yes. You're right to cry. But even righter, not to give way, back in there. Oh that was even righter. Now, cry, cry. I shall see you soon—and so will someone else.

KATE. Must—go. Bless you.

NOGGS. You too. Yes, yes, of course, must go. (*Noggs takes her towards the door.*) Oh, you were right, in there, right not to let him see you cry. (*Kate goes out. Noggs returns to his desk. A determined look on his face. "Newman Noggs stood at a little distance from the door, with his face towards it. And, with the sleeves of his coat turned back at the wrists, was occupied in bestowing the most vigorous, scientific, and straightforward blows upon the empty air. At first sight, this would have appeared merely a wise precaution for a man of sedentary habits, with the view of opening the chest and strengthening the muscles of the arms. But the intense eagerness and joy depicted in the face of New-man Noggs, which was suffused with perspiration: The surprising energy with which he directed a constant succession of blows towards a particular panel about five feet eight from the ground, and still worked*

*away in the most untiring and unpersevering manner, would have
sufficiently explained to the attentive observer, that his imagination
was threshing, to within an inch of his life, his body's most active employer, Mr. Ralph Nickleby". Noggs recovers from his exertion. He goes
to his desk. He finds a sheet of paper. He looks round, to doublecheck
he is alone. He begins to write a letter.)*
NOGGS. My dear young man. (*He crosses out.*) Dear Nicholas.

Scene Nine

*Portsmouth. Miss Snevellicci's apartments. The company is gathering
for the party. It is simplest to describe how they end up when Mr.
Snevellicci calls for silence. There are tables of various heights and
sizes, all covered with white cloths, jugs of wine, and glasses, arranged in a rectangular shape, with one side—the audience's side—
of the rectangle missing. There is thus a long, central section, and
two shorter sections coming downstage. Eventually, the set-up will
be that Mr. Snevellicci is dead centre, with Mrs. Snevellicci on one
side, and Mr. and Mrs. Crummles on the other. The rest of the Company fan out from there, with, as a general rule, the Women on stage
left and the men on stage right. The exceptions to that rule are Nicholas, who will sit next to Miss Snevellicci, Mrs. Grudden, who sits at
the downstage end of the Stage Right table, Mr. Lillyvick, who sits
near, but not next to, his wife, the erstwhile Miss Petowker, and
Smike, who hovers around pouring drinks and being helpful.
At this point, however, not everyone is here: those not here appear
in the next few moments. Downstage of the tables are, in three
groups: Nicholas, Smike and Folair; Mr. and Mrs. Snevellicci and
Miss Snevellicci; and Mr. and Mrs. Lillyvick. Mr. Snevellicci is red-
faced, bombastic, irritable and on the way to being drunk.*

FOLAIR. Well, there he is.
NICHOLAS. That's Mr. Snevellicci?
FOLAIR. Yes, it is.
NICHOLAS. And he—he is theatrical as well?
FOLAIR. Oh, certainly. Been in the business since he first played the
ten-year-old imps in the Christmas pantomime. He can sing a little,
dance a little, fence a bit, and act, but not too much . . . And since
he's took to so much rum and water, tends to play the military visitors

and speechless noblemen, you know . . . Ah, dear Mr. Snevellicci.
(*For Mr. Snevellicci has come over to Folair, with Miss Snevellicci.*)

MISS SNEVELLICCI. Ah, mamma, papa, please do meet Mr. Johnson.

MR. SNEVELLICCI. Oh, a privilege, a privilege.

MRS. SNEVELLICCI. Indeed.

NICHOLAS. The pleasure's mine.

MR. SNEVELLICCI. And have to say, dear boy, that haven't seen a hit
like that since my great, dear friend Mr. Glavormelly played the
Coburg.

FOLAIR. (*Drifting off.*) Glavormelly. (*The rest of the Company still arriving.*)

MR. SNEVELLICCI. Ever see him, sir?

NICHOLAS. No, I'm afraid I never did.

MR. SNEVELLICCI. What, never saw old Glavormelly? Not seen acting,
then, dear boy. If he had lived—

NICHOLAS. He's dead?

MR. SNEVELLICCI. Oh, yes, completely. Pushing up the daisies now, the
bourne from which no traveller, etcetera, and least can hope the poor
old boot's appreciated there. Ah, there he is. Old bricks and mortar.
Go and do my stuff. Excuse us, sir. (*And indeed, the Crummles family
have entered, with last of the Performers, and Mrs. Grudden. As Mr.
Snevellicci goes over to greet him, Mrs. Snevellicci takes the opportunity for a little word.*)

MRS. SNEVELLICCI. My daughter speaks, quite strongly of you, sir.

NICHOLAS. Oh, does she?

MRS. SNEVELLICCI. Yes, she does. Quite, quite uncommon strong.

NICHOLAS. Well, I assure you—

MRS. SNEVELLICCI. Yes, I know. (*Mrs. Snevellicci looks at Nicholas,
and gives a little wink and a smile, and goes off to join her husband.
Nicholas turns to see Mr. Lillyvick, whose wife is engaged in animated
chatter with the other women.*)

NICHOLAS. Well, Mr. Lillyvick. And how are you?

LILLYVICK. Quite well, sir. There is nothing like the married state,
depend on it.

NICHOLAS. Indeed!

LILLYVICK. How do you think she looks, sir? Mrs. Lillyvick, tonight?

NICHOLAS. She looks as handsome as she ever did. You are a lucky
man.

LILLYVICK. You're right there, sir, you're right. I often think, I couldn't
have done better if I'd been a young man, could I? You could not have
done much better, could you? (*Jabbing Nicholas with his elbow.*) Eh?

NICHOLAS. Oh, no, I—(*He is interrupted by Mr. Snevellicci, who has finished greeting the Crummleses, has had another drink, and feels it's time to get this jamboree on the road.*)

MR. SNEVELLICCI. Right then! Silence! Class to order. (*The stragglers sit, including Nicholas, whose closeness to Miss Snevellicci is noticed by the others.*) Ladies! Gentlemen. All welcome. In particular, the first. (*The ladies blush, the gentlemen applaud.*) And so, raise glasses. To the ladies. May God bless 'em. All of 'em. Unspliced and spliced, and those who are now in the former state, and who knows, very shortly, in the latter. (*This is so obvious a reference to Miss Snevellicci and Nicholas that the actress reacts.*)

MISS SNEVELLICCI. Oh, papa!

MR. SNEVELLICCI. But then, who knows? I don't. Does anyone?

MISS SNEVELLICCI. Papa! (*And Miss Snevellicci turns and runs, but is caught up with by the ladies, who cluster round her, covering her confusion.*)

MR. SNEVELLICCI. What's this? (*Miss Ledrook runs from the cluster to Mr. Snevellicci.*)

MISS LEDROOK. Oh, don't take any notice of it, sir. Say, that she exerts herself too much.

MR. SNEVELLICCI. She whats?

MRS. LILLYVICK. (*Approaching.*) She's only weak, and nervous. She has been so since this morning.

MR. SNEVELLICCI. Weak?

MRS. SNEVELLICCI. They mean—don't make a fuss of it, my dear.

MR. SNEVELLICCI. A fuss? What do you mean? (*Miss Snevellicci, recovered, comes over from the dispersing cluster.*) What? I'm to be instructed? Given marching orders? Told what I may do and say?

MISS SNEVELLICCI. Oh, pa, please don't—

MR. SNEVELLICCI. Don't what?

MISS SNEVELLICCI. Talk in that manner.

MR. SNEVELLICCI. Manner? Talk in any manner that I please. (*Miss Snevellicci and Mrs. Snevellicci look at each other.*) I'm not ashamed. The name is Snevellicci. Found in Broad Court, Bow Street, when in town. If out, inquire at the stage door. Look, dammit, had me portrait in cigar shops round the corner. Mentioned in the papers. Tell you what, if I found any chap was tampering, affections of me daughter, wouldn't talk. I would astonish him. In silence. That's my way. That is —my manner. (*He downs his drink.*) Hmph. What was I saying?

MRS. CRUMMLES. You were toasting everyone.

MR. SNEVELLICCI. (*Remembering.*) Oh, yes. The ladies. All of 'em. I love 'em, every one. (*All the men, for the sake of getting it over with, raise their glasses. Mr. Lillyvick has been growing agitated for some little time.*)

THE MEN. The la—

LILLYVICK. Not all of them, sir, surely?

MR. SNEVELLICCI. Oh, yes. Every one.

THE MEN. The la—

LILLYVICK. But that includes the married ladies, sir.

MR. SNEVELLICCI. Oh course! The memsahibs, certainly.

THE MEN. The—

MR. LILLYVICK. What, including Mrs. Lillyvick?

MRS. SNEVELLICCI. (*Impatiently.*) Why, yes, of course, including Mrs. Lillyvick. If I may say so, Mrs. L. especially. (*And Mr. Snevellicci winks at Mrs. Lillyvick. Then he blows her a kiss.*) Eh, what? (*Mrs. Lillyvick blushes. Mr. Lillyvick strikes Mr. Snevellicci on the nose.*) Hey, what this? Fisticuffs? (*The Company reacts as Mr. Snevellicci tries to hit Mr. Lillyvick.*) You strike me, sir?

LILLYVICK. I do. (*Nicholas, Smike one or two other actors rush in to separate them.*)

MRS. BRAVASSA. What's this?

MISS GAZINGI. What's happening?

MRS. LILLYVICK. Oh, lor.

LILLYVICK. (*Still struggling.*) You see that, sir? Here's purity and elegance combined, whose feelings have been violated—

MRS. LILLYVICK. Lor, what nonsense, Lillyvick. He ain't said nothing to me. (*Pause. The men let Lillyvick go. He turns to Mrs. Lillyvick.*)

LILLYVICK. Said, Henrietta? It was how he looked—

MRS. LILLYVICK. Well, d'you suppose that nobody is ever going to *look* at me again? A pretty thing, it would be, to be married, if that was the law!

LILLYVICK. You didn't mind it?

MRS. LILLYVICK. Mind it? What I minded was . . . You know, you ought to go down on your knees, I tell you, Lillyvick, and beg for everybody's pardon, that you ought.

LILLYVICK. Pardon, my dear?

MRS. LILLYVICK. Yes, and mine first. Do you suppose I ain't the best judge of what's proper and what's improper. (*Pause.*)

MISS BRAVASSA. Well, to be sure.

MISS LEDROOK. We'd notice.

MISS GAZINGI. If there'd been anything that needed to be taken notice of.

MR. SNEVELLICCI. Hm. Absolutely right. Spot on. There. So now that's settled—charge your glasses, one and all. (*And Mr. Snevellicci goes round the ladies, starting with Mrs. Lillyvick, giving them kisses. Lillyvick, broken, stumbles to the side.*)

MRS. GRUDDEN. (*Hiccups.*) Beg pardon. (*We realise that Mrs. Grudden is slightly inebriated. She reaches into her reticule for a handkerchief and finds a letter.*) Oh. Mr. Johnson.

NICHOLAS. Yes?

MRS. GRUDDEN. There's a letter for you. Sorry, it completely slipped my mind. (*Mrs. Grudden a little giggle. Nicholas a quizzical look, takes the letter. Increasingly worried look. Mr. Snevellicci has finished kissing all the ladies.*)

MR. SNEVELLICCI. So—a toast.

MRS. GRUDDEN. Toast.

MR. SNEVELLICCI. To—to the brightest, male, star in your, way blue yonder—Mr. Johnson.

EVERYONE. Mr. Johnson.

FOLAIR. Speech! Speech!

MRS. GRUDDEN. Speech. (*Applause. Nicholas steps forward.*)

NICHOLAS. My dear friends, I am very sorry.

CRUMMLES. Sorry?

NICHOLAS. That I must—in a nutshell, I must leave your company. (*Pause.*)

MISS SNEVELLICCI. What? Leave?

MRS. GRUDDEN. Oh, hoity-toity.

FOLAIR. Stuff.

NICHOLAS. There are some—circumstances, that call me away.

CRUMMLES. But to return, sir, surely?

NICHOLAS. No.

CRUMMLES. (*Quietly.*) Not even if, your salary was—

NICHOLAS. No. (*Pause. Everyone looks at Mrs. Crummles, who has been building up to her reaction.*)

MRS. CRUMMLES. This is Astounding.

NICHOLAS. I am sorry that I could not have prepared you for it, Mrs. Crummles.

MRS. CRUMMLES. So am I. (*Pause.*)

CRUMMLES. Well, then. . . . Well then. . . . We will announce it. Monday. Positively last appearance. Posters, first thing in the morning.

NICHOLAS. Sir, I'm—

MRS. CRUMMLES. Yes, of course. And then, on Tuesday, reengagement for just one night more, and then on Wednesday, Thursday, yielding to the wishes of our numerous and influential patrons—

NICHOLAS. Ma'am, I must be off tonight.

MRS. CRUMMLES. Tonight?

NICHOLAS. Immediately. At once.

MRS. CRUMMLES. No positively last appearance?

NICHOLAS. No.

MRS. CRUMMLES. Not one night more, by popular demand?

NICHOLAS. No, sorry.

MRS. CRUMMLES. There's nothing we can do or say, to move you from this awesome pass? There's nothing I can do or say, to melt your stern, unyielding heart?

NICHOLAS. There isn't, I'm afraid.

MRS. CRUMMLES. Then—there's, no more to say. (*She turns. Turns back.*) Except—farewell.

CRUMMLES. Farewell, my noble, lion-hearted boy! (*Crummles embraces Nicholas. The Phenomenon bursts into tears. Others dab their eyes with handkerchiefs.*)

MR. HETHERINGTON. Farewell.

MISS BELVAWNEY. Farewell.

MR. BANE. Farewell.

CRUMMLES. If nothing can detain you with us. . . .

MISS SNEVELLICCI. Nothing?

CRUMMLES. Then—

MRS. CRUMMLES. (*Embracing Nicholas.*) Farewell. (*The Great Embrace is still occurring when Mrs. Grudden makes an announcement.*)

MRS. GRUDDEN. I shall. Now sing. A song. (*Consternation.*) I shall require. A player at the pianofort. (*More consternation.*) To sing it.

MRS. CRUMMLES. Mrs. Grudden, what is going on?

MRS. GRUDDEN. I am. (*To the musicians.*) Thank you. (*Nicholas collars Smike.*)

NICHOLAS. Come, Smike, let's go—

SMIKE. (*Fascinated.*) But—look—(*Mrs. Grudden is getting her note. She begins to sing an extraordinarily sentimental ballad. During it, various members of the Company come to Nicholas and shake his hand. Lenville's shake is reconciliatory, but he is clearly delighted. The penultimate shaker is Miss Snevellicci. As they finish shaking, the Company members join Mrs. Grudden's song, or burst into tears, or something.*)

MRS. GRUDDEN & COMPANY—SONG.*

> O stay but for an hour;
> If any power I have in pleading,
> No way but only this to yield a kiss
> And feel my death succeeding,
> O how can I be strong
> As you would have me be
> Though duty calls I long to keep you here with me,
> But no, go, and hold this memory
>
> Farewell, my dear, farewell,
> For ever let us part:
> But don't, I pray you, tell the news to my aching heart.
> Be kind, my dear, be kind: Though hope at last be gone,
> And even my love be blind,
> O let it go hoping on. (*During the next verse as the attention has completely transferred, Nicholas taps Smike's arm, and nods regretfully, and Smike realises they have to go. Nicholas is nearly out when he is confronted by Mr. Lillyvick.*)

LILLYVICK. Sir. I can—I can see nothing.

NICHOLAS. What?

LILLYVICK. I can see nothing, more, in Mrs. Lillyvick. Of Miss Petowker. (*Pause.*)

NICHOLAS. I'm—so sorry. (*Nicholas and Smike leave. The song reaches a tumultuous climax.*)

MRS. GRUDDEN & COMPANY.

> Farewell, my dear, farewell.*
> For ever we must part
> But don't I pray yoy, tell the news to my aching heart.
> Be kind, my dear, be kind:
> Though hope at last be gone,
> And even my love be blind,
> O let it go hoping on.
> Farewell, my dear, farewell,
> For ever we must part:
> But don't, I pray you, tell the news to my aching heart.
> Be kind, my dear, be kind:
> Though hope at last be gone,

* See special note on copyright page.

And even my love be blind,
   O let it go hoping on. (*And, miraculously, the chairs and tables, and the Company of Mr. Vincent Crummles, have all disappeared.*)

Scene Ten

The Wititterlies'. The chaise-longue, and one chair. Enter Kate and Mrs. Wititterly.

MRS. WITITTERLY. Now, child, you must tell me how you came to know Lord Frederick, and all those other charming gentlemen.
KATE. Oh, I met them at my uncle's.
MRS. WITITTERLY. I was so glad—if surprised—at the opportunity which that respectable person, your dear mother, gave us of being known to them.
KATE. Yes, I, too, was surprised.
MRS. WITITTERLY. Though, of course, we have been nearly introduced a dozen times. (*A bell.*) Ah, that will be them now. Alphonse! (*Alphonse goes out. Kate agitated.*) I naturally told them they could call. Miss Nickleby . . . You cannot think of going.
KATE. You are very good. But—
MRS. WITITTERLY. Please, please don't upset me, make me speak so loud, Miss Nickleby, I beg—(*Enter Alphonse.*)
ALPHONSE. Uh, Mr. Hawk, Lord Mulberry Pyke, Sir Frederick Pluck, and Mr. Verisopht. Or something. (*Enter the above-named.*)
MRS. WITITTERLY. Gentlemen, I am delighted, I am sure. Please, gentlemen, my lord, sit down. (*As they do so:*)
HAWK. And how are you today, Mrs. Wititterly?
MRS. WITITTERLY. Well, I must own, Sir Mulberry, that I am still quite torn to pieces.
HAWK. (*With a look at Kate.*) Mm?
MRS. WITITTERLY. (*To Verisopht.*) I am always ill after drama, my lord, and after the opera I scarcely exist for several days.
VERISOPHT. Yes . . . I'm, the same. (*Mr. Wititterly bursts in.*)
MR. WITITTERLY. (*To Lord Frederick Verisopht.*) My lord, I am delighted, honoured, proud. I am indeed, most proud. (*To Mrs. Wititterly.*) My soul, you'll suffer for this thrill tomorrow.
VERISOPHT. Suffer?
HAWK. Pray, whatever for?
MR. WITITTERLY. Oh, the reaction, sir this violent strain upon the ner-

vous system, what ensues? A sinking, a depression, lowness, lassitude, debility. My lord, if Sir Tumley Snuffim were to see that frail creature at this moment, he'd not give a—(*With a toss of snuff.*) this, for her continued life! (*Mrs. Wititterly sighs.*)

PYKE. It's obvious that Mrs. Wititterly's a martyr.

MR. WITITTERLY. Oh, she is.

PLUCK. Perhaps, in fact . . . the other room, in order to escape the draught . . . ?

MRS. WITITTERLY. (*Less faintly.*) What draught . . . ? (*Pyke and Pluck leading Mrs. Wititterly to the "other room."*)

PYKE. A constitution like a flower, just the slightest puff of wind, it's clear—

MRS. WITITTERLY. (*Vaguely.*) Sir Mulberry, my lord . . .

(*Hawk gestures to Verisopht that they must follow. Verisopht stands, annoyed, and follows Mrs. Wititterly, her husband, Pluck and Pyke. Kate is trying to follow too, when Hawk turns, and stands in her way. This during:*)

MR. WITITTERLY. You're right, sir, you're so right. If anybody will produce to me a greater martyr than my wife . . . (*And, as Mrs. Wititterly is fussed round, Kate is in the first room alone with Sir Mulberry Hawk.*)

HAWK. Don't hurry, now, don't hurry—(*Kate tries to pass. Hawk prevents her.*) Now, then, stay—

KATE. You'd better not detain me, sir.

HAWK. Why not? Oh, my dear creature, why d'you keep up this show of anger with me, eh?

KATE. Show? Show? How dare you, to presume to speak to me, sir—to address me—

HAWK. You look pretty in a passion, dear Miss Nickleby.

KATE. I hold you, I must tell you, in the bitterest detestation and contempt. If you find looks of, disgust, aversion, if you find such looks attractive—let me go, sir, let me join—

HAWK. Oh, I will let you join, Miss Nickleby, I promise you. (*Kate, speechless, looks at Sir Mulberry Hawk.*) And I will see you very often, we're invited here, whenever and however we—desire. (*Kate makes another attempt to get past Hawk, who tries, roughly, to embrace her. Meanwhile, both Mrs. Wititterly and Lord Verisopht have realised the device that has been used on them. Mrs. Wititterly is insisting to her husband on going back into the first room. Kate pulls herself back from Hawk. He decides to leave it there.*) I will be joining you, Miss Nickleby. (*Kate turns to go. Then, she decides to turn back, to speak to Hawk. During this, Mrs. Wititterly appears in between the two rooms, followed by Verisopht, Pluck, Pyke and Mr. Wititterly.*) Now, my lord. We should not outstay our welcome.

VERISOPHT. No. (*Pause.*) We shouldn't.

HAWK. We hope, Mrs. Wititterly, to find you soon in better health. Don't we?

PLUCK. Certainly we do.

PYKE. Indubitably. (*Enter Alphonse.*)

MR. WITITTERLY. My lord, Sir Mulberry, I trust that you will—

HAWK. Oh, yes. Very soon. (*Mr. Wititterly, who doesn't understand the atmosphere, fusses round as Verisopht, Hawk, Pyke and Pluck depart. Then Mr. Wititterly moves towards his wife, who has not moved. She dismisses him with a gesture. Mr. Wititterly goes out. Mrs. Wititterly takes a step towards Kate.*)

MRS. WITITTERLY. Miss Nickleby, I wish to speak to you. I'm sorry, but you leave me no alternative. (*Kate says nothing.*) Your—this behaviour, is so very far from pleasing me . . . I'm very anxious that you should do well, Miss Nickleby, but you will not, if you go on as, as you do. (*Kate turns away. Mrs. Wititterly stridently.*) And you needn't think that looking at me in that way, Miss Nickleby, will stop me saying what I'm going to say, which I regard as a religious duty. You will not look at me, in that, that manner. I am not Sir Mulberry, no, nor Lord Frederick Verisopht, Miss Nickleby; nor am I Mr. Pluck, nor Mr. Pyke. If such things had been done when *I* was a young girl—I don't suppose it would have been believed.

KATE. I don't—

MRS. WITITTERLY. Please, I will not be answered! I will not, Miss Nickleby. D'you hear?

KATE. I hear you, ma'am.

MRS. WITITTERLY. And I must tell you, once, for all, I must insist upon your altering your forward manner with those gentlemen, who visit at this house. It's not becoming. It's improper. It's—unchaste.

KATE. Oh. Is not this, too cruel, too hard to bear? It's not enough, that I should suffer as I do, from contact with these, people, but I am exposed to this unjust and most unfounded charge!

MRS. WITITTERLY. You'll have the goodness to recall, Miss Nickleby, that when you use such terms as 'unjust' and 'unfounded', you are implying, in effect, that I am stating that which is untrue.

KATE. I do. I say that. It is vilely, grossly, wilfully untrue. Oh, is it possible! That someone of my own sex can sit by, and not have seen the misery those libertines have caused me! Is it possible that you can't see the disrespect, contempt they hold for both of us? And can I not expect from you, another woman, and so much my senior, a little—female aid and sympathy? I can't believe it.

MRS. WITITTERLY. What? Disrespect? Contempt? What, senior? (*Mr. Wititterly and Alphonse run into the room.*)

MR. WITITTERLY. What's the matter? Heavens, Julia! Look up, my life, look up!

MRS. WITITTERLY. Sir Tumley! Get Sir Tumley!

MR. WITITTERLY. (*To Alphonse.*) Run, run quickly—fetch Sir Tumley. Go! (*Alphonse scuttles out. To Kate.*) I knew it, knew, Miss Nickleby. All that society, it's been too much for her. This is, this is all soul, you know, soul, every bit of it. Come, help, to get her to her room. (*Kate to the aid of Mr. Wititterly. Mrs. Wititterly looks up at Kate.*)

MRS. WITITTERLY. Please, take your hands off me. (*Mr. Wititterly looks surprised and confused. He picks up his wife and carries her out. Kate left alone. Enter Sir Mulberry Hawk. Kate sees him. He picks up a cane that he has left behind.*)

HAWK. Oh, poor Miss Nickleby. Where can you look, now, for protection.

Scene Eleven

The streets of London. Bare stage. Narrators burst on to the stage. Amidst them are Smike and Nicholas.

NICHOLAS. London at last! (*Narrators tell us and show us of the Great City.*)

NARRATORS.

And there they were in the noisy, bustling, crowded streets of London,

Now displaying long double-rows of brightly-burning lamps, and illuminated besides with the brilliant flood that streamed from the windows of the shops.

Streams of people apparently without end poured on and on, jostling each other in the crowd, and hurrying forward, scarcely seeming to notice the riches that surrounded them on every side;

Emporia of splendid dresses, the materials brought from every corner of the world;

Vessels of burnished gold and silver, wrought into every exquisite form of vase, and dish, and goblet;

Screws and irons for the crooked, clothes for the newly-born, drugs for the sick, coffins for the dead, and churchyards for the buried—

Pale and pinched-up faces hovered about the windows where was tempting food,

Hungry eyes wandered over the profusion guarded by one thin sheet of brittle glass—

Life and death went hand in hand—

Wealth and poverty stood side by side—

Repletion and starvation laid them down together—

But, still—

It was—

London! (*The music changes. More urgent, darker. The streets more threatening than gaudy, as Nicholas and Smike rush through them, to knock on a door. Crowl appears above.*)
NICHOLAS. Oh, Mr. Crowl. Is Newman here.
CROWL. Oh, no. But you're expected. Laid out food and drink as well.
NICHOLAS. D'you know when he'll be home?
CROWL. A troublesome affair of business, keeps him. Not be home, he says, till twelve o'clock.
NICHOLAS. Then, sir, look after this young man for me? And see he's fed and rested?
CROWL. Of, of course I will. Make sure he's fed, and warmed. (*Music again, and Nicholas runs round through the ever-darkening streets, as*

if to another front door. He knocks. Hannah—Miss La Creevy's maid—appears above.)

NICHOLAS. Oh, Hannah. Is your mistress in?

HANNAH. Who? Miss La Creevy?

NICHOLAS. Yes, of course.

HANNAH. Oh, no. She's out.

NICHOLAS. Where out?

HANNAH. Out at the theatre.

NICHOLAS. Which? And when will she return?

HANNAH. Dunno. (*And Nicholas runs off again, through the streets till finally he comes to another "door" and beats on it.*)

NICHOLAS. (*Banging on the door.*) Hey, mother! Mother! Kate! Kate, are you there? (*He leans against the door, exhausted.*) What *is* this? Where *are* they? *All* of them!

NARRATORS.

And then Nicholas suddenly recalled, from Newman's letter, that his sister's new employers lived in Chelsea,

And with the firm resolve to leave no stone unturned, he set his course to Sloane Street,

And such was his state, confused and tired and desperate,

He hardly saw, outside the fashionable coffee-house, the cabriolet that juddered to a halt before him.

Scene Twelve

Inside and outside a fashionable coffee-house. During the following, the coffee-house is set up: three tables, two with customers dining, being served by two Waiters and a Serving-Girl, whom we shall call Walter, Wilbur and Wanda. But, for the moment, our attention is on Nicholas, downstage, as Hawk, Verisopht, Pluck and Pyke enter, on their way to the coffee-house. We imagine that the door to the coffee-house is behind Nicholas, and the entering Revellers need to pass round him to get to it.

HAWK. Now, gentlemen, another pint or two of wine?

VERISOPHT. Why not? Another toast?

PLUCK. Oh, yes.

PYKE. Indeed. (*Pyke is already in the coffee-house, Pluck following. Verisopht needs to be kept upright by Hawk.*)

PLUCK. Hey, waiter, magnum!

HAWK. To whom, my lord?

VERISOPHT. Who else? The lady we've been drinking to all evening. That damned, enchanting little . . .

HAWK. (*Promptly.*) Kate.

VERISOPHT. Kate Nickleby. (*Hawk and Verisopht enter the coffee-house. Nicholas follows.*)

HAWK. Hey, waiter! Magnum!

PLUCK. Where is that girl? Girl with the magnums? Is there no service here? (*Wanda hurries in with the bottles on a tray. Walter hurries up with a corkscrew. Hawk, who is sitting on the edge of the empty table with Lord Verisopht, grabs the screw.*)

HAWK. I'll do it myself, dammit. Doubtless you'll take half-an-hour, and break the cork. (*To Wanda.*) You—glasses! (*Walter bows obsequiously, and nods to Wanda, who hurries out, having her bottom pinched by Hawk on the way. Nicholas has entered. The place is rather richer than he is used to patronising, and he is aware that he is dusty and travel-stained.*)

PYKE. (*To a terrified Customer.*) Excuse me, sir, but could I— (*Taking glasses from the table.*) Thank you ever so.

HAWK. (*Opening the magnum and spilling its contents.*) The thing is, my dear lord, about this little Nickleby, is that she is, in fact, quite similar to that old crow, her uncle. (*Hawk pours wine into the glasses which Pyke and Pluck have liberated from the other Customers.*)

VERISOPHT. Damned sight prettier. (*Wanda enters with the glasses. The party raise their glasses to her. She looks to Walter, who nods at her, and she goes out, having her bottom pinched by Mr. Pluck. One of the other customers gestures to Walter, and they whisper about the intrusion.*)

HAWK. Indeed. But, nonetheless, in essence, quite the same. You need something from her in the way of—interest, she holds back, to be more sought after—as he does; and when she/he relents, at last, the bargain's doubly hard, but the, advance, is more than doubly welcome.

PLUCK. The advance.

PYKE. Let's have some oysters, dammit! (*Walter has gone to Nicholas.*)

WALTER. Yes, can I help you?

NICHOLAS. No. (*And Nicholas marches over to Sir Mulberry Hawk. Hawk looks up at Nicholas.*) Sir, may I have a word with you?

HAWK. With me?

NICHOLAS. That's what I said. (*The rest of the coffee-house becoming aware of what's going on.*)

HAWK. Well. A mysterious intruder.

NICHOLAS. Will you step apart with me, or d'you refuse?

HAWK. Sir, name your business, and then go away. (*Wanda coming in with a tray of food. Nicholas takes a card from his pocket and throws it on the table.*)

NICHOLAS. There, sir. My business you will guess. (*Wanda stops in her tracks, turns to go, Walter gestures to her, and she puts down the tray as far as possible from the hostilities, and goes out.*) Now, sir. Your name, and your address.

HAWK. Sir, I will give you neither. (*The customer who has paid his bill gets up and leaves.*)

NICHOLAS. Then—if there's—one gentleman, among this party, he will tell me who you are, and where you live. (*Nicholas is talking too loudly.*) I am the brother of the lady who has been the subject of this conversation. I demand—some satisfaction. (*Pluck and Pyke a step towards Nicholas.*)

HAWK. Oh, no, let the fellow talk. I've nothing serious to say to a boy of his station, and his pretty sister shall save him a broken head, at least.

NICHOLAS. I'll follow you. All night, if need be. I will know you.

HAWK. (*Laughs.*) Hm. (*Hawk pours another drink. Another customer gestures to Wilbur, who goes and takes his money. Nicholas to Walter.*)

NICHOLAS. Do you know this person's name?

WALTER. This gentleman? No, sir, I don't, sir.

HAWK. (*To Walter.*) Do you know *this* person's name?

WALTER. I don't know anyone.

HAWK. (*Tossing Nicholas's card to Walter.*) Then you will find his name, there, sir. And when you've mastered it, then you can burn it.

WALTER. Burn it. Right. (*Walter picks up the card and withdraws. Walter, Wilbur and Wanda now in a little huddle by the kitchen door.*)

HAWK. (*To Nicholas.*) You are an errand boy, for all I know. And now, be off with you. (*Hawk turns to his friends.*)

NICHOLAS. I am the son of a country gentleman. Your equal in birth and education, and your superior, I trust, in everything besides. (*Hawk laughs.*) (*Blurted.*) Miss Nickleby's my sister, sir! I will not leave. (*The last customer hurries out.*)

HAWK. Well, then, we'll go.

NICHOLAS. I'll follow you.

HAWK. Well, then, we'll stay. (*Long pause.*)

VERISOPHT. I think, perhaps, I will go. It's very late.

HAWK. Oh, is it? Very well, my lord.

PLUCK. Perhaps my lord would like a travelling companion.

PYKE. Or two.

HAWK. Then all of you—do go. (*Slight pause. Verisopht goes to Walter, and signs the instantly proffered bill.*)

VERISOPHT. Good night, then. (*Verisopht, Pluck and Pyke go out. Hawk picks up the magnum, goes to another table. He sits and drinks. Nicholas is watching Hawk like a hawk. A very long pause. A clock chimes. Walter, Wilbur, and Wanda look at the clock and at each other. Another long pause. Hawk finishes his wine.*)

HAWK. Waiter—my cane. (*He stands. Wilbur brings Hawk's cane. Hawk takes it, and throws some coins on the table.*)

NICHOLAS. So, will you make yourself known to me, sir? (*Pause.*)

HAWK. No. (*Hawk goes, Nicholas follows. Walter, Wilbur and Wanda walk forward and deliver their lines out front, as the chairs and tables of the coffee-room disappear, and the cabriolet is set up in the darkness.*)

WILBUR. And there was a private cabriolet in waiting,

WANDA. And the groom opened the apron,

WALTER And jumped out to the horse's head,

WILBUR. Who was a thoroughbred,

WANDA. And consequently Very Highly Strung. (*Now we can see the cabriolet. It is a small, private carriage, represented by a chair, carried by four actors and pointing upstage, on which Hawk sits with his whip. Upstage of that are more actors, covered with a long black cloth, to represent the horse, as, in a moment, it rears and bolts. This effect relies on careful lighting, so that we hardly see the other actors, but only Hawk, Nicholas and the head of the horse.*)

WALTER. And the young man walked up to the older gentleman,

WILBUR. And grasped his arm, and spoke: (*Nicholas, held up by actors, as if on the footboard of the carriage.*)

NICHOLAS. So, will you make yourself known to me?

HAWK. No, damn you. (*To his Coachman.*) Barton!

NICHOLAS. I'll hang on to the footboard.

HAWK. You will be horsewhipped if you do. Barton, let go her head.

NICHOLAS. (*Clinging on to Hawk.*) You shall not—shall not go—I swear—till you have told me—

176

HAWK. Now! Leave go! (*The "horse" plunges and rears.*) Will you let go?

NICHOLAS. Will you tell me who you are?

HAWK. No!

NICHOLAS. No! (*Hawk strikes Nicholas with his whip. Nicholas grabs the whip and strikes Hawk. The "horse" is rearing wildly. Screams of passers-by. Nicholas strikes Hawk again. The horse bolts: in other words, the horse actors rush upstage, outside of the light, followed by the actors carrying Hawk. Nicholas reels away. A huge crash and darkness.*)

Scene Thirteen

Noggs' garret and the Nicklebys' house in Thames Street. Bare stage. Early morning. Noggs and Smike enter one side, Nicholas the other. He is bleeding.

NICHOLAS. Don't be alarmed. There's no harm done, beyond what a basin of water will repair.

NOGGS. No harm! What have you been doing?

NICHOLAS. I know everything. I have heard a part, and guessed the rest. But now we must go and see them. You see, I am collected. Now, good friend.

NOGGS. Your clothes are torn. You're walking lame. Please, let me see to you.

NICHOLAS. No. No. I must go to them. (*Pause. Noggs nods to Smike, who is looking upset by Nicholas's appearance. To Smike.*) Smike, we're going to my home.

SMIKE. We—home? Your home?

NICHOLAS. Our home. (*And Nicholas takes Smike's hand, leading him, to Kate. Noggs goes out. We are now in the Nicklebys' house in Thames Street.*)

NICHOLAS. So Kate, this is my faithful friend and fellow-

KATE. (*Going to Smike.*) Dear Smike. I've been so looking forward, after all my brother's told me. And to thank you, for the comfort you have been to him.

SMIKE. I'm—very pleased to meet you. Uh—he's my only friend. I would lay down my life, to help him. (*Enter Mrs. Nickleby, and Miss La Creevy, with luggage.*)

MRS. NICKLEBY. Well, Lord bless my life. To think that Sir Mulberry

Hawk should be such an abandoned wretch; when I was congratulating myself every day on his being an admirer of our dear Kate's. . . .

MISS LA CREEVY. Now, come, dear Mrs. Nickleby, please try to cheer up, do.

MRS. NICKLEBY. Oh, I dare say, dear Miss La Creevy, that it's very easy to instruct someone to cheer up, but if you had had as many reasons to cheer down as I have—and, oh mercy, think of Mr. Pyke and Mr. Pluck, two of the perfectest true gentlemen that ever lived. . . .

KATE. But come now, mother, there's a coach outside, to take us to the Strand. To Miss La Creevy's.

MISS LA CREEVY. Everything is ready, and a hearty welcome too. Now let me go with you downstairs. (*Miss La Creevy and Mrs. Nickleby turn to go and see Smike.*)

MRS. NICKLEBY. Oh, uh—uh, Nicholas—

NICHOLAS. Oh, mother, Miss La Creevy. This is Smike. My friend—who came with me from Yorkshire. You remember?

MRS. NICKLEBY. Smike.

NICHOLAS. That's right.

SMIKE. I'm very—

MRS. NICKLEBY. Oh, dear . . .

KATE. Uh, mother—

MRS. NICKLEBY. Oh, it's so like Pyke. I shall be better presently. (*She makes to go. Then turns back, trying hard to be a good hostess.*) I don't suppose, that, while in Yorkshire, Mr. Smike, you might have taken dinner with the Grimbles, of Grimble Hall?

SMIKE. The Grimbles.

MRS. NICKLEBY. A most proud man, Sir—Sir Hadley Grimble—with six quite lovely daughters, and the finest park in the North Riding.

NICHOLAS. Oh, mother. D'you suppose that this—unfortunate poor outcast would receive an invitation to the finest house in the North Riding?

MRS. NICKLEBY. Finest park, dear. The house was not, I think . . .

MISS LA CREEVY. Now, please come, Mrs. Nickleby. (*Mrs. Nickleby a last look, and then she goes out. Miss La Creevy realizes that brother and sister wish to talk to each other, so:*)

MISS LA CREEVY. And, Mr. Smike? (*She takes Smike's hand.*)

SMIKE. New home. (*Miss La Creevy takes Smike out. Nicholas and Kate left together.*)

NICHOLAS. I'd thought, to run away would help you. Thought, if I stayed here, you'd be without protection. (*Pause. Kate runs and embraces Nicholas.*)

KATE. Oh, I've been so unhappy.

NICHOLAS. Oh, my darling girl.

KATE. Don't leave me any more. You promise me?

NICHOLAS. Of course. I'll never leave you. (*Slight pause.*) Tell me—tell me that I acted for the best.

KATE. Why should I tell you what we know so well? (*They part to go out. Nicholas stops her.*)

NICHOLAS. I will write to him. I will tell him we renounce him, and will not be beholden to him any more. (*Pause.*)

KATE. We are just beholden to each other. (*Smike enters to pick up the last of the luggage.*)

SMIKE. I'm very pleased to meet you, Kate. Kate Nickleby. (*Kate and Nicholas, smiling, lead Smike out.*)

Scene Fourteen

The apartments of Sir Mulberry Hawk. Verisopht tending to the broken form of Sir Mulberry, who lies on a couch, "with a shattered limb, a body severely bruised, a face disfigured with half-healed scars, and pallid from the exhaustion of recent pain and fever." Enter Pluck and Pyke, with newspapers.

HAWK. Well, then?

PLUCK. It is—it's noised abroad in all directions.

PYKE. Every club and gaming room has rung with it.

PLUCK. There's even been a song composed, we hear, and printed too—

PYKE. With most—unfunny lyrics, wouldn't you agree, Pluck?

PLUCK. Yes, Pyke, in the very worst of taste.

HAWK. When I, am off, this cursed bed—I will have, such revenge, as never man had yet. By God, I will. He's—this damned accident—has marked me for a week or two, but I'll put such a mark on him that he will carry to his grave. I'll slit his nose and ears—I'll flog him—maim him—(*Verisopht, nervously.*)

VERISOPHT. Yes, you might. Might try. But if you did—I should try to prevent you.

HAWK. What?

VERISOPHT. I have—been thinking. (*Slight pause.*) And—It is my

view, in fact—that you—you should have told him who you were. And
given him your card. For as it is—you did wrong. I did too. Because I
didn't interfere. What happened afterwards was more your fault than
his, and it should not, shall not, be cruelly visited upon him. It shall
not, indeed.

HAWK. You pale, green boy, you parsonage, what's this?

VERISOPHT. I do believe, too, on my honour, that the sister is as virtuous and modest a young lady as she is a handsome one: and, of the
brother, I say that he acted as a brother should. And I wish, with all my
heart and soul, that any one of us came out of this—thing, half as well
as he does. (*Exit Lord Frederick Verisopht.*)

HAWK. Well, Well, there's a thing. Well, there's a turnaround. (*He
turns, and screams at Pluck and Pyke, who have been notably silent
and unsupportive over the last few moments.*) Don't you agree?

PYKE. Don't you agree that there's a turnaround, then, Pluck?

PLUCK. Pyke, don't you think that there's a—thing? (*Hawk looks at his
lieutenants. They look at each other. They go out.*)

Scene Fifteen

The street. Bare stage. Enter Nicholas.

NICHOLAS. And the next morning, Nicholas went once more to the
General Agency Office, in search of a position. (*Nicholas goes downstage, and mimes looking in the window of an employment exchange.
He is joined by Poor People, who narrate the following sequence.*) The
office looked just the same as when he had left it last,

NARRATORS.

And indeed, with one or two exceptions, there seemed to be the
very same placards in the window that he has seen before. (*They
are joined, looking at the placards, by a short, elderly Gentleman,
dressed in a somewhat untidy, old-fashioned, comfortable style.*)

There were the same unimpeachable masters and mistresses in
want of virtuous servants,

And the same virtuous servants in want of unimpeachable masters
and mistresses.

And the same magnificent estates for the investment of capital,

And the same enormous quantities of capital to be invested in estates,

And, in short, the same opportunities of all sorts for people who wanted to make their fortunes. (*The Poor People disperse. The old Gentleman, who is smiling, and even chuckling a little at the placards, is still there. His name is Mr. Charles Cheeryble.*)

LAST NARRATOR. And a most extraordinary proof it was of the national prosperity, that people had not been found to avail themselves of such advantages long ago. (*Nicholas and Mr. Charles looking at the cards, and, occasionally, when they think the other isn't, at each other. This pantomime carries on for a few moments, when Mr. Charles turns to go, and Nicholas catches his eye, and stammers out, in embarrassment.*)

NICHOLAS. Oh, I'm sorry, I——

MR. CHARLES. (*Who is Welsh.*) Oh, no offence. Oh, no offence, at all. (*They both smile. Nicholas waves at the cards.*)

NICHOLAS. A great many opportunities here, sir.

MR. CHARLES. A great many people, willing and anxious to be employed, have thought so very often, I dare say. (*Pause. They both smile again.*)

NICHOLAS. Yes, I, um——

MR. CHARLES. Yes you um what, young sir?

NICHOLAS. (*At a rush.*) I merely hoped, or, thought, I mean to say— you had some object in consulting these advertisements?

MR. CHARLES. You mean, you thought that I was seeking a position? Eh? Hm? Eh?

NICHOLAS. Un—no.

MR. CHARLES. A very natural thought. Whatever. A highly comprehensible opinion. And, in fact, you'll split your sides at this, young sir, I thought the same of you.

NICHOLAS. Well sir, if you had, you'd not be too far from the truth.

MR. CHARLES. Eh? What? Dear me. No, no. A well-behaved young gentleman, reduced to such necessities. Can such things be?

NICHOLAS. (*Turning to go.*) I'm sorry, but they are, in my case; you'll forgive me.

MR. CHARLES. Stay. What do you mean, forgive you? What in heaven's name should I forgive you for? (*Nicholas turns back.*)

NICHOLAS. Oh, merely that your face and manner—both so unlike any I have seen—tempted me into an avowal, which to any other stranger

BONNEY:...My lords, ladies, and gentlemen: I must state that I have visited the houses of the poor, and have found them destitute of the slightest vestige of a muffin, or a crumpet, which there appears to be much reason to believe some of these persons do not taste from year's end to year's end. It is this melancholy state of affairs that the company proposes to correct...firstly, by prohibiting under dire penalties all private muffin and crumpet trading of every description.

TILDA: Well, I never had such luck. It's all you, Mr. Nickleby, I'm sure. I should like to have you for a partner always.

NICHOLAS: Well, I wish you had.

TILDA: Though if you win at cards, of course, you'll have a bad wife, sure as sure.

NICHOLAS: Not if your wish is gratified, Miss Price.

NICHOLAS: Oh, Smike. Oh—Smike. Why do you kneel to me?

SMIKE: To go. Go anywhere. Go everywhere. The world's end. To the churchyard grave. I can. You'll let me. Come away with you. You are my home.

MISS SNEVELLICCI: My darling Led—Miss Ledrook, from the company—was taken so ill in the night, we had to all move rooms. I thought she would expire, there, in my arms!
NICHOLAS: Well, such a fate is almost to be envied.

KATE: Don't leave me any more. You promise me?
NICHOLAS: Of course. I'll never leave you. Tell me—tell me that I
acted for the best.
KATE: Why should I tell you what we know so well?

NICHOLAS: (prompting) Such mortal drugs I have—
SMIKE: Such mortal drugs I have...
NICHOLAS: But Mantua's law—
SMIKE: But Mantua's law...
          Is death to any—one who utters them.

CRUMMLES COMPANY: See upon our smiling land,
Where the wealth of nations stand,
Where Prosperity and Industry walk ever
hand in hand,
Where so many blessings crowd,
'Tis our duty to be proud:
Up and answer, English yeomen, sing it joy-
fully aloud!

POOR PEOPLE: From day to day
In the same unvarying way
How crafty avarice grew rich, and manly honest
hearts were poor and sad
How few they were who tenanted the stately homes,
And how many those who lay in foul and rancid
tenements...

PHOTOGRAPHS BY MARTHA SWOPE

in this wilderness of London, I should not have dreamt of making. (*Slight pause.*)

MR. CHARLES. Now, that's very good. That is most aptly put. Yes, yes, a wilderness. As it was once to me.

NICHOLAS. It was?

MR. CHARLES. (*Sticking out a foot.*) Bare feet.

NICHOLAS. I beg your pardon?

MR. CHARLES. Came here. They did. Bare and naked. I remember to this day. So what brings you to London?

NICHOLAS. Well, my father—

MR. CHARLES. Died? And left a widowed mother?

NICHOLAS. Yes.

MR. CHARLES. And little brothers, sisters?

NICHOLAS. Sister. One.

MR. CHARLES. And you a scholar too, I dare say?

NICHOLAS. Well, I have been tolerably educated—

MR. CHARLES. (*Looking at his watch.*) Oh, a great thing, education. I have often wished that I'd had more of it myself. So, shall we go?

NICHOLAS. Go?

MR. CHARLES. Yes.

NICHOLAS. Go now?

MR. CHARLES. That's right.

NICHOLAS. Go where?

MR. CHARLES. Why, dear young man, go to the omnibus. And while we're travelling, you can be telling me the story of your life. (*He is striding out. Nicholas stops. Mr. Charles turns back.*)

NICHOLAS. Please, sir. I must ask one question.

MR. CHARLES. Ask away.

NICHOLAS. Who are you, sir?

MR. CHARLES. My name's Charles Cheeryble.

NICHOLAS. Charles Cheeryble.

MR. CHARLES. That's right. Now, please, sir, not another word.

Scene Sixteen

Ralph's office. Ralph sits at his desk, alone.

RALPH. I am not a man—the world knows—to be moved by a pretty face. I look and work beneath the surface, and I see the grinning skull beneath. (*Pause.*) And yet . . . And yet, I almost like the girl. If she had been less proud, less squeamishly brought up . . . And if the mother died . . . Who knows. This house might be her home. (*He stands.*) It is a splendid house. The rooms are costly. Glorious. But yet —a little still. And rather cold. (*Pause.*) A young girl's voice. Her laughter. And, when she's not there, a hundred little tokens of her presence. To remind . . . (*Ralph sits.*) But still. The world knows. That I know it. And myself. (*Enter Noggs.*) Yes? What?

NOGGS. You in?

RALPH. To whom?

NOGGS. To him.

RALPH. Who's him?

NOGGS. He is. (*Noggs turns to go. Turns back, correcting himself.*) They are. (*He turns to go. Turns back.*) And there's a letter come for you. Marked urgent.

RALPH. Give it here. And then get out. (*Noggs gives Ralph the letter.*)

NOGGS. See? Urgent. (*Noggs potters out. He is given an odd look by the entering Squeers and Young Wackford.*)

RALPH. Well, this is a surprise. I should know your face, Mr. Squeers.

SQUEERS. Ah, and you'd know it better, sir, if it hadn't been for all I've been a-going through.

RALPH. Ah, yes, sir, I trust you are now fully recovered from my nephew's scoundrelly attack?

SQUEERS. Well, if I am, it's only just, sir. I was one blessed bruise, sir, right from here to there. Vinegar and brown paper, sir, from morning to night. As I lay there, all of a heap in the kitchen, you might have thought I was a large brown paper parcel, chock full of nothing but groans. Did I groan loud, Wackford, or did I groan soft?

WACKFORD. Loud. (*Ralph a quizzical look at the boy.*)

SQUEERS. My son, sir, little Wackford. I've brought him up, on purpose, to show the parents and guardians. I've put him in the advertisement this time, too: Look at a boy—himself a pupil. So, what do you think, sir?

RALPH. Think of what?

SQUEERS. Of him, sir, for a specimen of our feeding? Ain't he fit to burst right out of his clothes, and start the seams, and make the very buttons fly off with his fatness? (*Poking and pinching. Wackford.*) Ooh, here's flesh, here's firmness, and here's solidity. Why, you can hardly get enough of him between your finger and your thumb to pinch him anywhere.

WACKFORD. Ow!

SQUEERS. Oh, well, been a long time since he had his breakfast. Ooh, but look, sir, at those tears. There's oiliness!

RALPH. He certainly looks fit and well.

SQUEERS. In fact . . . D'you have such a thing as twopence, Mr. Nickleby?

RALPH. I—think I have. (*Ralph produces "after much rummaging in an old drawer, a penny, a half-penny, and two farthings".*)

SQUEERS. I thankee. (*He gives the money to Wackford. Ralph looking at the letter Noggs brought him.*) Now, you go and buy a tart—and mind you buy a rich one. What d'you say?

WACKFORD. Yes, thank you, father. (*Wackford goes out.*)

SQUEERS. Pastry makes his flesh gleam a good deal, and parents think that that's a healthy sign. (*Turning back to Ralph.*) So, Mr. Nickleby. (*Ralph still immersed in the letter.*) Um—Mr. Nickleby? (*Ralph looks up, darkly. Something in the letter has made him angry.*)

RALPH. Sit down. Attend to me. (*Squeers sits.*) I am not to suppose, that you are dolt enough to have forgotten or forgiven very readily the violence that was committed on you?

SQUEERS. Never.

RALPH. Or to lose the chance to pay it back, with interest.

SQUEERS. Try me.

RALPH. And maybe, it was some such object brought you here?

SQUEERS. Well . . . I had thought, perhaps, some compensation—

RALPH. Who's the boy? The boy that he took with him?

SQUEERS. Name of Smike.

RALPH. And is he old, young, healthy, sickly, tractable, rebellious?

SQUEERS. Well, wasn't young. Young for a boy, that is.

RALPH. That is, he's not a boy.

SQUEERS. I think, 'bout twenty. But—a little wanting, here, (*Taps forehead.*) like, nobody at home.

RALPH. How did he come to you?

SQUEERS. Oh, fourteen years ago, a strange man brought him to my place, and left him there. The money came some six or seven years. But then it stopped. I kept him, out of—

RALPH. Charity?

SQUEERS. That is the word. Though he's been useful, in the recent years.

RALPH. Yes, yes. Now, Mr. Squeers, we'll talk of this again, when I've had time to think about it. So, where are you staying?

SQUEERS. (*Presenting a card.*) With a Mr. Snawley, Somers Town. I've got two lads of his, and he's that pleased with how they're being treated, that—

RALPH. (*Stands.*) We are alone, sir. There's no need to advertise to me. (*A thought.*) This Snawley got two boys, you say, with you?

SQUEERS. That's right. Remarried, wife's two sons, you know.

RALPH. I do. (*Noggs brings in Wackford, stuffing his face with a tart. Squeers stands.*)

SQUEERS. Ah, Wackford. He's a fine boy, ain't he, Mr.—

NOGGS. Very.

SQUEERS. Pretty swelled out, eh? The fatness, twenty boys.

NOGGS. Oh, yes, he has. The fatness—twenty, thirty even. More. He's got it all. Ha! Ha! Oh, Lord.

SQUEERS. (*To Ralph.*) Is this man drunk? Or mad? (*Ralph shrugs. Noggs cracking his knuckles.*) We'll speak then, Mr. Nickleby. (*Squeers and Wackford go out.*)

NOGGS. God help the others.

RALPH. What? Get out.

NOGGS. Get out. (*Noggs goes out. Ralph alone, furious, with the letter.*)

RALPH. Yes. Yes. To wound him through his own affections. Yes. To strike him, through this boy.

Scene Seventeen

The offices of the Brothers Cheeryble. In fact, Ralph's office, with its desk and Noggs' high desk and stool, remains downstage—it will become Mr. Charles' office later. Upstage, in a mirror-effect, is another high desk and stool, on the opposite side from Noggs', and another desk with two chairs, on the opposite side to Ralph's. This upstage area represents the counting-house of the Cheerybles'; their old, round, white-haired clerk Tim Linkinwater sits at the high desk working: above him hangs a birdcage with a blackbird inside. At the desk sits, facing upstage, Mr. Ned Cheeryble, and, upstage of him, a beautiful, if distressed, Young Woman. Charles Cheeryble enters Tim's section of the office, with his new friend Nicholas Nickleby.

MR. CHARLES. Ah, Tim, you knave, God bless you. Is my brother in.

TIM. Yes, he is, sir, but someone's with him.

MR. CHARLES. Then we will not disturb him for the moment. Tim. This young man is called Mr. Nicholas Nickleby.

NICHOLAS. I'm pleased to meet you, sir.

TIM. And you. Hm, sir.

MR. CHARLES. And, this, dear Nicholas, is Mr. Tim Linkinwater, possibly the most ferocious lion in the general region of Threadneedle St. Am I not right, Tim Linkinwater? Hm? (*Tim shrugs and allows himself a little smile.*)

MR. CHARLES. (*To Nicholas.*) Note, sir, at first, the order. Paper, pens, inks, ruler, sealing wax, Tim's hat, Tim's glove, Tim's other coat, Tim's blackbird and Tim himself; and you shift any one of them, without a by-your-leave or even with it, and you do so at your peril. Isn't that correct? (*Mr. Ned Cheeryble opens his door. To let his visitor out. Mr. Ned looks exactly the same as his brother Mr. Charles. Nicholas double-takes.*)

MR. NED. Ah, dear brother Charles. And how are you?

MR. CHARLES. I am in quite outrageous health, dear brother Ned. And how are you?

MR. NED. I am in precisely the same condition, brother Charles.

MR. CHARLES. Now, brother—(*Mr. Ned puts his finger to his lips. The beautiful Young Woman comes out of the office.*)

MR. CHARLES. My dear Miss Madeline. Has Brother Ned explained to you our view—has he expressed our most sincere entreaty?

YOUNG WOMAN. Yes, he has. But my opinion is, and must remain, the same. Your generosity, your kindness, is quite unsurpassable. But still —I cannot do what you would have me do. I cannot . . . For reasons that I know you understand.

MR. CHARLES. Of course . . . Of course, we understand. (*Mr. Ned guides the Young Woman to the door. She goes out. Nicholas following her with his eyes. Mr. Ned turns back to his brother.*) Now, Brother Ned, are you busy, or can you spare time for a word or two with me?

MR. NED. Brother Charles, my dear fellow, don't ask me such a question. (*Mr. Charles notices that Nicholas is still looking after the Young Lady.*)

MR. CHARLES. Um— Mr. Nickleby—

NICHOLAS. I'm sorry.

MR. CHARLES. P'raps you'd grant us the inestimable privilege of entering my room.

NICHOLAS. Of course. (*They go into Mr. Charles' office, which is Ralph's office.*)

MR. CHARLES. Now, brother Ned, here is a young friend of mine we must assist. You will wish, of course, to have his statements, made to me, repeated, and then—

MR. NED. Brother Charles, it is enough that you say he should be assisted. When you say that, no more statements are required. It would be churlish to demand them. Assisted he shall be. What are his needs, and what does he require? Where is Tim Linkinwater? (*Mr. Ned is striding back towards the working Tim Linkinwater.*)

MR. CHARLES. Stop, dear brother, stop. Before we—um, involve Tim Linkinwater—who, as I have said, dear sir, is quite a veritable tiger—I've a plan to put to you.

MR. NED. Then put it, brother Charles.

MR. CHARLES. I shall, dear brother Ned. Now, Tim is getting old, and Tim has been a faithful servant, and I don't think pensioning his mother and his sister and the buying of a little tomb when his poor brother died, was a sufficient recompense for all his services.

MR. NED. Sufficient! It was miserly.

MR. CHARLES. Exactly, so if we could somehow lighten old Tim's duties—

MR. NED. (*To Nicholas.*) Parsimonious.

MR. CHARLES. Prevail on him to go into the country now and then, and sleep in the fresh air—

MR. NED. Cheeseparing.

MR. CHARLES. And then come in, an hour later in the morning—

MR. NED. Niggardly.

MR. CHARLES. Then who knows, he'd grow young again in time.

MR. NED. He would indeed. I'll go and tell him so. (*Mr. Ned strides Upstage and confers with Tim Linkinwater as Mr. Charles talks to Nicholas.*)

MR. CHARLES. If Brother Ned, whom I hold dearer than I hold myself, has but a fault, it is an eagerness, enthusiasm, quickness of response, that sometimes edges close to the impulsive. Now, sir, what I had in mind was taking you on as a clerk, assistant to Tim Linkinwater, at a salary of one hundred and twenty pounds a year, which pennypinching churliness will without a doubt provoke you to depart my presence at an instant. So, good morning, sir.

NICHOLAS. Oh, sir.

MR. CHARLES. What's this? Not gone?

NICHOLAS. Sir, I do not know how I can begin to thank you. (*Tim and Mr. Ned enter Charles' room.*)

MR. CHARLES. Start by keeping quiet. Now, Tim Linkinwater, do you understand that we intend to take this gentleman into the Counting-Room?

TIM. Hm. Yes. I do.

MR. CHARLES. Subject of course, to your inspection and investigation and interrogation.

TIM. Hm. So I should think.

MR. CHARLES. And what is your opinion of this course of action?

TIM. Hm. Not coming in an hour later in the morning, that's for sure. Not going to sleep out in the fresh air, or be packed off to the country. Hm! A pretty thing to make a man do, at my time of life. The country. Phoo.

MR. CHARLES. What's this?

MR. NED. Phoo?

MR. CHARLES. Damn your obstinacy, Tim.

MR. NED. What do you mean, sir?

TIM. It is three and thirty, next May, since I first kept the books of the Brothers Cheeryble. There ain't—I've said it again and again—such a square as this in all the world. There's not such a spring in England as the pump under the archway. There's not such a view in England as the view out of my window. I have slept in that room for three and thirty years, and if it isn't inconvenient, and doesn't interfere with the business, I shall request leave to die there.

MR. CHARLES. Damn you, Tim Linkinwater.

MR. NED. How dare you talk of dying? Do you hear that, Brother Charles?

TIM. That's all I've got to say. It's not the first time, Brother Edwin, Brother Charles you've talked of superannuating me; but I'd appreciate it if it was the last. (*Tim Linkinwater goes back to his desk. Pause.*)

MR. CHARLES. He must be done something with, dear Brother Ned.

MR. NED. That's true, dear Charles;

MR. CHARLES. We must disregard his old scruples.

MR. NED. They cannot be tolerated. He must be made a partner, Brother Charles.

MR. CHARLES. And if he won't submit to it peaceably:

MR. NED. We must have recourse to violence.

MR. CHARLES. Quite right. Quite right, dear brother. If he won't listen to reason, we must do it against his will, and show him that we are determined to exert our full authority. We'll quarrel with him, Brother Ned.

MR. NED. We'll quarrel with him now. (*Mr. Ned is striding out, as Mr. Charles is giving a look to Nicholas, as if to say: "Impulsive!". Mr. Ned bumps into the re-entering Tim Linkinwater.*) Now, then Tim Linkinwater, curse you—

TIM. I've been thinking.

MR. CHARLES. Yes?

TIM. That if the young man measures up—

MR. NED. He will, of course he will—

TIM. Then it's all right. As long—

MR. CHARLES. Yes, what's—as long?

TIM. As there's No Country.

MR. NED. (*Pumping Tim's hand.*) Well, then, Tim Linkinwater, devil take you sir, God bless you.

MR. CHARLES. (*To Nicholas.*) Sir, you are approved. (*Mr. Charles takes Tim back into the counting-room as Mr. Ned takes Nicholas's arm.*)

MR. NED. Now would it be beyond the bounds of the conceivable, for you to suffer the intolerable inconvenience of starting work on Monday? (*Pause.*)

NICHOLAS. Sir, sir, I—Yes. (*Mr. Ned goes after his brother, Nicholas turns out front.*) And Nicholas' heart was so full up with gratitude, that he could hardly speak, and he felt, more than at any time since he had come to London, truly happy.

NARRATOR. But his heart was even fuller, with a matter he could not reveal, still less show thanks for to his benefactors. For, since he had seen her, he had found it hard to think of anything except the dark-eyed lady who had walked so sadly through the counting-room.

NICHOLAS. I would, he thought, I would . . . I'd know her in ten thousand.

Scene Eighteen

Ralph's office. Nicholas remains there, as Ralph strides into what is now his own office again. Nicholas is quoting from the letter Ralph is reading.

RALPH. So, this is it. He's loose again.

NICHOLAS. Your brother's widow and her orphan children spurn the shelter of your roof, and shun you with disgust and loathing.

RALPH. So, I'm to be defied, am I? And held up in the worst and most repulsive colours?

NICHOLAS. We, your kindred, now renounce you, and your riches—

RALPH. And, of course, she will be taught to hate me, and to feel there is infection in my touch and taint in my companionship . . .

NICHOLAS. Let them corrupt and rot you, we'll be free of their infection—

RALPH. And always. Always. When my brother was like him, the first comparisons were made; he, open, liberal, gallant; and I cold and cunning, with no spirit but the thirst for gain:

NICHOLAS. I know you.

RALPH. Well, let it be so. If he, if they both, affect to despise the power of money, I must show them what it is. (*Ralph goes out, as Nicholas, rapt:*)

NICHOLAS. I would, he thought, I would: I'd know her in ten thousand . . .

Scene Nineteen

The streets of the city of London. Just after dark. Smike is wandering round. There are sellers of everything, and buyers of it too: There are Street-hands, and Balladeers, and Buskers. Smike is entranced.

(*"He had been gazing for a long time through a Jeweller's window, wishing he could take some of the beautiful trinkets home as a present, and imagining what delights they would afford if he could, when the clocks struck three quarters past eight. Roused by the sound, he hurried on at a very quick pace, and was crossing the corner of a byestreet when he was violently brought to, with a jerk so sudden that he was obliged to cling to a lamppost to save himself from falling." Smike has been collared by Mr. Squeers and Young Wackford.*)

WACKFORD. Oh father, father—

SQUEERS. Well. Well, here's a go! Here's a quite delicious go. (*Onlookers are looking on. Mr. Snawley, who has been with the Squeerses, but has become detached in the hubbub, hurries up.*)

SNAWLEY. What's happening? Who's this?

SQUEERS. This is the boy I told you of, dear Snawley, one that ran away. Hey, Wackford, fetch a hackney coach!

WACKFORD. A coach! (*Wackford runs out.*)

A LABOURER. Hey. What's this lad been a-doing of?

SQUEERS. What doing of? Why, everything! Like running off, and joining in bloodthirsty attacks upon his master—oh, there's nothing he ain't done. Oh, what a most delicious go! (*Hitting Smike.*)

SMIKE. I must—

SQUEERS. Yes, sir? What must you?

SMIKE. Must go home.

SQUEERS. Oh, will. You'll go home very soon. A week, locked up, our lodgings, Eh Snawley, and then to that delightful village, Dotheboys, in Yorkshire. That's your home.

SMIKE. Go home. (*Re-enter Wackford.*)

WACKFORD. I've found a coach! I've found one, father!

SQUEERS. Right. (*He is dragging Smike out when Snawley speaks.*)

SNAWLEY. Hard-heartedness and evil-doing never prosper, sir.

SQUEERS. That's true. That's very true.

SMIKE. Home!

SQUEERS. What a go! What a delicious go! (*Smike is dragged out by Squeers. Snawley and Wackford follow.*)

Scene Twenty

The garden of the Nicklebys' new home at Miss La Creevy's. A pair of flats represent a wall. There is a bench. Enter Kate and Mrs. Nickleby. It's afternoon.

MRS. NICKLEBY. No, Kate, before your dear papa and I, and even after for a while, we met at least, I was besieged by suitors. Quite besieged, and it was certainly a matter of some comment and occasionally a little jealousy.

KATE. Well, I am convinced of it, mama.

MRS. NICKLEBY. It must have been, suitors I mean—at least a dozen.

KATE. Oh, mother, surely not!

MRS. NICKLEBY. Well, yes, indeed, my dear, and that is not including your papa, or the young gentleman who used to go to the same dancing school and would send round gold watches to our house in gilt-edged paper—all returned, of course—and who, unfortunately, was sent out to Botany Bay, in a convict ship, and then escaped into a bush and started killing sheep—I don't know how they got there—and was going to be hung, until he accidentally choked himself, and so they pardoned him. No, there was Lukin— (*A bunch of radishes flies over the wall. Kate astounded.*) Mogley—(*A cabbage.*) Tipslark—(*A turnip.*) Cabbery—(*A bunch of carrots.*) Young Smifser—

KATE. Uh—mama—

MRS. NICKLEBY. Good heavens. What can all these be?

KATE. They're vegetables, ma'am.

MRS. NICKLEBY. Well, so they are indeed. They must be from the gentleman.

KATE. What gentleman?

MRS. NICKLEBY. The one next door. It appears to be his custom, to communicate his feelings in this—charmingly eccentric way.

KATE. So this intrusion has occurred before?

MRS. NICKLEBY. Oh yes, why, certainly. The cucumbers we ate at dinner yesterday—

A VOICE. A-hem!

KATE. That's him?

MRS. NICKLEBY. Yes, yes, it must be, but I wouldn't say intrusion, dear, in fact, you will recall the cucumbers were excellent and I am seriously considering pickling the rest for winter, and—

THE VOICE. A-hem!

KATE. Mama, he's—

MRS. NICKLEBY. Now, don't be alarmed, my dear. It's not intended to scare anyone; we must give everyone their due—

KATE. What do you mean, mama? (*The Gentleman Next Door has climbed up a ladder behind the wall and appears above it. He is quite old, and wears a nightcap. He looks—and is—crazy.*)

KATE. Now, mother. We are going to stand up and very calmly walk back to the house.

MRS. NICKLEBY. Oh, Kate, you're such a coward. (*To the Gentleman.*) Sir, what do you want? How dare you look into this garden?

THE GENTLEMAN. Queen of my soul. This goblet—sip. (*He empties a basket of more vegetables into the garden.*)

MRS. NICKLEBY. Nonsense, sir.

THE GENTLEMAN. Won't you sip the goblet? Oh, do sip the goblet.

MRS. NICKLEBY. Go away, sir!

THE GENTLEMAN. Go away? Go quite away?

MRS. NICKLEBY. Yes, certainly.

THE GENTLEMAN. Go now?

MRS. NICKLEBY. Exactly now!

THE GENTLEMAN. Without the chance of asking you one question?

MRS. NICKLEBY. Well—

KATE. Mama!

MRS. NICKLEBY. One must be civil, dear.

THE GENTLEMAN. The question is—are you a princess?

MRS. NICKLEBY. Sir, you mock me.

THE GENTLEMAN. No, but really.

MRS. NICKLEBY. I am not, sir. Obviously.

THE GENTLEMAN. Then are you a relation to the Archbishop of Canterbury? Or the Pope of Rome? Or the Speaker of the House of Commons? Forgive if I err, but I was told you were the niece to the Commissioner of Paving, which would account for your relationship to all three.

MRS. NICKLEBY. Whoever has spread such reports has taken a great liberty, and one which I am sure my son, were he aware of it, would not allow one instant. The idea! Niece to the Commissioner of Paving.

THE GENTLEMAN. Beautiful madame—

KATE. Now, mother. Come away.

MRS. NICKLEBY. Be quiet, dear.

THE GENTLEMAN. I am no youth, ma'am, but I venture to presume that we are fitted for each other.

MRS. NICKLEBY. Oh, dear, Kate—

THE GENTLEMAN. I have estates, ma'am—jewels, lighthouses, fishponds, and a whalery of my own in the North Sea, and several oyster-beds of great profit in the Pacific Ocean. But I've enemies about me, ma'am—the Messrs. Gog and Magog—who would poison me and steal my property. But if you bless me with your hand and heart, we'll have the Lord Chancellor call out the military, and so clear the house before the service is performed. Then, bliss and rapture! Bliss and rapture! Love, be mine, be mine! (*Pause.*)

MRS. NICKLEBY. (*To Kate.*) I don't know what to say.

KATE. Surely, mama, you need only say one word.

MRS. NICKLEBY. Sir, just one word. While I acknowledge that your peroration—if only to a small extent—is quite agreeable—

KATE. Mama, inside.

MRS. NICKLEBY. I have made up my mind to stay a widow, and devote myself to my two children. It's a painful thing, of course, rejecting a proposal—but—

KATE. Now!

MRS. NICKLEBY. As I'm, somewhat rudely, summoned, sir, good day. (*The Gentleman slumps suddenly, as if the ladder had been pulled. He looks down.*)

KEEPER. Oi!

THE GENTLEMAN. Oh. You. (*The voice of the Gentleman's keeper.*)

KEEPER. That's right.

THE GENTLEMAN. How's the Emperor of Tartary?

KEEPER. Oh, much the same as usual.

THE GENTLEMAN. In that case. Perhaps I'd best descend.

KEEPER. Well, yes. Perhaps you had. (*The Gentleman descends. His keeper then appears.*)

KEEPER. Ah. Beg your pardon, ladies. Has this gentleman been making love to either of you?

KATE. Yes.

KEEPER. Oh, dear. He always will, you know. There's nothing will prevent him making love.

KATE. Out of His Mind?

KEEPER. Way out.

KATE. A long time?

KEEPER. Very long.

KATE. And there's no hope for him?

KEEPER. No, none at all. And don't deserve to be. I tell you, he's a great deal pleasanter without his wits than with 'em. (*Pause.*) Well. So sorry you've been troubled, ladies. Afternoon. (*And he climbs down the ladder out of view.*)

KATE. (*Firmly.*) Out of his mind. (*Mrs. Nickleby picking up all the vegetables except one cucumber.*)

MRS. NICKLEBY. Oh, Kate! You don't think—you don't believe the gentleman is mad?

KATE. Of course I do. You heard—

MRS. NICKLEBY. Oh, yes, I heard. Oh, yes, dear, I heard everything. (*Mrs. Nickleby sails into the house.*)

KATE. Mama! (*Kate, in frustration, picks up the cucumber and throws it back over the wall. Nicholas stands there.*)

NICHOLAS. Kate, what are you doing?

KATE. Oh, Nicholas—

NICHOLAS. Kate, do you know where Smike is?

KATE. Why, isn't he—I thought he'd gone to meet you.

NICHOLAS. No. Well, at all events . . . Kate. (*Nicholas suddenly panics, and runs into the house. Kate follows. The rumble of thunder.*)

Scene Twenty-One

Outside the Saracen's Head. Bare stage. Enter Tilda and John Browdie. John is carrying an immense amount of luggage, which he puts down.

JOHN. So did tha see that, Tilda? See that Post-Office? Ecod, if that's a

Post-Office, I'd like to see the house of the Lord Mayor of Lunnon. Wouldn't tha?

TILDA. I would indeed, John.

JOHN. (*Shouts off.*) Come on, Fanny! Raise thissen! We're here! (*And Fanny Squeers shuffles on. She looks as if it's been a very long journey.*) Eee, lass, tha looks like summat that's been dragged from Yorkshire, 'stead of coming on a big clean coach. Ee, don't tha think so, Tilda?

FANNY. Tilda. How you have been kicking me throughout this blessed night.

TILDA. Well, I like that! When you had nearly the whole coach to yourself. (*Enter William the waiter.*)

FANNY. No, don't deny it, Tilda, for it's true, although of course you won't have noticed it, as being fast asleep, but I've not closed my eyes a single wink, and so I think I am to be believed.

WILLIAM. Good morning, ladies. Sir. Welcome to the Saracen's Head.

JOHN. Eh. I were right. I said that it were Sarah, Sarah Summat.

FANNY. What.

JOHN. Sarah-Son's head. I told 'ee, Fanny.

FANNY. (*Clocking William.*) Tilda, dear, please stop him, we'll be taken for I don't know what.

JOHN. Oh, let 'em take us how they find us. I'm a married man. Here be the wedding party: bride and bridesmaid, and the groom, and we've not come to Lunnon for another purpose but to 'joy oursens, now have we? (*Fanny looks at John. John elbows Fanny.*) Have we, Fanny. Eh?

FANNY. (*To William.*) I wonder, sir, if you could tell me if my father's in.

WILLIAM. Your father? Who may that be, Miss?

FANNY. (*Impatiently.*) It's Mr. Wackford Squeers. He should be stopping—staying—in this here establishment.

WILLIAM. Oh, him. Oh, he's not stopping here, Miss. Stopping somewhere else, entirely, with some friends of his, to save on the expense, I would imagine. But he comes in every day. I'll go and tell him he's been asked for. (*Enter Squeers.*)

SQUEERS. Eh. Fanny. Mr. Browdie. Tilda Price. Well, who'd have thought of this? (*Exit William.*)

TILDA. It's Tilda Browdie now, sir. John and I are wed.

JOHN. And come down for our honeymoon.

SQUEERS. Well, Fanny, here's a thing. It's your turn to be married now. You must make haste.

FANNY. Oh, I am in no hurry, dear papa.

TILDA. No, Fanny?

FANNY. No, dear Tilda. I can wait.

TILDA. So can the young men, it appears.

FANNY. Oh, *Tilda.*

SQUEERS. Eh. Eh, Fanny. Who do you suppose we laid our hands on yesterday?

FANNY. Oh, pa! Not Mr. Nick—

SQUEERS. No. But just about next door.

FANNY. You can't mean, Smike?

SQUEERS. I can. I do. I've got him hard and fast.

JOHN. What's that? You got that poor, damned scoundrel? Where?

SQUEERS. Why, at the top back room, my lodging. Him on the one side and a great key the other.

JOHN. (*Greatly amused*): At tha lodging! Got him at the lodging! Eh, I'm damned, but I must shake tha hand for that. (*He pumps Squeers' hand.*) Eh. Got him at tha lodging. (*He punches Squeers merrily on the chest.*)

SQUEERS. Yes. That's right. My lodging. Thankee—and please don't do that again.

FANNY. Where are your lodgings, father?

SQUEERS. Oh, a place called Somers Town. It's quite a way but you must come to tea and meet the Snawleys, Fanny.

JOHN. 'Course we will. We'd come if it were 20 mile. Eh. Tilda? (*Tilda, a shruggy smile.*)

SQUEERS. Uh—

JOHN. (*Picking up the baggage.*) We can go and see the sights, tomorrow, can't we?

TILDA. Uh, John—

JOHN. Oh, certainly. We'll be there. Now. Where is that fellow? (*He turns back. He is still amused.*) Be there. At tha lodging. Come on, Tilda! (*He takes the bags out. Fanny and Squeers look at Tilda.*)

TILDA. (*Nervously.*) I think—perhaps he's sickening for something. I have seen him—just the same. When he's been sickening. (*She goes out.*)

SQUEERS. I think he's lost his wits.

FANNY. Poor Tilda. (*Squeers looks at his daughter. Thunder rumbles again, and they run indoors.*)

Scene Twenty-Two

A park. Bare stage. Thunder. Ralph runs on, his collar up against the rain. He stops centre stage, looks up. We imagine he's under a tree. A beggar passes. The beggar turns back, looks at Ralph. Then he speaks. It's Brooker.

BROOKER. Oh, you. At last. (*Pause.*)

RALPH. What's that?

BROOKER. At last, I've found you.

RALPH. What do you want?

BROOKER. What do I want? You see me. I'm a miserable and wretched outcast, nearly sixty years of age, and destitute and helpless, wanting even one dry crust of bread. So, what'd you think I want?

RALPH. I'm sixty, and neither destitute nor helpless. Work, sir, work. Don't beg for bread, but earn it. (*Ralph makes to go.*)

BROOKER. Do you not know me? (*Ralph turns back.*)

RALPH. No. Why, should I?

BROOKER. Do you not remember, 30 years ago, a man you threw in jail for owing you some paltry sum of money?

RALPH. Well, I've had many debtors in my time, and have arrested many, too.

BROOKER. But the one who you released—and took into your service? As a clerk, who wasn't overnice, and knew a little of the trade you drove? (*Pause.*)

RALPH. Oh, yes. Perhaps I do remember.

BROOKER. And how I served you always faithfully?

RALPH. Well, yes. You had your wages, and you did your work. You owed me money, and you owe it still. Now, tell me what you want.

BROOKER. I've been looking for you, now, two days.

RALPH. Well, now you've found me. What d'you want?

BROOKER. I want to pay you back.

RALPH. Oh, yes? What with?

BROOKER. With interest. With something—that will interest you.

RALPH. Yes? What?

BROOKER. I know, there's something that I know. I took advantage of my place, with you. There's something that I did, to get at you. And you would, you'd give half of what you own to know it.

RALPH. Would I, now.

BROOKER. (*Forcefully.*) I've been a convict now, for seven years. For some small trickery that lay outside the law, a nothing to the trickery you money-makers do within it. I have now returned, the broken creature that you see before you. (*Slight pause.*) I haven't come to beg. I've come to sell. My expectations are not monstrous, but I have to live. (*Pause.*)

RALPH. Well, Mr.—I don't know the name to call you.

BROOKER. By my old one. I don't care.

RALPH. Then hear this, Mr. Brooker. You have claimed you have a hold on me. My answer is: you keep it, or publish it, for *I* won't care.

BROOKER. That wouldn't serve me.

RALPH. Sir, I know the world, the world knows me. Whatever sin of mine you've gleaned, the world knows it already. You could tell it nothing that would shock it about me. I am reviled and threatened every day.

BROOKER. You're proud of that.

RALPH. Indifferent. For all the rank contempt in which I'm held, things roll on just the same, and I grow richer by them. So, now, go.

BROOKER. I won't.

RALPH. Then I will.

BROOKER. Then I tell you—you will hear from me again.

RALPH. Then I tell *you,* that if I do, and you so much as notice me by one small begging gesture, you shall see the inside of a jail once more, and contemplate your hold on me in there! That is my answer to your trash. So, take it! (*Ralph strides off.*)

BROOKER. Oh, you'll hear from me again. (*"The man remained upon the same spot with his eyes fixed upon the retreating figure until it was lost to his view, and then drawing his arms about his chest, as if the damp and lack of food struck coldly to him, lingered with slouching steps by the wayside, and begged of those who passed along".*)

Scene Twenty-Three

The top back room of the Snawley's house in Somers Town. Smike is there, locked up. A rattle of keys, and John Browdie enters. Smike shrinks in terror. John grabs Smike, and puts his hand over Smike's mouth. Note: this scene is peculiarly effective if a trapdoor is available, and the "door" is the trap.

JOHN. My name is Browdie. I'm from Yorkshire. I'm a friend of your friend, lad who beat the schoolmaster. Don't say a word. (*Pause. Smike nods. John lets him go and takes a screwdriver from his pocket.*) I've snuck up, making out I'm poorly. When you gone, I'm going to prise the lock off, make it look as how you did it.

SMIKE. Go where?

JOHN. Where? Go away. Go home. (*Smike looking confused.*) Escape. Do you understand?

SMIKE. Yes, yes. I understand. (*Smike is beginning to go. Then he suddenly grabs John.*) He brought me back, before. He'll do again. I know he will.

JOHN. He won't. Now, come on, quickly, off with 'ee. (*Smike can't move.*) Oh, th'art a broken-down old chap. I shouldn't shout at thee. Go down the stair, go quiet past the door t'where they are's tight shut, I swear they'll never hear thee. (*Smike releases John.*)

SMIKE. Now?

JOHN. Yes, now. One more thing. Just tell young master, when tha sees him, as I'm spliced to Tilda now, and staying at the Saracen's. Tha can remember that?

SMIKE. Yes, yes. Spliced to Tilda.

JOHN. Now, go, go. (*Smike a look at John, then he goes. John with his screwdriver, goes to prise off the lock. But something is preventing him holding it steady. He is shaking, as if in a strong convulsion. It gradually becomes apparent that John Browdie is even more vastly amused than he has ever been vastly amused before.*)

Scene Twenty-Four

The roads to and from the country. Enter Smike, desperately running on the spot.

NARRATOR. And without pausing for a moment to reflect upon the course he was taking, he fled away with surprising swiftness, borne upon such wings as only fear can wear. (*Smike is in a spot running. Behind him, through the darkness, we see, as a fantasy, a nightmare vision of Dotheboys Hall: Mrs. Squeers, ringing her bell, Mr. Squeers with his cane, Wackford laughing, Fanny, the Boys. We hear lines too, echoed and distorted: "And a pretty thing it is". "O.U.T.C.A.S.T.". "Foresaken". "Homeless". "In here, you haven't finished". "I'll flog you within an inch of your life". And gradually, the noises coalesce, and become the swishes of a cane, growing louder and louder. Smike puts his hands to his ears. The sounds grow even louder: they're inside his head. Finally, the nightmare fades, Smike stops, takes his hands from his ears, and there is silence. An owl hoots. Silence.*)

NARRATORS.

And it was not until the darkness and quiet of a country road recalled him to the world outside himself,

And the starry sky above him warned him of the rapid flight of time,

That, covered with dust and panting for breath, he stopped to listen and look about him.

All was still and silent.

A glare of light in the distance, casting a warm glow upon the sky, marked where the huge city lay.

It was late now.

He turned back, and taking the open road, made again for London. (*Smike turns and walks. Passers-by cross the stage, and continue the Narration.*)

NARRATORS. And by the time he re-entered it at the western extremity, the greater part of the shops were closed. Of the throngs of people who had been tempted abroad after the heat of the day, but few remained. (*Suddenly, out of the passers-by leaps Newman Noggs, who grabs Smike. Smike nearly jumps out of his skin.*)

NOGGS. Dear fellow; oh, dear fellow.

SMIKE. Uh—uh—

NOGGS. Smike, it's only me.

SMIKE. Oh, Mr. Noggs—

NOGGS. Where have you been? They've been half mad about you.

SMIKE. Who have?

NOGGS. (*Obviously.*) Mr. Nicholas. His mother. And Miss Nickleby. And I must take you home at once.

SMIKE. Yes. Yes. (*Noggs is striding off. Smike not. Noggs turns back, looks, questioningly.*) Miss Nickleby.

NOGGS. That's right.

SMIKE. Miss Nickleby . . . Half mad about me too? (*Pause. Noggs a little nod, goes and takes Smike's arm. They go out together.*)

END OF ACT ONE.

ACT TWO

Scene One

The coffee-room of the Saracen's Head. Nicholas sits at a table with a white cloth. Two other chairs. Enter John Browdie, Tilda and William the waiter.

JOHN. A gentleman? What gentleman? (*Sees Nicholas.*) Eh! Schoolmaster's assistant.

NICHOLAS. Mr. Browdie.

JOHN. (*To William.*) Well, din't stand there—gentleman has come to see us. Fetch some food, some pies, some cuts of beef, a tongue or two, a fowl, some ale. Come on, sir, bustle.

TILDA. John, we have just had dinner—and, p'raps, Mr. Nickleby as well—?

JOHN. What? Call that dinner? Come now, bustle, bustle.

WILLIAM. Yes, sir, certainly. (*William goes out.*)

JOHN. Well, then.

NICHOLAS. Sir, I have come here with three purposes. The first is to express my heartfelt thanks to you, releasing that poor lad, at such a risk—

JOHN. Oh, weren't no risk.

NICHOLAS. Well, I am sure that's not the case, but still. The second, naturally, is to express my most sincere congratulations on your recent nuptials.

JOHN. Oh, ay.

NICHOLAS. And trusting that I'll be allowed to take the usual license, Mr. Browdie.

JOHN. Oh, ay—take whatever—dinner's coming soon.

NICHOLAS. I thank you. Mrs. Browdie. (*Nicholas kisses Tilda.*)

TILDA. Mr. Nickleby!

JOHN. Oh, I see. Do, do make thaself at home.

NICHOLAS. I shall, of course—on one condition.

JOHN. Ay, what's that?

NICHOLAS. That when you have occasion for one, you'll make me a godfather.

TILDA. Oh, Mr. Nicklcby.

JOHN. (*Hugely tickled.*) Wha's that? A godfather? Oh, ay. Oh, don't say another word. Tha'll not beat that. A godfather. Eh, Tilda, hast tha ever heard the like? Wha's going on? (*And indeed, during the last few moments, we have become aware of a disturbance.*)

TILDA. I don't know, John. (*Enter a gaggle of people, including an angry fellow with a bleeding nose and torn collar, William, a Young Man, rolling up his sleeves, and a number of Customers and Waitresses.*)

ANGRY FELLOW. (*To William.*) Police! I want the police. (*Pointing to the Young Man.*) I want that man arrested.

1st CUSTOMER. Right, so he should be.

1st WAITRESS. What a thing to do!

WILLIAM. Now, sir, please, if we could just keep calm about this—

ANGRY FELLOW. Calm? He asks me to be calm!

2nd CUSTOMER. (*To 1st Waitress.*) He asks him to be calm.

ANGRY FELLOW. The police, sir! Now!

JOHN. What's going on here, then?

ANGRY FELLOW. I'll tell you, sir, what's going on, that if a fellow sitting quietly with a drink, conversing with his friends, is liable to be assaulted by a perfect stranger—

2nd WAITRESS. Well, it's certainly a scandal.

ANGRY FELLOW. Sitting, quietly, doing nothing but conversing—

1st CUSTOMER. Nothing else.

ANGRY FELLOW. And then to have some great young lout come up to him, and tear his collar, punch him on the nose—

NICHOLAS. Could one inquire—what is the explanation of the gentleman concerned?

ANGRY FELLOW. Well—do you hear that! "Gentleman". "An explanation". Hmph!

2nd CUSTOMER. "Could one inquire".

1st WAITRESS. "The gentleman concerned". (*The Young Man steps forward. He is Welsh.*)

YOUNG MAN. One could inquire, sir, and I would be pleased to give an explanation. I have just returned, sir, from a journey of some distance, and was sitting in the coach-house with a pint of wine, when I could not but overhear that person, choosing to express himself in very disrespectful and familiar terms, of a young lady. I informed him, with considerable civility, that I was sure he was mistaken in his vile conjectures, which were of a most offensive nature, and demanded he withdraw them unconditionally. This he refused to do, and so I took his collar and I punched him on the nose. (*Pause.*)

NICHOLAS. I see. Well—that does sound, it seems you did have cause, sir, certainly—you know the lady, I presume?

YOUNG MAN. Oh, no, I never heard of her.

NICHOLAS. But, um—

YOUNG MAN. But it would be a pretty state of things, if names of ladies could be bandied round the town, without a let or hindrance, merely for the want of some acquaintance of the bandied person being present to defend their honour. Wouldn't it?

1st WAITRESS. Well, now—

2nd WAITRESS. That certainly sounds reasonable.

1st CUSTOMER. If not, I mean, uh—

1st WAITRESS. Where would be the end of it?

YOUNG MAN. My view entirely. (*To the Angry Fellow.*) Now, sir, I'd suggest we both allow our tempers to cool down. I can be contacted, at this address. (*He hands the Angry Fellow a card.*) if you should wish to bring a charge. But now, I'd seriously advocate, that everyone proceeds about their business with no more ado.

1st CUSTOMER. Right, then.

2nd WAITRESS. Yes, back to business.

1st CUSTOMER. What an excellent idea. (*They have all gone, except for the Angry Fellow.*)

YOUNG MAN. Good evening, sir. (*The Angry Fellow goes out. To Nicholas.*) Well, I must thank you for your intervention, sir, and ask to know where I may find you to express my formal gratitude. Here is my card. Good evening, sir. (*Nicholas gives the Young Man his card, as he accepts the Young Man's.*)

NICHOLAS. Good heavens. You're a Cheeryble.

FRANK CHEERYBLE. (*For it is he.*) That's right, sir.

TILDA. (*To John.*) What's a Cheeryble?

NICHOLAS. But surely not—that Cheeryble, who's nephew to the other Cheerybles, who has been for the last four years establishing an agency in Lancashire, and is expected back tomorrow?

FRANK. Yes, I am that Cheeryble, indeed, sir. And may I presume to ask if you are that same Mr. Nickleby whom I have learnt was recently employed by my two uncles, and of whom I've heard, by letter and by wire, the most complete and constant good report?

NICHOLAS. Well, of the good report, I cannot speak. But I am Mr. Nickleby.

FRANK. Well, there's a thing.

NICHOLAS. Yes, isn't it.

FRANK. You, Mr. Nickleby. Do call me Frank.

NICHOLAS. You, Mr. Cheeryble. Please call me Nicholas.

JOHN. (*To Tilda.*) D'you s'pose the dinner'll have come?

NICHOLAS. (*Suddenly.*) Oh, Mr. Browdie. I said I had come with a threefold purpose, and I did not complete my mission. Would you and Mrs. Browdie do us the great honour of calling on us at our house tomorrow night. And if you would forgive me making one addition to the party, I would hope that Mr. Cheeryble might join us too.

FRANK. I would be most delighted.

TILDA. So would we.

NICHOLAS. Right, then. That's settled. (*Enter William.*)

WILLIAM. (*To John.*) Sir, I have laid out what you ordered in your room. I would point out, though, that I didn't realise your party was—of only four. There is enough for twice or thrice that number, sir.

JOHN. In that case. It'll do.

Scene Two

The Kenwigs' front room. Chairs, tables, a clothes-horse with towels hanging. Downstage, kettles and teapots. At least three Married Ladies, Mrs. Cutler, Miss Green, and Morleena, who is nursing Little Lillyvick, the baby. Mr. Kenwigs himself is standing looking nervous, for Mrs. Kenwigs, offstage, is having another baby. The Narrators fill us in as the scene is set up:

NARRATORS.

And after a substantial supper with the Browdies,

Nicholas walked on to Golden Square,

And to the house of Newman Noggs,

Not knowing that downstairs from his old friend,

There had been an addition to the family of the Kenwigs,

An event which half the neighborhood had come to witness and to celebrate.

(*Enter a Nurse from Mrs. Kenwigs' room of confinement. All the Ladies eagerly move towards her. The Nurse looks quickly round to select the most suitable people for the tasks in hand. Behind her enters Dr. Lumbey, the doctor, whose task is completed, and is rolling down his sleeves.*)

NURSE. Morleena. Fetch your ma a cup of something hot. And— Madam, will you fetch more salts. (*Kenwigs stepping forward.*) No, not yet, Mr. Kenwigs! (*The Nurse goes back into the other room. Morleena puts Little Lillyvick in his crib, goes to the hob, pours a hot drink, and takes it in. Dr. Lumbey talks to Kenwigs and goes to pick up the abandoned Little Lillyvick.*)

DR. LUMBEY. It's a fine boy, Mr. Kenwigs, there's no doubt about it.

KENWIGS. Oh, Dr. Lumbey, do you think so?

DR. LUMBEY. Now this is—

KENWIGS. Little Lillyvick. (*Enter the Nurse.*)

NURSE. Please, madam, put more water on to boil. And—(*To Miss Green.*) Miss, please run down to the corner shop and get a bottle of sal volatile. In a few moments, Mr. Kenwigs! (*Miss Green goes out to the shop.*)

KENWIGS. (*To Dr. Lumbey.*) Morleena was a fine child as well.

DR. LUMBEY. Oh, they all were, sir. (*To the Baby.*) Goo goo goo goo.

KENWIGS. She'll be a treasure to the man she marries. Did you ever see her dance?

DR. LUMBEY. No, I haven't had that privilege. (*To the Baby.*) Gob gob gob gob.

KENWIGS. Not to speak of course, about her expectations.

2ND MARRIED LADY. What, expectations?

MRS. CUTLER. Mm.

KENWIGS. Well, ma'am; it's not perhaps for me to say. It's not for me to boast of any family with which I have the honour to be linked—but shall we say, my children might come into a small matter of a hundred pounds-a-piece. Perhaps. P'raps more; but certainly that much.

1st MARRIED LADY. A very pretty little fortune.

KENWIGS. I will make mention of no names, but many of my friends have met a relative of Mrs. Kenwigs in this very room, as would give dignity to any company, that's all.

MRS. CUTLER. I've met him. In this very room.

KENWIGS. And it's naturally most gratifying—(*Enter the Nurse.*)

NURSE. Morleena, dear, the kettle.

KENWIGS. To my feelings as a father—

NURSE. (*To Kenwigs.*) You—stay there! (*Nurse goes out. Morleena goes and fills a teapot from the kettle.*)

KENWIGS. To see a man like Mrs. Kenwigs' uncle, Mr. Lillyvick, a man like that a-kissing and a-taking notice of my—(*Enter Miss Green.*)

MISS GREEN. Well, now, Mr. Kenwigs, look who I found, coming up the stairs.

KENWIGS. (*Irritated.*) Who is it? (*Enter Nicholas. He is slightly breathless.*) Why, Mr. Johnson! What a privilege.

NICHOLAS. I fear, sir, that in fact my purpose was to Mr. Noggs and must be, very soon, but having heard about your circumstance—

KENWIGS. Ah, yes. My circumstance. And, as I was saying, it is naturally very gratifying to my feelings as a husband and a father, to consider how dear Mr. Lillyvick, how he will feel when he is made acquainted with this—happy circumstance.

NICHOLAS. Uh—Mr. Lillyvick.

KENWIGS. That's right. (*To 1st Married Lady.*) The Collector of the Water-Rate.

NICHOLAS. I wonder—if you've heard from him at all.

KENWIGS. No, not for several weeks. Oh, a week or two. (*To 2nd Married Lady.*) And Mrs. Kenwigs' uncle.

NICHOLAS. Or had a message.

KENWIGS. Why? Is there a cause for one?

NICHOLAS. Well. . . .

KENWIGS. Well what? (*Pause.*)

NICHOLAS. Sir, you remember Miss Petowker?

KENWIGS. Yes, of course I do.

NICHOLAS. He's married her. (*Long pause.*)

KENWIGS. He's married Miss Petowker.

NICHOLAS. Yes, that's right. In Portsmouth.

KENWIGS. Portsmouth. Mr. Lillyvick has married Miss Petowker.

NICHOLAS. That's correct. (*Pause. Morleena drops the kettle.*)

KENWIGS. My children! My defrauded, swindled infants!

FIRST MARRIED LADY. What's this? (*Morleena goes rigid and starts screaming.*)

NICHOLAS. Um—

KENWIGS. Villain! Cur! And traitor!

SECOND MARRIED LADY. Hmph! (*Enter the Nurse and the Third Married Lady.*)

NURSE. What's all this? What's going on? What is this noise?

KENWIGS. Be silent, woman!

NURSE. You be silent, sir. Have you no feelings for your baby?

KENWIGS. No!

EVERYONE. Oh! Oh!

NURSE. Then, shame on you. Unnatural monster!

KENWIGS. Let him die! He has no expectations, and no property to come into. We want no babies here—take 'em away! Take all of them —off to the Foundling! (*Morleena screaming. Dr. Lumbey trying to attend to Morleena.*)

MRS. CUTLER. Mr. Kenwigs!

KENWIGS. Oh, the attention. The attention, that I've shown that man. The oysters he has eaten, and the pints of ale he's drunk, here in this house—

MRS. CUTLER. Now, Mr. Kenwigs, naturally, it's most upsetting—

KENWIGS. The presents that I've given him. The pipes, the snuff-boxes, a pair of india-rubber galoshes, costing six-and-sixpence—and then, for this—for this—Be quiet, Morleena! (*Morleena stops screaming.*)

MORLEENA. Sorry, Pa.

NURSE. Oh, drat the stupid man! (*The Nurse goes out.*)

KENWIGS. That man! His wild and careless passion—it has ruined us. (*He goes out, dramatically.*)

NICHOLAS. Uh, I appear to be . . . the bearer of bad tidings. Please— excuse me. (*Nicholas goes out.*)

FIRST MARRIED LADY. *Well.*

MRS. CUTLER. What a performance.

SECOND MARRIED LADY. What a vulgar man.

DR. LUMBEY. Goo goo. Goo goo.

Scene Three

Noggs pottering round his garret. Nicholas bursts in.

NICHOLAS. Newman, I've come to thank you.

NOGGS. What?

NICHOLAS. For finding him, and bringing him to us.

NOGGS. Oh, don't, please don't.

NICHOLAS. And Newman, and to tell you something. Something I've been bursting with for days and cannot tell another living soul.

NOGGS. What's that?

NICHOLAS. It is—it is—oh, Newman, if you'd only seen her!

NOGGS. Seen her? Who?

NICHOLAS. Her lips, her eyes, her hair—

NOGGS. Uh—it's a lady?

NICHOLAS. Yes, of course, it is a lady. And, oh, what a lady. And—I had to tell you. (*Pause.*) There. (*Pause.*)

NOGGS. Uh—tell me all about her.

NICHOLAS. I know nothing of her.

NOGGS. Nothing?

NICHOLAS. No. Except her first name. Which is Madeline. But now, I must—oh, if you saw her, Newman! (*He runs out.*)

NOGGS. If. (*Slight pause.*) Oh, Nick. (*Pause.*) In Love. With lips and eyes and hair. With Madeline.

Scene Four

The Cheerybles' offices, upstage, and Ralph's house, downstage. For the Cheerybles, all we need as Mr. Ned's desk and three chairs; for Ralph's house, Noggs' desk, his high stool, and a low stool as well. Narration, as Noggs enters and sits at his desk.

NARRATORS.
The next morning, in his little office

And on the top of his little stool,

Newman Noggs heard the chime of a neighbouring church clock,

Looked up,

And clicked his tongue,

And soliloquised.

NOGGS. Three quarters past! My dinner is at two. And him not back. And told to wait. Three quarters of an hour. (*Pause.*) It's done on purpose. Just like him. (*Pause.*) I don't believe he has an appetite. Except for pounds, shillings and pence. I should like to have him made to swallow one of every English coin. (*Pause. Noggs relishes the idea.*)

208

The penny. (*He laughs.*) Ha—two shillings. (*He laughs.*) And—the crown!

NARRATORS.

His humour being in somes degrees restored, Newman brought forth a little bottle,

Shook it,

Opened it,

And drank,

And restored it even more. (*Mr. Charles, Mr. Ned and Nicholas assembling. Narration cont.*)

While at the same time,

At the offices of the Brothers Cheeryble,

Nicholas was asked by Mr. Charles and Mr. Ned

If they could beg the quite immeasurable delight

Of having one quick word with them

In the privacy of their room.

NICHOLAS. Well, yes. Of course. Indeed. (*Nicholas, Mr. Charles and Mr. Ned sit at the table.*)

NARRATOR. While Newman, having put away his bottle, heard the door, and voices—(*The Narrators withdraw.*)

NOGGS. Well, that's it. There's someone with him. It'll be—"Stop till this gentleman has gone." Well, I won't do it, and that's flat. (*Noggs hides and Ralph enters with Arthur Gride, an old, wizened miser.*)

RALPH. Noggs! Where are you, Noggs? (*To Gride.*) He must have gone to dinner. Hm. (*Gride shrugs and grins. Noggs a look out of his closet. He sees the two men aren't going.*) Well, we'll use his room. It's cool and in the shade. (*Another look from Noggs. He realises he's stuck. Gride shrugs and grins.*) So, sit down, Mr. Gride, and tell me what's your business. (*Gride sits on the low stool, Ralph on the high one. Gride laughs.*) Hm. What's this?

GRIDE. Oh, you're bold and deep one, Mr. Nickleby. (*Transfer focus to Cheerybles.*)

MR. CHARLES. Now, sir, we would like to employ you, on a confidential and delicate mission.

MR. NED. The object of the mission is a—um, young lady.

MR. CHARLES. Nay, a very beautiful young lady, whom, I think you caught sight of in these very offices the first day you came here.

NICHOLAS. Ah, yes, I do remember, certainly. (*Transfer to Ralph and Gride.*)

RALPH. So, then?

GRIDE. I'm going to be married.

RALPH. Hm. Some old hag with a fortune?

GRIDE. No, a pretty, dainty and bewitching little creature, of not yet nineteen. Do you remember Walter Bray?

RALPH. Oh, yes, indeed. The man about town, for whom the town became beyond his means. He owes me money. As I recall, nine hundred and ten pounds, four and—something.

GRIDE. Yes. And he owes me money too. A little more. And he is dying. And he has a daughter. (*Transfer to Cheerybles.*)

MR. CHARLES. The lady's father, sir, was married to a friend of ours. He was a wastrel and a profligate.

MR. NED. His wife died, oh, about a year ago. He was committed to the King's Bench Prison.

NICHOLAS. So—she is destitute.

MR. CHARLES. She is.

NICHOLAS. Can such a—is this possible?

MR. NED. Well, yes, Mr. Nickleby, I'm afraid it is. (*Transfer to Ralph and Gride.*)

RALPH. So what you plan is this. You offer to release Bray from his debts, perhaps you give him an allowance, so he can live out his dying days in reasonable comfort, and, in exchange, you have his dainty daughter for your wife.

GRIDE. That's right.

RALPH. And as I'm the other creditor, you come here to ask me what I would accept.

GRIDE. Just so. I'd thought, nine shillings in the pound. . . .

RALPH. Gride, tell me the whole story.

GRIDE. What? (*Pause.*) Oh, well . . . (*Transfer to Cheerybles.*)

MR. NED. And so, good brother Charles and I considered, and debated, and resolved, that we must undertake a harmless subterfuge.

MR. CHARLES. That someone, feigning to be dealing in small ornaments and drawings and the like, should go to her and purchase what she makes for cash.

NICHOLAS. Uh—someone?

MR. NED. So, then, there being no time like the present, can you go there now?

NICHOLAS. (*Going quickly to the door.*) Yes, yes. At once, without delay. (*He runs out. Transfer to Ralph's.*)

GRIDE. Oh. Well. Supposing I was in possession of a deed, concerning some small property to which this pretty lady was entitled, of which nobody knows anything, except for me, and which her husband would lay to claim to, would that, p'raps, account for—

RALPH. For the whole proceeding. Yes. You have the deed about you?

GRIDE. Oh, very well. If I'm to have my bride. (*He hands over the deed. Ralph reads it.*) My dainty bride. (*Ralph reads.*) Her eyelashes, and lips, and hair the fingers itch to play with . . .

RALPH. I've little eyes for beauty, I'm afraid. But if you choose to think you're buying her for love, then I can't stop you.

GRIDE. Buying her.

RALPH. Oh, Mr. Gride, you have your dainty creature, Bray has his debts paid off, and I *my* debt, the full amount, and my share of your inheritance. (*Gride looks up in alarm.*) And so we're all content. Now, shall we go? (*Gride and Ralph go. Noggs emerges.*)

NOGGS. I think . . . I think I've lost my appetite. (*Transfer to Cheerybles. Nicholas bursts back in.*)

NICHOLAS. Oh—Mr. Charles.

MR. CHARLES. What, back so soon?

NICHOLAS. You haven't told me where she lives. Or who she is. Or anything.

MR. NED. Oh, please forgive us. (*Handing over a slip of paper and an envelope.*) Here is the address; the money; and the order. The young lady's name is Madeline. Her father's name is Walter Bray. (*As the scene disperses:*)

NICHOLAS. And Nicholas, repressing every feeling that he should perhaps have stated his emotions with regard to the young lady, turned and left the chambers of the Brothers Cheeryble, and set a sprightly pace for the King's Bench Prison, and the meagre debtors' houses that surround it.

Scene Five

Near the King's Bench Prison. Bare stage, but full of beggars, criminals, the poor and the mad. For the first time, we are seeing London's super-poor, the lowest of the low. As Nicholas walks through

*them, he is grabbed and begged. Into the middle come Madeline,
pushing her father Walter Bray in his wheelchair. The beggars and
criminals withdraw, but their presence remains with us for this and
the next scene.*

BRAY. Madeline, what's this? Who told a stranger that we could be
seen? Who is it?

MADELINE. I believe—

BRAY. Oh, yes, you always do, believe. What is it?

NICHOLAS. Sir, I've called with a commission. For a pair of hand-
screens, and some painted velvet for an ottoman. I have a sum here, as
deposit, of five pounds. (*He hands the envelope to Madeline.*)

BRAY. Hm. See it's right then, Madeline.

MADELINE. I'm sure it's absolutely right, papa.

BRAY. You're sure? How can you be. "I'm sure". (*Madeline takes a
five pound note out of the envelope.*)

MADELINE. Well, I was right to be, papa.

BRAY. Now, go and get a newspaper, some apples, and two bottles of
that port I had last week, and—and—I can't remember half of what I
want. Well, you can always go out twice. And you can go too, sir, as
soon as you've had your receipt.

NICHOLAS. It is no matter, sir.

BRAY. No matter? What d'you mean, sir? Do you think you bring your
paltry money as a gift? It's business, sir, return for value given. Damn
you, sir, d'you know that you are talking to a gentleman, who at one
time could buy up fifty of such men as you, and all you have?

NICHOLAS. I merely meant that as I shall have many dealings with this
lady, I'll not trouble her with forms.

BRAY. Well, we will have all the forms we need. My daughter, sir,
requires no charity, and will not be the object of your pity. Business,
sir! Now, Madeline, receipt! (*Madeline writing a receipt.*)

NICHOLAS. (*To Madeline.*) When shall—when shall I call again?

BRAY. When you're requested, sir, and not before.

MADELINE. Oh, not for three or four weeks, sir. It is not necessary, I
can do without.

BRAY. What? Not for three or four weeks, Madeline?

MADELINE. Then, sooner—sooner, if you please.

NICHOLAS. A week?

MADELINE. (*Giving Nicholas the receipt.*) Yes, then, a week. Here's
your receipt, sir.

NICHOLAS. Thank you. In a week's time, then. Goodbye. (*He goes out.
Madeline, after a moment, following.*)

BRAY. Where are you going, my dear?

MADELINE. Oh, he's left his—

BRAY. What?

MADELINE. I—I'll be a moment, father—

BRAY. (*Unable to move without assistance.*) What has he left? (*Madeline catches up with Nicholas.*)

MADELINE. Oh, sir, I don't know if I'm doing right, but pray—don't mention to your masters what has happened here this morning. He has suffered much. Today he's very bad. I beg you, sir.

NICHOLAS. You only have to hint a wish, and I would risk my life to gratify it. (*Madeline turns away.*) Oh, I speak the truth. I can't disguise my heart from you. I'd—I would die to serve you. What else can I say?

MADELINE. Say nothing. (*She goes out.*)

NICHOLAS. A week. How can I stand a week.

Scene Six

The same, a little later. Bray has been joined by Ralph and Arthur Gride. Nicholas and Madeline have gone.

RALPH. It must be in a week, sir. And we must know in five days. (*Pause.*) Now, sir, it's Mr. Arthur Gride. An offer any father would be proud of! Think what a haul it is. (*Bray looks at Gride.*) Come, sir. Mr. Gride has money but no youth. Miss Madeline has youth and beauty but no money. Tit for tat. A deal of heaven's making. Hm?

GRIDE. Matches are made in heaven, so they say.

RALPH. So, what do you reply? (*Pause.*)

BRAY. It's not for me to say. It's for my daughter.

RALPH. Yes, of course. But you have still the power to advise.

BRAY. Hm. Hm. Advise. I tell you, Nickleby, there were times when my will carried against everyone: her mother's family and friends, whole pack of 'em. With power and wealth on their side, and just my will on mine.

RALPH. Well, there we are. Your wish is her command, I'm sure. But if it isn't . . . (*Bray looks miserably at Gride. Ralph nods to Gride, who withdraws a little.*)

BRAY. What? If I can't convince her?

RALPH. Well, shall we say . . . I see two pictures. One of Walter Bray, the fashionable fellow, as he once was, shining in society, in freer air, and under brighter skies, who knows, in France, but certainly in luxury. Another lease of life. (*Moving closer.*) Or else, another picture. In a churchyard, with a gravestone and a date. Perhaps two years, perhaps a little less, not more. Now, is it really not for you to say? It's really for your daughter to decide? (*Pause.*) You'll have cheated nature, Mr. Bray. (*Pause.*)

BRAY. But, Nickleby. Is this not cruel?

RALPH. Cruel? If he were younger, yes. But think, how long is it before your daughter is a widow?

BRAY. Yes, but still—

RALPH. By this, she is made rich. And you'll be young, and bright, and blazing once again.

BRAY. Yes, yes. (*Pause.*) You're right. It is for her, as well as me. (*Ralph gestures Gride back.*)

RALPH. Exactly. And she'll live to thank you. (*Sound of Madeline returning.*)

BRAY. Hush. It's her. (*Enter Madeline with apples, two bottles of port, and a newspaper.*) Ah, Madeline. Here are two gentlemen.

MADELINE. I see them, father.

BRAY. (*Trying to make a joke.*) Huh. She used to say, Gride, that the very sight of you would make me worse. Well, p'raps she'll change her mind on that point; girls can change their minds, you know—you look so tired, my dear.

MADELINE. I'm not, indeed.

BRAY. Oh, yes, you are, you do too much.

MADELINE. I wish I could do more.

BRAY. I know. But still you overtax yourself, this wretched life, my love, it's more than you can bear, I'm sure of it. . . . (*Pause.*) It's more than I can bear. (*Slight pause. Madeline goes and kisses her father.*)

RALPH. Five days, then, Mr. Bray.

BRAY. Yes, very well. Five days. (*Ralph turns to go. Gride trying to take Madeline's hand to kiss it.*)

GRIDE. And if the lady . . . if the lady condescends. . . . (*Madeline shrinks from Gride. Gride looks to Ralph, who gestures him to go. Ralph and Gride leave Bray and Madeline. Gride a feeble grin to Ralph before scuttling off.*)

RALPH. Oh, Lord, how do people dupe themselves. (*Noggs is there. The Brays have gone.*) They're here?

NOGGS. They've been here half an hour.

RALPH. Two men? One Mr. Squeers?

NOGGS. That's right. In your room now.

RALPH. Good. Get a coach.

NOGGS. A coach. Whatever for?

RALPH. To ride in. To the Strand. (*Ralph goes Upstage. We can see him greet Snawley and Squeers. Noggs gesturing vaguely.*)

NOGGS. A coach. The Strand. Coach! The Strand! The Nicklebys. Oh, I should follow—but he'd see me. (*He waves, agitatedly. We see Brooker groping along.*) Coach! Oh, the Strand, there's mischief in it. There must be! (*He spots Brooker.*) Are you a coach?

BROOKER. No.

NOGGS. (*Searching in his pocket.*) Uh—

BROOKER. Are you the clerk of Mr. Nickleby?

NOGGS. Oh—no. Mean—yes.

BROOKER. Get him his coach. And see him off in it. And then, I want a word with you.

NOGGS. Coach!

Scene Seven

The Nicklebys' rooms in the Strand. A party. Mrs. Nickleby, Kate, Nicholas, Smike, Miss La Creevy, John and Tilda Browdie, Frank Cheeryble and Tim Linkinwater. A rug on the floor. Narration as the scene is set up:

NARRATORS.
And meanwhile, at the Strand,

At Miss La Creevy's,

The evening party was well under way,

And it was universally agreed by all the guests

That they could not remember when they had had such a time,

And, in particular, John and Tilda Browdie wished it to be known by one and all that they

JOHN. Would not have missed it for the world. (*The Narrators withdraw.*)

MISS LA CREEVY. Well, thank you *so* much, Mr. Browdie, as it happens, I can't think—

MRS. NICKLEBY. Well, yes, indeed, it's very good of you, dear Mrs. Browdie too, because of course you come to see us in a very plain and homely manner. As I said to Kate—

MISS LA CREEVY. I just can't think of when I've had a better—

MRS. NICKLEBY. As I said "Kate, dearest, you will only make the Browdies feel uncomfortable, if we indulge in great display, and how very inconsiderate that would be". But that is not to say—

MISS LA CREEVY. Of when I've had a better time myself.

MRS. NICKLEBY. To say, of course, that we have no experience of high society, Kate, d'you recall those parties at Peltiroguses? They used to live about a mile from us, not straight you understand, but turning sharp left by the turnpike at the point the Plymouth mail ran over someone's donkey, Kate, you do recall those parties at the Peltiroguses?

KATE. (*Very firmly.*) Mama. I entertain of them the most distinct and vivid memory. (*Slight pause.*) But also, I recall that earlier this evening Mr. Browdie promised us that he would sing a song, and I am sure we are all most impatient that he should redeem his promise, and I'm certain that it will afford you much more pleasure and amusement than it's possible to think of.

MISS LA CREEVY. Oh, now, what a treat.

MRS. NICKLEBY. Sing a song?

KATE. That's right, mama. Now, Mr. Browdie?

JOHN. Oh, well, uh—

TIM. Oh, yes.

MISS LA CREEVY. Oh, Mr. Browdie, please—

JOHN. Well, um—(*To Tilda.*) Sam Tansey's Fancy?

TILDA. No, John.

JOHN. Ballad of John Barleycorn?

TILDA. I think that's better.

JOHN. Right. (*He stands, clears his throat.*) Aye, right. (*He sings.*)
   There came three men from out the west
   Their victory to try—(*A very loud knocking.*)

TILDA. What's that?

NICHOLAS. Must be some mistake. There's no-one who would come here at this hour.

MRS. NICKLEBY. Perhaps it's—some—

KATE. I'll answer it. (*Nicholas going to stop Kate, for fear that it's some malefactor, but Kate has got there, and Ralph Nickleby walks in.*) Oh, uncle.

MRS. NICKLEBY. Brother-in-law. Why, what on earth—

RALPH. Now, stay, before that boy speaks, you will hear me, ma'am.

NICHOLAS. You won't, mama. Don't hear him. I will not have it. I do not know that man.

JOHN. (*Restraining Nicholas.*) Come now, come now.

NICHOLAS. I cannot bear his presence, it's an insult to my sister, and I will not—

KATE. Oh, please, Nicholas—

NICHOLAS. This is my house, am I a child? Oh, this will drive me mad!

FRANK. Who is this man?

MISS LA CREEVY. It's Nicholas' uncle. Calls himself Ralph Nickleby.

SMIKE. Ralph Nickleby. (*Pause.*)

RALPH. Ah. So this is the boy. (*He goes and speaks outside.*) Please come in, gentlemen. And Miss.

SMIKE. Ralph Nickleby! (*Enter Squeers, Snawley and Fanny.*)

JOHN. Eh, school master!

TILDA. Oh, Fanny!

SMIKE. (*Clinging to Miss La Creevy.*) Huh. The enemies.

NICHOLAS. Am I to stand here and allow this? To allow my house to be invaded by these people?

RALPH. It will not last long, sir. I have come here on a simple mission, to restore a child to his parent—

NICHOLAS. What!

RALPH. —his son, sir, kidnapped and waylaid by you, with the base design of robbing him some day of any little wretched pittance which he might inherit.

SQUEERS. Oh, I bet you didn't think of this, eh? Got a father, has he?

RALPH. And as a proof, this is the father. Mr. Snawley, there's your son. (*Pause.*)

KATE. Oh, no.

SNAWLEY. Oh, yes. Yes, there he is. My son! My flesh and blood!

JOHN. Not that much flesh.

SNAWLEY. Come to me, boy. (*Pause. Smike rigid with terror.*)

MISS LA CREEVY. Stay here.

RALPH. Then it is clear we must have further proof. You had a son by your first marriage, Mr. Snawley?

SNAWLEY. Yes, I did, and there he stands.

RALPH. You and your wife were separated, and then you heard after a year or two, the boy had died.

SNAWLEY. Yes, I did. And now, the joy of—

RALPH. Whereas, in fact, you have discovered that your son's death was an invention by your former wife, to wound you, and in fact the boy had lived but was of an imperfect mind, and she had sent him to the school of Mr. Squeers. Is that not so?

SNAWLEY. You talk like a good book, sir, that's got nothing inside it but the truth.

NICHOLAS. I am expected to believe this fantasy? (*Ralph producing documents from a case.*)

RALPH. Certificates of marriage, birth, the letters of the wife, and other documents. Perhaps you'd like to read them, sir.

NICHOLAS. Frank, Tim, please help me look at these. (*Frank, Tim and Nicholas put documents on the table and read them. Ralph sits.*)

SQUEERS. Well, sir, it seems you're reunited with your child. Oh, what a blessed moment!

SNAWLEY. Sir, I knew the very moment when you brought him to my house. I felt—at once—a tingling, a burning, and a palpitation.

SQUEERS. That's parental instinct, sir.

SNAWLEY. That's what it was, no doubt about it. My heart yearned.

SQUEERS. It only shows what nature is, sir. She's a rum one, nature.

SNAWLEY. She's a holy thing. (*Tim, Nicholas and Frank have finished.*)

FRANK. I'm afraid there's little doubt about it. Everything's in order.

TIM. It's a shame to say it, but it's so.

KATE. Oh, Nicholas, this can't be true. (*Nicholas shrugs. Ralph goes to the table and collects the documents.*)

KATE. (*Quickly, to Snawley.*) Sir, if you are the father of this boy, then look, sir, at the wreck he has become, and tell us if you plan to send him back to that vile den my brother took him from.

SQUEERS. Vile den! You hear that, Mr. Nickleby?

RALPH. Now, there's a carriage waiting. Everything is proved. Let's take young Master Snawley and begone. (*Pause.*)

NICHOLAS. There is—the documents speak clearly. If our pleas won't move this man, there's nothing to be done.

SNAWLEY. They won't indeed. Hmph! Have a father to abandon his own child? (*Snawley goes and takes Smike's arm.*) Come, son. The coach is waiting. (*Miss La Creevy looks away as Smike walks halfway towards Snawley. He stops.*)

SMIKE. O.U.T.C.A.S.T. A noun. Substantive. (*Snawley looks bemused. He turns to Squeers who shrugs and smiles, as if to imply that Smike is delirious. Nicholas turns away.*)

SMIKE. Cast. Out. Home. Less. No! (*He runs back to Miss La Creevy.*) I won't. Won't go away again.

KATE. You hear that? Smike has chosen for himself.

SNAWLEY. Oh, this is cruel. Do parents bring children into the world for this?

JOHN. (*Nods to Squeers.*) Do they bring 'em into the world for *that?*

SQUEERS. Now, come on, blockhead, clear the way, and let him take his boy.

RALPH. Yes, sir, you have all blustered long enough.

JOHN. What, blockhead! Bluster? Well, I tell 'ee—I've released this poor chap from your clutches once—and I'll not stand by and see 'im going back to 'em again.

FANNY. Oh, Father, it was him! It was him let Smike go!

JOHN. Ay, 'twere, Fanny, and I tell 'ee—Get tha hands off me! (*For Squeers has been trying to get past John and at Smike. John elbows Squeers in the chest.*) I've had enough of this. The lot of you, get out, and leave the poor chap be. (*And he starts pushing Squeers and Snawley to the door.*)

SQUEERS. I tell you, sir—

JOHN. I'm telling you! Out! Out!

FANNY. Oh, Tilda! Stop him!

TILDA. Stop him what?

FANNY. He's beating up my father. Stop him!

TILDA. How?

SNAWLEY. I want my son! Ungrateful boy!

SQUEERS. Oh, he always was sir—he never loved me, never loved our Wackford, who is next door to a cherubim—

JOHN. Out, now, out!

SQUEERS. I warn you, sir—(*But John has got Squeers and Snawley out.*)

JOHN. Well, done for two of 'em—(*To Ralph.*) You'd best get to your carriage, too, sir. And you, Fanny.

FANNY. Tilda.

SQUEERS. Eh, Fanny, s'got me hat! (*Tilda shrugs.*) Tilda, I renounce you. I—I throw you off, for ever, I—I wouldn't have a child named Tilda—not to save it from its grave.

JOHN. Come on, now, Fanny—

FANNY. Don't you meddle with my Christian name. Don't you—

SQUEERS. Eh, me hat, or else he'll steal it!

FANNY. (*To Tilda.*) Viper! False friend! Vixen! Artful—vulgar—myrmidon!

TILDA. Oh, don't be silly, Fanny.

NICHOLAS. Yes, Miss Squeers, your father's gone—

SQUEERS. Not going. Not without me hat, I'm not.

FANNY. Oh, don't you speak to me. (*Fanny runs out. Squeers runs back in, grabs his hat.*)

SQUEERS. I'll have you, Knuckleboy! (*And John ejects him once again.*)

RALPH. Well, sir. If reason and good feeling fail you, it will have to be the law. (*Slight pause.*) But one thing can be said. I take it your romance about this boy has been destroyed. No, unknown, lost descendant of a man of high degree; but the weak, imbecilic son of some poor tradesman.

NICHOLAS. Sir. Now. Leave this house!

RALPH. I know you, sir. At least, do not delude yourself. I know your nature. Ma'am, goodnight. (*Ralph goes out. Pause.*)

TIM. Well, what a business.

MRS. NICKLEBY. I don't know—he's right of course, we should be reasonable. If only it was possible to settle it in a friendly manner—say, if Mr. Snawley would agree to furnish something certain for Smike's board and lodging. . . . wouldn't it be very satisfactory and pleasant for all parties?

KATE. No, mama. It wouldn't. You don't understand. (*Slight pause.*)

MRS. NICKLEBY. No, well—perhaps I don't. Perhaps I do—from time to time—find things a little hard to understand. (*Pause. A hiatus. Then Smike runs to Kate and embraces her. Pause. Miss La Creevy goes to Smike.*)

MISS LA CREEVY. Now, Mr. Smike, it's very late, and with all that excitement—shouldn't you be off to bed? (*She takes Smike's hand and leads him towards the door. Smike turns back, to John Browdie.*)

SMIKE. I am so grateful. Everything went black. I couldn't see. (*He turns and goes out with Miss La Creevy.*)

JOHN. Well, now, don't this call for a celebration? Come on, gentlemen. . . . (*The Men pouring drinks for everyone.*)

NICHOLAS. Well, yes, indeed, Frank.

FRANK. Now, Mrs. Browdie—(*The rug begins to move. Note: This effect relies on a trap door. In the book, this incident involves an intrusion down the chimney.*)

TILDA. What's that?

FRANK. What's what? (*The rug is beginning to stand up.*)

TILDA. Oh, just, I thought I—oh, I did!

TIM. It's—under—

KATE. Oh, it's—from the cellar—

MRS. NICKLEBY. From the—(*The rug stands up. Under it is the Gentleman From Next Door.*) Oh, good heavens!

FRANK. What's this?

TIM. An intruder!

MRS. NICKLEBY. Oh, it's him!

NICHOLAS. Mama, you know this person?

THE GENTLEMAN. (*Revealing himself.*) Oh maid! Oh maid, I thee entwine! (*He presents Mrs. Nickleby with a cucumber.*)

KATE. Oh, it's the man—the madman from next door!

MRS. NICKLEBY. Now, Kate, I won't have that.

KATE. You won't?

MRS. NICKLEBY. No, not at all. And I'm surprised at you. This is a most unfortunate and persecuted gentleman, in my view, to be aided rather than abused.

THE GENTLEMAN. That's excellent. So, bring the bottled lightening, one clean tumbler, and a corkscrew. Fetch the thunder sandwiches! (*No-one fetches the thunder sandwiches. Enter Miss La Creevy.*)

MISS LA CREEVY. What's going on?

KATE. Oh, Miss La Creevy, it's—

THE GENTLEMAN. Ah, she is come!

MRS. NICKLEBY. What's this?

THE GENTLEMAN. She's come! Take all three graces, all nine muses, melt 'em down with fourteen of the biscuit-bakers daughters of Oxford Street and make a woman half as lovely. Phoo! I defy you! (*"After uttering this rhapsody, the old gentleman subsided into an ecstatic contemplation of Miss La Creevy's charms." He takes the cucumber from Mrs. Nickleby and gives it to Miss La Creevy.*)

FRANK. He seems to, um . . . have changed his mind.

MRS. NICKLEBY. Oh, nonsense. He's mistaken me, that's all. It's often so. I am mistaken, frequently, for Kate. Now, sir—

THE GENTLEMAN. (*To Mrs. Nickleby.*) Avaunt ye, cat.

MRS. NICKLEBY. I beg your pardon? (*The Men move in to eject the Gentleman.*)

JOHN. Right now, that's enough.

THE GENTLEMAN. Cat! Puss! (*Mrs. Nickleby faints quite away.*)

THE GENTLEMAN. Tit! Kit! Grimalkin!

FRANK. Or we may use force upon you.

THE GENTLEMAN. Tabby! Brindle! Whoosh! (*As he departs, to Miss La Creevy.*) Miss Milky Way—I am your puppet and your slave. (*The Gentleman and the Men have gone.*)

MISS LA CREEVY. Well.

MRS. NICKLEBY. (*Reviving.*) Kate. Is he gone?

AKTE. He is, mama.

MRS. NICKLEBY. Oh, Kate, how dreadful.

KATE. It is that.

MRS. NICKLEBY. I do believe the gentleman has lost his mind.

KATE. You do?

MRS. NICKLEBY. And I am the unhappy cause.

KATE. You are?

MRS. NICKLEBY. Of course. You saw him, just the other day, you see what he is now. You've heard the dreadful nonsense he has talked this evening, oh, can anybody doubt that he has gone quite mad and it is my refusal of him that has made him so. (*Exit Mrs. Nickleby. The Men returning.*)

KATE. And with this, Mrs. Nickleby turned tail, and, apologising to her guests, went off to bed.

NICHOLAS. And soon the gentlemen came back, the old man having been returned to his custodian.

TILDA. And John and Tilda, having to depart tomorrow morning, took their leave, with many thanks, and invitations to the company, if ever in North Yorkshire, to drop by.

ALL. North Yorkshire. (*Exit John and Tilda.*)

NICHOLAS. And although it was past midnight, Frank and Tim remained a moment more.

TIM. Dear Miss La Creevy, please assure me you've recovered from your terrible ordeal.

MISS LA CREEVY. Oh, yes. Certainly, dear Mr. Linkinwater.

FRANK. Dear Miss Nickleby, I trust that all these violent altercations have not too disturbed your constitution.

KATE. No, I assure you, Mr. Cheeryble. (*And as the lights fade, we see Smike, behind them, looking fixedly at Kate and Frank Cheeryble.*)

Scene Eight

The house of Arthur Gride. Bare stage. Gride enters, dragging an old, battered, metal trunk, which is all the set we will need. He is singing "the fag end of some forgotten song."

GRIDE.
Tarantarantoo
Throw the old shoe
And may the wedding be lucky . . . (*He opens the trunk, and takes out a bottle-green jacket.*)

Young, loving and fair . . .

Oh, what happiness there . . . (*He looks at the jacket.*)
The bottle green? Now, that's a famous suit, for when I bought it at the pawnbroker, there was a tarnished shilling in the waistcoat pocket. So, it's a lucky suit . . . I'll marry in the bottle green. (*He calls.*) Peg! (*Pause.*) Peg! Peg! Peg Sliderskew! (*This call, loudly repeated twice or thrice, brought into the apartment a short, thin, sweasen, blear-eyed old woman, palsy-stricken and hideously ugly. It is Gride's deaf housekeeper, Peg Sliderskew. She is Scottish.*)

PEG. Wha's that?

GRIDE. Ah, there you are, Peg. I've decided. I'll—

PEG. Wha's that you calling?

GRIDE. Yes, of course, I wanted—

PEG. Or was't just the clock? It must ha' been one or the other—nothing else stirs in *this* house, that's for—

GRIDE. (*Tapping his chest.*) Me, Peg, me.

PEG. Oh, you. What do you want?

GRIDE. I want, Peg, to be married in the bottle green.

PEG. Huh? (*Slight pause.*) What's this, dress up to be married? Why, what's wrong with what you usually wear?

GRIDE. But look my best, Peg, look my best.

PEG. What for? I tell ye, master, she's as handsome as you say, she won't look much at you, whatever you'se decked up in: bottle-green, sky-blue or tartan-plaid, won't make a fig of difference.

GRIDE. Now, Peg, I've told you, I've decided—

PEG. Och, I know—

GRIDE. And after, there'll be only she and me, and you, and we can live, the three of us, as cheap as you and I have always done . . .

PEG. Oh, is that so?

GRIDE. So take up the loose stitches in the bottle-green, Peg, best black silk, and put new buttons on the coat, you'll do this for me, Peg? My wedding day? (*Pause.*)

PEG. Och, aye. I'll do't. (*She takes the coat. The bell rings. Peg laughs.*) Och, who'd have thought.

GRIDE. The bell, Peg.

PEG. That old Arthur Gride—(*Bell rings.*)

GRIDE. The bell. Peg.

PEG. (*Still laughing.*) Falling for a wee—

GRIDE. The bell! (*Slight pause.*)

PEG. You what?

GRIDE. Go to it!

PEG. Go to what? What's wrong, me stopping here?

GRIDE. (*Gesturing a ringing bell.*) It Is The Bell. (*Slight pause.*)

PEG. Och. Aye. Well—I'll go answer it. (*Peg goes out.*)

GRIDE. Hm. Half a witch that woman, I believe. But very frugal, very deaf, her living costs me next to nothing. Oh, she'll do, she'll do. (*Calls.*) Who is it, Peg? (*Peg leads in Noggs.*)

PEG. It's him.

GRIDE. Ah, Mr. Noggs, my good friend, so what news d'you bring for me? (*Exit Peg.*)

NOGGS. (*Handing over a letter.*) No news. A letter. Mr. Nickleby. The bearer waits.

GRIDE. (*Opening it eagerly.*) A letter? Then it's news. (*Quickly reading.*) Oh, yes, and good news, too. The very best there could be.

NOGGS. The bearer waits.

GRIDE. And will not wait much longer—a verbal answer. Tell him: "Yes".

NOGGS. Just "Yes"?

GRIDE. That's right. He'll understand.

NOGGS. (*Turning to go.*) I'm sure he will. (*Noggs going.*)

GRIDE. Oh— Mr. Noggs?

NOGGS. Got the answer. "Yes."

GRIDE. I wondered—

NOGGS. Yes?

GRIDE. If you would like to join me in a little drop. To celebrate. (*Pause.*)

NOGGS. Oh, well . . .

GRIDE. I know you're partial. Mr. Noggs.

NOGGS. Oh. Very well. (*Gride opens the trunk to find a bottle and two small glasses. The hand which holds the letter is on the top of the trunk so Noggs can read it.*)

NOGGS. Poor girl. Poor girl. (*Gride has got the bottle and glasses, and suddenly shuts the trunk. Noggs, to cover, stares "at the wall with an intensity so remarkable that Arthur was quite alarmed."*)

GRIDE. Oh. Do you see anything in particular, Mr. Noggs?

NOGGS. Only a cobweb.

GRIDE. Oh. Is that all?

NOGGS. No. There's a fly in it.

GRIDE. There's a good many cobwebs here.

NOGGS. So there are in our place. And flies too. (*"Newman appeared to derive great entertainment from this repartee, and to the great discomposure of Arthur Girde's nerves, produced a series of sharp cracks*

*from his finger-joints, resembling the noise of a distant discharge of
small artillery." Then:)* Sorry. *(He looks balefully at the bottle.
Gride's grin reappears.)*

GRIDE. I tell you, you have never tasted anything like this, I swear.
Called eau d'or. It means "golden water". Water—turned to gold. I tell
you, it's a sin to drink it. *(Gride looks at Noggs, who looks balefully at
him.)* Still. *(He pours two small measures. Noggs picks up his glass.)*
Oh, wait a minute, Mr. Noggs. Don't drink it yet. I've had this bottle
twenty years. And when I take a little taste, and that's not often, I do
like to look at it. And think about it. For a moment. Tease myself.
(Pause.)

NOGGS. Uh—

GRIDE. Yes?

NOGGS. Uh—bearer waits.

GRIDE. Well, then. We'll drink it. Drink a toast. We'll drink it—to a
lady.

NOGGS. To the ladies?

GRIDE. No—a lady. Little Madeline. *(Slight pause.)*

NOGGS. What's that?

GRIDE. What's that? Oh, Mr. Noggs, that is the prettiest, and daintiest,
and—

NOGGS. Madeline?

GRIDE. That's right. With eyelashes, and—

NOGGS. *(Suddenly.)* Bearer waits. You hea—, her health. To Little
Madeline. *(He knocks the drink back in one.)* I pray it can't be—But
I fear it is. Good night. *(He runs out, bumping into Peg as she comes
in.)*

PEG. So. Who's that lunatic?

GRIDE. He's Nickleby's.

PEG. He's who's?

GRIDE. Oh, doesn't matter. *(Gride gestures with Noggs' glass, to indicate Noggs is a tippler.)*

PEG. Oh. I see.

GRIDE. Peg. Peg. It's Wednesday. Two days time.

PEG. What is?

GRIDE. My wedding day. *(Pause.)*

PEG. It's time for bed. *(Peg shuffles off.)*

GRIDE. Huh. There's a change come over you, Mrs. Peg. I don't know
what it means. But if it lasts, shan't be together long. You're turning
crazy, Mrs. Peg, and if you do, I'll turn you out. All's one to me. *(He
comes across a document in the trunk.)* Oh, here it is. Oh, here it is,

my little beauty. "To Madeline." "To come of age or marry." Oh, my darling, dainty little deed. (*He kisses the document and puts it away. Locking up.*)

    Young, loving and fair,
    Oh, what happiness there.

    The wedding is sure to be happy. (*Gride goes out. We are aware that, in the gloom, Peg stands there. She has, if not overheard, at least overseen, Gride with the document. She potters forward.*)

PEG. Huh—huh. A wedding, eh? A precious wedding. Huh. (*Pause.*) Wants someone better than this old Peg, eh? Take care of him. (*Pause.*) And wha's he said? So many times. Keep me content wi' short food, little wages and no fire? "My will, Peg, Peg, I've nobody, but you. Just think—my will." (*Pause.*) And now it's a new mistress, is it? Baby-faced young chit. (*Pause.*) She won't come in my way. Says you. Well, no she won't. I tell ye, Arthur, boy. She won't. But you— you don't know why. (*Pause.*) You're stuck to me, old Arthur Gride, You'll never throw out old Peg Slider. (*Slight pause.*) 'Cos she's stuck to you. (*Fade.*)

Scene Nine

A street. Bare stage. Enter Nicholas, followed by Noggs.

NICHOLAS. Tomorrow!
NOGGS. Yes—I didn't—never told me what her second name was—
NICHOLAS. But—*tomorrow*—
NOGGS. Had no way to know, you see; now, we must think—
NICHOLAS. I will go straight to Bray's. I'll see this man. And if there's one—small feeling of humanity, still lingering—
NOGGS. I doubt it.
NICHOLAS. Then what am I to do? You are my best friend, Newman, and I must confess I don't know what to do.
NOGGS. The greater need, then, for a cool head, reason and consideration. Thought.
NICHOLAS. There's only one thing. I can go to her. And try to reason with her, and point out the horrors she is hastening to.
NOGGS. Yes, yes, that's right! You see? That's bravely spoken.
NICHOLAS. Entreat her, even now, at least to pause. To pause! (*Nicholas runs out.*)
NOGGS. He is a violent man. He has a violent streak. But still—I like him for it. There is cause enough. (*Noggs potters out.*)

Scene Ten

The King's Bench Prison area. Beggars, criminals etc. around again.
Madeline wheels in Bray. Nicholas arrives.

NICHOLAS. Sir. Miss Madeline.

BRAY. Well, sir, what do you want?

NICHOLAS. I, um—I have come to—

BRAY. Hm. I s'pose you think you can burst in on us without a with-
your-leave, because without the—paltry sums you bring, we'd starve?

NICHOLAS. My business, sir, is with the lady—

BRAY. With the daughter of a gentleman! Your business, sir! We didn't
look to see your face again till Thursday, at the earliest.

NICHOLAS. (*With a piece of paper.*) Yes, but . . . My employers would
appreciate, Miss Madeline, if you could undertake—

BRAY. Oh, I see, you have brought more orders, sir? (*Bray takes the
paper from Nicholas.*)

NICHOLAS. That's not the term I would prefer to use. Commissions, yes.

BRAY. Well, you can tell your master that they won't be undertaken;
you can tell him that my daughter—Miss Madeline Bray—condescends
no longer, that we don't need his money, and that this is my acknowl-
edgement of your "orders", sir! (*He tears the paper.*) So, unless you've
any further "orders," sir . . .

NICHOLAS. No, I have none. Except . . .

BRAY. Yes, what?

NICHOLAS. I do have fears. And I must state them: fears, that you are
consigning that young lady to something worse, worse even than to
work herself to death. Those are my fears, sir. (*Bray furious, hitting
the side of his chair.*)

MADELINE. For heaven's sake, sir, please remember that he's ill—

BRAY. I am not ill! Out, out! I will not see his face a moment longer.
Take me out of here! Please. (*Slight pause.*) Please, Madeline. (*Madeline wheels Bray out. She returns to Nicholas.*)

MADELINE. If you are charged with some commission to me, please
don't press it now. The day after tomorrow—come here then.

NICHOLAS. It will be too late, then, for what I have to say, and you will
not be here. Please listen to me.

MADELINE. No, I can't, I won't.

NICHOLAS. You will. You must. I must beseech you, contemplate again this fearful course to which you've been impelled.

MADELINE. What's this? What course?

NICHOLAS. This marriage. Yours. Fixed for tomorrow, by two men who have never faltered in a bad intent, and who have wound a web around you, and betrayed you, and bought you for gold.

MADELINE. I will not hear this.

NICHOLAS. But you must, you must. I know you don't know half of what this evil man has done—Think of the mockery of pledging yourself to this man, at the altar—solemn words, against which nature must rebel and, think, too, of the days and days with him that stretch before you . . . Oh, believe me, that the most degraded poverty is better than the misery you'd undergo as wife to such a man as this. Believe me, Madeline. (*Madeline looks at Nicholas.*)

MADELINE. Believe me, sir. This evil, if it is an evil, is of my own seeking. I'm impelled by nobody, but follow this course of my own free will. It is my choice.

NICHOLAS. How *can* you say this?

MADELINE. Because it is true. (*Slight pause.*) I can't disguise—although perhaps I ought to—that I've undergone great pain of mind, since you were last here. No, I do not love this gentleman. He knows that, and still offers me his hand. Please don't think of me I can feign a love that I don't feel. Do not report this of me, for I couldn't bear it. He's content to have me, as I am. And I am happy for that. And I will grow happier.

NICHOLAS. You're crying with your happiness. Oh, just just one week, postpone this marriage, for a few days, even just a day—

MADELINE. Before you came here, my father was talking, of the new life that he would lead, the freedom that will come tomorrow. And he smiled—a smile I haven't seen for—he was smiling, laughing at the thought of open air, and freshness, and his eyes grew bright, his face lit up—I'll not defer it for an hour.

NICHOLAS. These are—just tricks to urge you on—

MADELINE. It is no trick, my father's dying, sir. By doing this, I can release him not just from this place, but from the jaws of death itself. How *can* you tell me to act otherwise? (*Pause.*)

BRAY. (*Off.*) Hey! Madeline!

NICHOLAS. There's nothing I can say that will convince you.

MADELINE. Nothing.

NICHOLAS. Even if I—knew a plot, that you might, be entitled to a fortune that would do all that this marriage can accomplish? More?

BRAY. (*Off.*) Where are you Madeline?

MADELINE. He's calling. What you say's a childish fantasy.

NICHOLAS. If I could prove to you the things I know—

MADELINE. It would mean nothing. I am happy in the prospect of what I'll achieve so easily.

BRAY. (*Off.*) Come, Madeline!

MADELINE. Now, I must go to him.

NICHOLAS. We'll never meet again?

MADELINE. No. No. Of course not. (*She goes, turns back.*) Sir, the time may come when to remember this interview might drive me mad. (*Slight pause.*) Please tell them I looked happy.

BRAY. (*Off.*) Madeline! (*Exit Madeline. Nicholas goes out.*)

Scene Eleven

A gambling house. At once, lights, music. Smoke, laughter. Downstage, are two tables, either side, with chairs. Upstage, a crowd of people, concealing a Croupier, upstage of them. He has a football rattle, with which to give the impression of a roulette wheel. At one of the tables sits Verisopht, Pluck, Pyke, and a Captain Adams, with Ladies of Leisure and bottles of wine. The crowd round the "table" upstage includes Men of Pleasure and Ladies of Leisure, and, in particular, a rival of Sir Mulberry Hawk called Handsaw, and a couple of his young male friends. As the scene assembles:

CROUPIER. The wheel of fortune, gentlemen. Place your bets on red or black, or odd or even, or a number. Double with a colour, gentlemen, and much, much more, if the wheel points to your number. How do you do, sir, can I take your bet. Bets till the wheel spins, gentlemen— and then it's just waiting till we see who's won. All bets in now. The wheel's about to spin. Your bets please, gentlemen! (*But the Croupier stops, as he, and shortly everyone else, has noticed the entrance of Sir Mulberry Hawk, attended by Mr. Westwood. Hawk gives his cape to an attendant. The Proprietor goes over to him.*)

PROPRIETOR. Why, Sir Mulberry. Good evening. This is—a great pleasure. Please, sir, let me escort you to a table. (*Verisopht looks at Hawk, but Hawk goes to the empty table, with Westwood, and sits. We see Hawk still has a slight limp. Verisopht whispers to the waitress, who takes a bottle to Hawk. The Proprietor nods to the Croupier.*)

CROUPIER. Last bets, gentlemen. And let the wheel of fortune spin!

(*Noise back in, as the wheel is spun, and the betters watch and shout eagerly.*) Number 27! Red! Red 27, gentlemen! (*The Croupier pays out as Handsaw, comes over to him. He has a couple of young men in tow.*)

HANDSAW. Well, Hawk, and how are you, sir? (*Verisopht stands and goes over to Hawk's table as:*)

HAWK. Well. I am very well.

HANDSAW. Still limping, I observe.

HAWK. But very nearly mended, I assure you.

HANDSAW. Yes, but still a little, ah, my Lord, a little pulled down, rather, still, out of condition, eh?

VERISOPHT. I'd say, still in very good condition. I'd say, nothing much the matter. Actually.

HANDSAW. Upon my soul, I'm glad to hear it. And to see, of course, your good friend back, so soon, into society. It's bold, it's game: To withdraw just long enough for people to get curious, but not for men to have forgotten that, unpleasant—tell me, Hawk, I've never understood why you didn't give the lie to all those damned reports they printed in the papers . . . looked there every day—

HAWK. Look in the papers, then, tomorrow, or the next day.

CROUPIER. Place bets. Place your bets, gentlemen!

HANDSAW. Oh. What will I find there?

HAWK. Something that will interest you, I'm sure.

HANDSAW. What's that? (*Hawk gestures towards the "wheel." Handsaw bows and he and his acolytes leave Hawk and Verisopht.*)

VERISOPHT. Good evening, Hawk.

HAWK. My Lord. (*He waves his glass.*) My thanks to you.

VERISOPHT. What should he look for in the papers?

HAWK. Oh . . . well, it won't be a murder. But, still, something near. If whipcord cuts and bludgeons bruise.

VERISOPHT. Bruise who?

HAWK. Who do you think?

CROUPIER. Last bets! Last bets please, gentlemen! (*Hawk stands, to go and place a bet. Verisopht stops him.*)

VERISOPHT. I'd hoped—that after all this time, you would have reconsidered.

HAWK. Well, sir, I have not. So, there is your answer.

VERISOPHT. Then I hope you will remember what I said. That if you were to take this course, I would try to prevent you.

HAWK. I'd mind your business, if I was you, and leave me to mind mine.

VERISOPHT. It *is* my business. I shall make it so. It's mine already. I'm more compromised by all this than I ought to be. (*Hawk turns to go, but turns back to Verisopht.*)

HAWK. My Lord, I will be straight with you. I am dependent on you, as you know. But, if that's so, then your dependence upon me is ten times greater. Do not interfere with me in this proceeding, I warn you; or else you'll force me to destroy you. And I will.

CROUPIER. Come on, now, gentlemen. Last bets. Last bets before the spinning of the wheel. (*Hawk turns and quickly goes to join the crowd round the wheel and places a bet.*) Ah, Sir Mulberry. Most privileged. A bet, sir? Thank you. And let the wheel of fortune spin—(*Verisopht pauses, then goes to his table. His party bobbing to their feet, when Verisopht, on a sudden impulse, turns, strides over to Hawk, and, as the wheel is spun, grabs his shoulder and pulls him round.*)

HAWK. What? What's this?

VERISOPHT. I will not have it, Hawk. I cannot have it.

HAWK. Let me go, boy.

VERISOPHT. No. (*Hawk tries to push Verisopht away. Verisopht hits Hawk across the face. Everyone's attention suddenly focussed. Westwood stands. The wheel clatters to a stop unneeded.*)

HAWK. He struck me. (*Pause.*) Do you hear? He struck me! Have I not a friend here? Westwood! (*Westwood to Hawk.*)

WESTWOOD. I hear, sir. Come away, now, for tonight.

HAWK. No, I will not, by God. A dozen men here saw the blow.

WESTWOOD. Tomorrow will be ample time.

HAWK. No it will not. Tonight—at once—here.

VERISOPHT. (*Turning to Adams, who has joined the group round the wheel.*) Captain Adams. I say, let this quarrel be adjusted now. (*Westwood whispering to Hawk.*)

ADAMS. My lord, an hour or so, at least.

VERISOPHT. Then, very well. An hour. (*He walks aside.*)

HAWK. (*Shouts, at the Company.*) No more. (*Hawk marches out. Westwood to Adams. Adams nods, to say, "In a moment." He goes to Verisopht.*)

WESTWOOD. Captain Adams.

ADAMS. You will not—

VERISOPHT. Only if he will retract. The things he said. (*Adams shrugs.*)

ADAMS. He is a splendid shot, my lord.

VERISOPHT. So I have heard. (*Slight pause. Verisopht laughs. Adams looks at him oddly.*) Oh, so I've heard. Are you a married man, dear Captain?

ADAMS. No, I'm not.

VERISOPHT. (*Still laughing.*) Well, nor am I. Oh, nor am I. (*He stops laughing.*) I'll see you in an hour, then. (*Verisopht goes out. The Proprietor nods to the Croupier.*)

CROUPIER. Uh—place your bets. Your bets, please, gentlemen. (*Adams to Westwood. They talk. The Proprietor whispers to the Croupier. The Croupier, with more enthusiasm.*) Sir Mulberry, this side! Lord Frederick, the other—place your bets now, gentlemen! (*And Pluck and Pyke move in to place their bets. And the wheel and the Gentlemen disappear. And Verisopht is there alone.*)

VERISOPHT. It was daybreak. And as they walked towards the place agreed, he saw the trees, and the fields, and gardens, and they all looked very beautiful, as if he'd never noticed them before. And young Lord Verisopht felt little fear; but more a sense of something like regret, that it should come to this.

Scene Twelve

Dawn. By the river. Bare stage. Enter Adams to Verisopht.

ADAMS. So here we are, my lord. My lord, you're shivering.

VERISOPHT. I'm cold.

ADAMS. It does strike cool, to come out of hot rooms. Do you want my cloak?

VERISOPHT. No, no. (*Hawk, Westwood, the Gentleman acting as Umpire, a Surgeon, one or two other Gentlemen, come in. Among the group, too, at the back, unnoticed, are Mr. Pluck and Mr. Pyke.*) Well, here they are. (*He laughs.*)

ADAMS. My lord?

VERISOPHT. It's nothing. (*Adams goes to Westwood and they talk. Verisopht jumpy, laughing to himself, light-headed. Adams returns to him.*)

ADAMS. My lord. They're ready.

VERISOPHT. Ready. (*As the Umpire opens the box of pistols, Verisopht comes over to him and Hawk.*)

VERISOPHT. Uh—Hawk.

HAWK. (*Gruffly.*) My lord?

VERISOPHT. Hawk, just one word.

HAWK. Yes? What? Speak, quickly.

VERISOPHT. I—you know, I owe Ralph Nickleby £10,000.

(*Pause. Everyone looking edgy.*)

HAWK. I know. (*Pause.*)

VERISOPHT. I am not married.

HAWK. That is true. Can we begin? (*Slight pause.*)

VERISOPHT. And being in that state, my debts die with me. (*Pause.*)

HAWK. What?

VERISOPHT. I don't mean . . . We must settle this, of course. But, just to let you know. (*Slight pause. He looks at the pistols.*) The terms. My father's will. I die unmarried—and I die a pauper. And my creditors live, paupers, too. (*A slight laugh. He takes a pistol from the case. Pause.*)

HAWK. What's this?

VERISOPHT. So. Either way, Hawk. I'll destroy you. Won't I. (*Verisopht laughs.*) Won't I. Eh? (*Pause. Hawk takes a pistol from the case. Verisopht turns his back to Hawk. Hawk turns his back on Verisopht.*)

HAWK. (*To the Umpire.*) Begin.

UMPIRE. Yes. Yes. Sir Mulberry. My lord. Proceed. One, two, three, four, five, six, seven, eight, nine, ten. (*Hawk and Verisopht take ten paces. They turn and fire. Verisopht falls. The Surgeon to Verisopht. He finds that Verisopht is dead. He nods. Quickly: Adams takes Verisopht's pistol, and Westwood gives it to Hawk, who shakes his head and pockets his pistol; the Umpire and the other Gentlemen depart. Only, still at a distance, Pluck and Pyke are left.*)

WESTWOOD. Now, Hawk, there's not a moment to be lost. We must leave here immediately—for Brighton, and then France. (*Pause. Hawk impassive.*) Come, Hawk. This is a dreadful business, and delay will make it worse.

HAWK. An hour. Meet you at the stage-coach: in an hour. (*Striding out.*)

WESTWOOD. But—but, Hawk—

HAWK. An hour! (*Exit Hawk. Westwood looks at Adams, shrugs and goes out. Adams nods to Pluck and Pyke. They come forward.*)

PLUCK. Well. Is this is a bad business, Pyke?

PYKE. Is this a dreadful business, Pluck.

ADAMS. You both know what to do. (*Adams goes out. Pyke and Pluck take Verisopht's watch, rings and all valuables. Then they pick him up by the arms and drag his body out.*)

Scene Thirteen

London. Dawn. Nicholas enters, on a bare stage. Kate stands to the side. During the following, we hear the hiss of gas lights, and a Lampman slowly crosses the stage with a long pole. He mimes shut-

ting off the gas at the top of an imaginary street lamp. Then, slowly, the stage fills with the Poor of London, at dawn: maids scrubbing doorsteps, blind men begging, street-sweepers sweeping, prostitutes soliciting, and pimps watching. There are mothers and fathers with babies and children, too. Gradually, the naturalistic evocation of a London morning turns into a Chorus: the Poor move forward into a phalanx around Nicholas, eventually surrounding and obscuring him.

NICHOLAS. And at the same daybreak, Nicholas arose,
KATE. And softly left the house,
NICHOLAS. And wandered into London. And as he paced the streets and listlessly looked round on the gradually increasing bustle of the day, everything appeared to yield him some new occasion for despondency. Last night, the sacrifice of a young, affectionate and beautiful creature to such a wretch had seemed a thing too monstrous to succeed. But, now, when he thought how regularly things went on:
POOR PEOPLE.
From day to day

In the same unvarying way

How crafty avarice grew rich, and manly honest hearts were poor and sad

How few they were who tenanted the stately homes,

And how many those who lay in foul and rancid tenements,

Or even

Lived

And died

Father

And son,

Mother,

And child,

HALF. Race upon race,
ALL. And generation upon generation, without a home to shelter them

PROSTITUTE. How in seeking, not a luxurious and splendid life, but the bare means of a most wretched and inadequate subsistence,

ALL. Subsistence.

PROSTITUTE. There were women and children in that one town, divided into classes,

PIMP. And reared from infancy to drive most criminal and dreadful trades—

YOUTHS AND CHILDREN. How ignorance was punished and never taught—

PROSTITUTES AND THIEVES. How jail-door gaped and gallows loomed for thousands.

ALL. How many died in soul, and had no chance of life—

NICHOLAS. How many who could scarcely go astray, turned haughtily from those who could scarce do otherwise,

ONE THIRD. How much injustice,

TWO THIRDS. Misery,

ALL. And wrong there was, (*Nicholas now surrounded and is obscured as:*)

NICHOLAS. And yet how the world rolled on from year to year, alike careless and indifferent, and no man seeking to remedy or redress it: —when he thought of all this, and selected from the mass the one slight case on which his thoughts were bent, he felt indeed that there was little ground for hope, and little cause or reason why it should not form an atom in the huge aggregate of distress and sorrow, and add one small and unimportant unit to the great amount. (*The poor look at us. And then they split and melt away. And Nicholas is left alone. Noggs appears.*)

NICHOLAS. Oh, Newman. Legal right, the power of money, everything is on their side. And I can't save her.

NOGGS. Don't say that. (*Nicholas looks at Noggs.*) Oh, don't say it, Nick. Never lose hope, never leave off it, it don't answer. *I* know that. If nothing else, I have learnt that. (*Pause.*) Don't leave a stone unturned. At least you know you've done the most you could. Or else— how could you bear to live with it? (*Pause. Nicholas looks at Noggs. Nicholas goes out.*) Hope. Always hope. (*Noggs goes out, too.*)

Scene Fourteen

Ralph's house. A room, set up for a wedding ceremony. All that is needed are two chairs, on one of which sits Madeline, and Bray's wheelchair behind. Bray looks very ill; he is dressed up in uncom-

fortable finery. A Minister stands waiting. Gride enters, and is met by Ralph.

RALPH. Well, good day, Mr. Gride. Congratulations, on your wedding morning.

GRIDE. Nickleby. Is everything prepared?

RALPH. It is. Your bride waits to receive you, sir.

GRIDE. And, how is she?

RALPH. Bray says that she accepts it. She is calm. She may be safely trusted, now. It won't be long.

GRIDE. What won't be?

RALPH. (*With a nod at Bray.*) Paying his annuity. You have the devil's luck in bargains, Gride. (*He turns to go to the ceremony.*)

GRIDE. Uh, Nickleby—

RALPH. Yes? What? (*Gride takes two crushed carnations from his pocket.*) What's this?

GRIDE. To wear. Your buttonhole. It is a wedding day. (*Slight pause. Ralph shrugs. The two men put on their buttonholes. Then they go to the Minister. Ralph nods at the Minister. Gride sits next to Madeline. The Minister begins the service.*)

MINISTER. Dearly beloved, we are gathered together here in the sight of God and in the face of this congregation to join together this man and this woman in Holy Matrimony, which is an honourable estate, instituted of God in the time of man's innocency, signifying unto us the mystical union that is between Christ and his church which holy estate Christ adorned and beautified—(*Ralph gestures to the Minister to hurry it along. The Minister turns the page.*) I require and charge you both, as ye will answer at the dreadful day of judgement, when the secrets of all hearts shall be disclosed, that if either of you know any impediment, why ye may not be lawfully joined together in matrimony, ye do now confess it. (*Nicholas' voice, from off.*)

NICHOLAS. Won't you? Won't you confess it, Madeline?

GRIDE. What's this? What, Nickleby?

BRAY. It's him—him, Madeline—

MADELINE. Oh—sir—(*Nicholas and Kate are in the room, Ralph to them.*)

RALPH. I don't believe it.

GRIDE. Who is this man? This girl? Why have they come here?

NICHOLAS. We know everything. We've come to stop this marriage. And we won't go till we have.

RALPH. Gride. This is my niece. And this, her brother. I'm ashamed to say, my brother's son.

NICHOLAS. Oh, *you're* ashamed—

KATE. Nicholas—

RALPH. Now you, my dear, retire. We can use force on him, and will if need be, but I would not hurt you if it could be helped. (*Slight pause.*) Retire!

KATE. I won't, and you misjudge me if you think I will. You may use force on me—and it would be most like you if you did; but I will not go till we've done what we have come to do.

NICHOLAS. Well said.

RALPH. Oh, yes. I see. This fellow here—he brings with him, you note, his sister, as protection. I shouldn't be surprised, in fact, Gride, if he doesn't have a mind to marry Madeline himself.

GRIDE. What's that?

RALPH. Well, why d'you think he's here? Philanthropy?

NICHOLAS. I tell you, both of you, that there has been no word of love, no contract, no engagement—

RALPH. Certainly, there's no engagement. This young lady is engaged already. And about to be a bride.

GRIDE. My bride!

NICHOLAS. And we demand to speak with her.

GRIDE. And how we'll laugh together, she and me, at how this little boy was jilted—

NICHOLAS. Will you let me speak with her?

GRIDE. And I wonder, is there anything of mine he'd like besides? He wants my bride, perhaps he'd like his debts paid, and his house refurnished, and a few banknotes for shaving paper, if he shaves at all? (*Nicholas tries to push past Gride. Kate is between Ralph and Nicholas, and Ralph, to get to Nicholas, clasps her arm. Nicholas turns and takes Ralph's collar, when they are all interrupted by the entrance of Sir Mulberry Hawk.*)

HAWK. Well, look at this. A family reunion. (*Ralph pulls himself free from Nicholas.*) And—a wedding, too? Well, I'm sorry, Nickleby, to interrupt, but I have urgent news about an opposite affair.

RALPH. What's that?

HAWK. A funeral.

RALPH. Whose funeral?

HAWK. Lord Frederick Verisopht's. (*Kate a step forward. Pause. Hawk takes out his pistol.*) He struck me—as a consequence of something I had said—concerned with a young lady. And her brother. So . . . I had my answer. (*There is something strange about the face of Walter Bray, Madeline wheels her father a little further apart, and looks at him, and loosens his collar. The Minister, seeing that no-one is noticing him, slips out.*)

RALPH. But—

HAWK. Oh, yes. You know. For you know everything. Unmarried. And his bills, and mine on his account, all guaranteed by you, all over town. What would you say? Ten thousand pounds? (*Ralph looking blank.*) You do—you understand?

RALPH. I understand.

NICHOLAS. (*Laughs.*) Oh, yes. At last you understand. (*Hawk quickly to Nicholas, with the pistol.*)

HAWK. I tell you. That this should have been for you. (*Madeline has left Bray. She looks at Hawk, bemused.*) I'm sorry, ma'am. To frighten you. (*He is going.*)

MADELINE. He's dead. (*It almost sounds like a question. Hawk doesn't understand.*)

HAWK. Oh, yes. He's dead. Indeed. (*Hawk goes out. The penny drops for Ralph, Gride, Kate and Nicholas, as they see Bray, slumped in his chair.*)

MADELINE. He looked at me. And whispered that he couldn't bear to see—And shut his eyes. And wouldn't open them again.

RALPH. What's this you say? (*Ralph and Gride rush to the body of Bray. Kate to Madeline.*)

KATE. Oh, I'm so sorry. (*Gride trying to get to Madeline.*)

GRIDE. Oh, Madeline. My pretty little Madeline.

NICHOLAS. Oh, no. Her obligation to you's ended, now.

RALPH. This man—she's still his wife-to-be. And he shall have her.

GRIDE. Oh, she still shall be my wife, my dainty—now—with no-one, she will need me, won't she—precious—

MADELINE. No. Of course not. You said you would save him. And you've killed him.

GRIDE. What is this? What, me, my chick?

MADELINE. Yes, Indeed. That's what he meant. He couldn't bear to see me married to you. (*Suddenly, furiously, to Gride.*) How *can* you think that I could bear it, now?

NICHOLAS. Kate, downstairs. (*Kate taking Madeline's arm.*)

RALPH. You will not take her, girl.

KATE. Uncle, I will.

RALPH. You have no right to do this—

KATE. I have more right to do this, uncle, much more right, than you had to allow what happened to me here. (*She makes to lead Madeline out. Madeline to Nicholas.*)

MADELINE. Please, sir—I want him taken from here. (*Nicholas nods. Kate takes Madeline out. Nicholas to the wheelchair.*)

RALPH. Just one word.

NICHOLAS. Not even one. Your bills are now waste paper. Your debts will not be paid—save this—the one great debt of nature. (*He takes out the body of Walter Bray. Long pause.*)

GRIDE. It's not my fault.

RALPH. Who said it was?

GRIDE. You look as if you thought I was to blame.

RALPH. I don't. I blame him. Bray.

GRIDE. What for?

RALPH. For not—not living an hour longer. (*Pause.*) Now, go Gride. (*To himself.*) Ten thousand pounds. (*Gride turns to go. He is suddenly aware of something in the movement. He pats his coat, outside a pocket. He feels inside the pocket. Nothing there. He feels in the other pockets. He rips his coat off, searching desperately for something.*) What are you doing, Gride?

GRIDE. Lost something.

RALPH. Something? What.

GRIDE. It's gone.

RALPH. What is?

GRIDE. The deed. She's taken it.

RALPH. Who has?

GRIDE. Peg Sliderskew. Old, mad and deaf Peg Slider. She has robbed me of the deed! (*He waves his coat.*) I had it in my pocket. And it's gone!

RALPH. Now, come, Gride, first go home—

GRIDE. Oh, Nickleby. I shouldn't have it. It's not mine. Someone will read it for her. And she'll take it to the police. And then—and then—I'm done for.

RALPH. Gride. At least go home, and see you didn't drop it somewhere. See it isn't locked up where you left it.

GRIDE. I tell you Nickleby. I know it's gone. And I tell you something else. You said you'd help me to be married. And it's been prevented, by your flesh and blood. I tell you, if I go down with this business, then you're going too. (*Pause.*)

RALPH. All right, Gride. Yes. Now, tell me all about it. And we'll try and get it back. (*And they go out together.*)

Scene Fifteen

The Nicklebys' Garden. Bare stage, with dappled light. Smike is tending pot plants in a tray downstage, helped by Kate who wears gardening gloves. Enter Nicholas.

NICHOLAS. How's Madeline?

KATE. She's sleeping.

NICHOLAS. But is she—

KATE. She's exhausted, nothing more. (*Enter Mrs. Nickleby.*)

MRS. NICKLEBY. Well, now, Nicholas, perhaps you can explain all this to me.

NICHOLAS. Mother, I thought we'd—

MRS. NICKLEBY. Well, you did, indeed, at length, but still I can't see why, in the name of wonder, Nicholas should go about the world forbidding people's banns? (*Nicholas flapping with frustration.*)

KATE. I don't think, mother, you quite understand.

MRS. NICKLEBY. Not understand? I have been married myself, Kate, and have seen other people married, frequently, and as to this Miss Magdalen marrying a man that's older than herself, I would remind you of Jane Dibabs, who—

NICHOLAS. Jane Dibabs!

MRS. NICKLEBY. Yes, that's right, who used to live in that attractive little cottage past the lunatic asylum, and she married someone twenty or so years above her, and who was so honourable and excellent, that she was blissfully content about the whole arrangement, and remains so to this day. (*Pause. Kate, very patiently.*)

KATE. Mama, the husband in this case is greatly older; he is not her own choice; his character is quite the opposite of that which you've described; mama, don't you see a broad distinction between the two cases?

MRS. NICKLEBY. Well, I daresay, I'm very stupid, Kate—

KATE. Mama! (*Kate runs to Smike, and helps him with the garden, to cover her anger and frustration.*)

MRS. NICKLEBY. Well, I don't know what that's about, I'm sure. (*Nicholas about to join his sister when enter Hannah.*)

MRS. NICKLEBY. Yes, Hannah, dear?

HANNAH. There are three gentlemen without.

MRS. NICKLEBY. Now, Hannah, dear, what gentlemen?

HANNAH. Uh . . . (*Enter Mr. Ned Cheeryble, Mr. Charles Cheeryble and Frank Cheeryble. Hannah goes out.*)

FRANK. Mrs. Nickleby.

MR. CHARLES. Oh, my dear young man, my dear young man. Miss Madeline is safe?

NICHOLAS. Yes, she is safe. (*Kate comes to the Cheerybles, followed by Smike.*)

MR. NED. And you, sir, we have had the scantiest of reports, have sustained no injury?

NICHOLAS. I am completely well.

FRANK. And your dear sister, sir, we hear that she too was involved in this heroic enterprise—(*Frank has moved to Kate.*)

KATE. And have survived my humble part in it, sir, I assure you.

MR. NED. May we inquire—if it is possible to see the lady? (*Kate smiles and goes out, followed by Mrs. Nickleby. Mr. Charles to Nicholas.*)

MR. CHARLES. We cannot express, sir, our full admiration of your actions on this day. We will, sir, at the earliest opportunity, relieve you of the burden of her upkeep. (*Slight pause.*)

NICHOLAS. Well . . . (*Re-enter Kate.*)

KATE. Miss Bray's awake—and would be most delighted to speak with you, gentlemen.

FRANK. (*Taking Kate's arm.*) Now, Kate, please tell me everything . . . I wish for every detail . . . (*The Brothers, followed by Frank and Kate, go out. Nicholas looks at Frank and Kate together. He stands a moment, and then goes into the garden. Smike is sitting clutching his knees, looking miserable.*)

NICHOLAS. Well, Smike. And how are you today? (*Smike doesn't reply.*) How are you feeling? (*Smike doesn't reply.*) Smike, please answer me. (*Smike looks at Nicholas.*) Smike, what's the matter.

SMIKE. It's my heart. It is so very full. I cannot tell you why. You cannot tell how full it is.

NICHOLAS. Come on, now, Smike. It's growing chilly. Stand up, and let's go in. (*Pause.*)

SMIKE. I can't. I feel so ill. (*Nicholas looks at Smike. Suddenly, he calls.*)

NICHOLAS. Frank! Kate! (*Frank and Kate appear to help Nicholas with Smike.*)

Scene Sixteen

The same. As Kate and Frank arrive, five Narrators, dressed in dark costumes, emerge from the darkness at the back of the stage. They walk forward together, obscuring Smike. Brooker enters behind them, and stands, staring at Smike, who is now dressed for travelling, surrounded by luggage.

NARRATORS.
There is a dread disease which so prepares its victim, as it were for death

In which the struggle between soul and body is so gradual, quiet and solemn,

That day by day

And grain by grain

The mortal part wastes and withers, and the spirit part grows light and sanguine with its lightening load,

A disease which medicine never cured, wealth warded off, or poverty could boast exemption from—which sometimes moves in giant's strides, and sometimes at a tardy, sluggish pace, but slow or quick

Is ever sure and certain. (*The Narrators disappear. Smike looks at Brooker.*)

BROOKER. I know you. Do you know me?

SMIKE. I—know you. (*Brooker hears something and scuttles away. Kate and Nicholas, dressed for travelling, enter, with Mrs. Nickleby, Miss La Creevy and Hannah.*)

NICHOLAS. Come, Smike. It's all right. Time to go.

SMIKE. To Devon. (*Smike looks at Miss La Creevy and Mrs. Nickleby.*)

MISS LA CREEVY. Oh, Mr. Smike. To your return.

MRS. NICKLEBY. Yes. Yes, dear Mr. Smike. Please. Soon. (*Nicholas and Kate help Smike to his feet. They leave with him, the other Women waving.*)

END OF ACT TWO

ACT THREE

Scene One

Upstage, the Kenwigs' front room. Mr. and Mrs. Kenwigs eating a meal at the table. The crying of the new baby. Mr. Lillyvick appears downstage. He looks nervous. From offstage, we hear his knocking.

MRS. KENWIGS. Morleena! Morleena!

MORLEENA. (*Off.*) Yes, Ma!

MRS. KENWIGS. Door, Morleena!

MORLEENA. (*Off.*) What, Ma?

MRS. KENWIGS. Door! (*Morleena runs on as baby cries.*) Shh, shh. Hush, baby. (*Moreena sees Mr. Lillyvick.*)

MORLEENA. Uh?

LILLYVICK. Morleena.

MORLEENA. Oh, it's—Uncle Lillyvick!

LILLYVICK. It is. It is. (*Pause.*) Morleena, tell me—did your mother have the child?

MORLEENA. Oh, yes. She did. A boy. That's him.

LILLYVICK. And was it—she said—that she hoped that he would look like me.

MORLEENA. Oh, yes. He does. I s'pose. At least.

LILLYVICK. I would like someone, looked like me. (*Pause.*)

MORLEENA. Oh, Uncle. Heard about your wedding, Uncle. Made Ma cry. And Pa got very low as well. And I was ill, too. But I'm better now. Oh, Uncle. (*Pause.*)

LILLYVICK. Would you—give your uncle—just one kiss, Morleena? (*Pause.*)

MORLEENA. Yes. I would. But not Aunt Lillyvick. I won't kiss her. She is no aunt of mine.

MRS. KENWIGS. Who is at the door, Morleena?

LILLYVICK. Take me to them. Take me up, Morleena. (*Morleena takes Lillyvick to the Kenwigs as:*)

MRS. KENWIGS. Morleena!

KENWIGS. Now, don't shout, dear.

MRS. KENWIGS. Suppertime, Morleena!

KENWIGS. Please, don't shout, dear.

MRS. KENWIGS. Oh, I do declare.

KENWIGS. Yes, what do you declare, dear?

MRS. KENWIGS. (*Pouring herself a drink.*) That there's nobody, in all the world, as tried as I am. Nobody. That's all.

MORLEENA. Uh—ma—

KENWIGS. Oh. Mr. Lillyvick.

LILLYVICK. Kenwigs, shake hands.

KENWIGS. (*Standing.*) Oh, sir, the time has been when I was proud to shake hands with the kind of man that now surveys me. Oh, the time has been, sir, when a visit from that man's excited in my and my family's bosoms feelings both uplifting and awakening. But now I look at him, and ask, where is his human nature. (*Pause.*)

LILLYVICK. Susan Kenwigs, will you speak to me?

KENWIGS. She is not equal to it, sir. What with the nursing of her child, and the reflecting on your cruel behaviour, four pints of malt liquor, daily, has proved insufficient to sustain her. (*Mr. Kenwigs looks away.*) Oh, I remember thinking, all the time it was expected, if the child's a boy, what will its uncle say. Will it be Pompey, he will ask it to be called; or Alexander, or Diogenes; and when I look at him, a precious, helpless, cut-off child . . . Was it the money that we cared for, Susan?

MRS. KENWIGS. No, it was not. I scorn it.

KENWIGS. Then what was it, Susan?

MRS. KENWIGS. It was seeing your back turned upon us, Uncle. It was feelings—mine have been quite lacerated.

KENWIGS. Poor Morleena's pined, the infant has been rendered most uncomfortable and fractious—

MRS. KENWIGS. I forgive all that, and with you, Uncle, we can never quarrel. But I won't receive her, Uncle. Never ask me. For I will not. No, I won't, I won't. I won't—(*Kenwigs ministering to his wife when Lillyvick intervenes.*)

LILLYVICK. You will not need to. Susan. Kenwigs. For a week ago last Thursday, she eloped.

KENWIGS. Eloped?

LILLYVICK. That's right. With three sovereigns of mine, eight silver teaspoons, and the proprietor of a travelling circus. (*Slight pause.*) With moustaches. And a bottle nose. (*Slight pause.*) 'Twas in this room—this very room—I first set sight on Miss Petowker. It is in this room I cast her off for ever. (*Pause.*)

KENWIGS. Oh, Mr. Lillyvick. What suffering have you endured.

MRS. KENWIGS. Oh, Uncle. You'll forgive our harshness, please.

KENWIGS. And furthermore, the fact that we have nurtured in our bosom that—that—

MRS. KENWIGS. Viper.

KENWIGS. Yes, and—

MRS. KENWIGS. Adder.

KENWIGS. Absolutely, and that—

MRS. KENWIGS. Serpent, snake and crocodile.

KENWIGS. Indeed. And all we pray now is that you, dear Mr. Lillyvick, won't give way to unprevailing grief, but seek for consolation in the bosom of this family, whose arms and hearts are ever open to you. (*Bursting into tears.*)

MORLENNA. Yes. (*She runs and puts her arms round Mr. Lillyvick.*) Yes, yes.

KENWIGS. Morleena, leave your uncle be. (*Morleena leaves Lillyvick.*)

LILLYVICK. I gave her everything she asked for. Humoured her in every whim. Those teaspoons, for but one example. (*Slight pause.*) I feel I'll never knock a double-knock again, upon my rounds. I can't see how I'll manage it. (*Slight pause.*) But still. Important matters. Kenwigs. Susan. First thing in the morning, I shall settle on your children all these moneys I once planned to leave them in my will. Don't argue, don't protest—that's my decision.

KENWIGS. Mr. Lillyvick!

MRS. KENWIGS. Morleena—quickly, kiss your uncle, beg his blessing, fall down on your knees.

LILLYVICK. Yes, yes. Let her approach.

KENWIGS. This is a happening on which the Gods themselves look down!

Scene Two

Ralph's house. Bare stage. Enter Ralph.

RALPH. Ten. Thousand. Pounds. How many years of scrimping, scraping, calculating. For ten thousand pounds. And what I would have done with it. How many proud dames would have fawned and smiled. How many spendthrift nobles would have cringed and begged. How many smooth-tongued speeches, courteous looks, and pleading letters. And how many mean and paltry lies would have been told, not by the money-lender, but by his debtors . . . All your thoughtless, generous, liberal, dashing folk, who wouldn't be so mean as to save a sixpence for the world! (*Pause.*) Ten—thousand—pounds. (*Pause. Noggs and Squeers appearing.*) But now. I'm firm. I must be. Come what may. (*Noggs coughs. Ralph turns.*)

RALPH. Ah, Mr. Squeers.

SQUEERS. You sent a letter.

RALPH. Yes, indeed.

SQUEERS. First, let me say—

RALPH. First, let *me* say, Noggs.

NOGGS. Yes? What?

RALPH. Go to your dinner.

NOGGS. But it isn't time.

RALPH. Your time is mine, and I say it is.

NOGGS. You change it every day. It isn't fair.

RALPH. Begone. (*Noggs withdraws.*) Now. What?

SQUEERS. I'm worried about Snawley.

RALPH. Why? Where is the risk?

SQUEERS. You know the risk as well as I do.

RALPH. No, I don't. There is no risk. The certificates are genuine, he *has* been married twice, his former wife *is* dead, and the only lie is Snawley's, and he'll stick to it, why should he not? He tells the truth, and he's in gaol for perjury. So where's *your* risk in this conspiracy!

SQUEERS. I say, don't call it that—just as a favour, don't.

RALPH. But now, attend to me. The purpose of the fabrication of this tale was to cause hurt and pain to someone who half-cudgelled you to death. Now, is that so?

SQUEERS. It is.

RALPH. And are your bruises at his hands forgotten and forgiven?

SQUEERS. They are not.

RALPH. So. There's an opportunity to hurt him once again. There is a deed—a will. If it is found by him, then it will make a girl he wants to marry very rich. If it is found by us, and then destroyed, then all his expectations crumble.

SQUEERS. Well. Go on.

RALPH. Together, we are going to find the person with the will. You're going to take it from this person, and I'm going to give you fifty pounds in gold. (*Squeers scratches his ear.*) A hundred pounds.

SQUEER. Well, in that case . . . I suppose, as you're a friend . . .

RALPH. Attend to me. (*Squeers is led out by Ralph. In the shadows, Noggs follows.*)

Scene Three

Devon. Bare stage, dappled light. Kate, Nicholas and Smike enter.

NARRATOR. Dividing the distance into two days' journey, in order that their charge might sustain the less exhaustion and fatigue from travelling so far, Nicholas and Kate found themselves at the end of the second day back in the village where they had grown up together.

NICHOLAS. Look, there's our garden, Smike. That's where we used to play, and run, and hide.

SMIKE. You used to hide?

NICHOLAS. Yes, Smike, you know, the game.

KATE. And Nicholas would climb that tree: that big one, over there, to look at young birds in their nests—and he'd shout down, look Kate, how high I've climbed.

NICHOLAS. And you'd be frightened, and you'd tell me to come down.

KATE. And you, you wouldn't come down. But climb even higher, waving all the time.

SMIKE. You climbed up there.

NICHOLAS. And that's the house, Smike, where we used to live, that was Kate's room, behind that tiny window.

KATE. I remember still, the way the sun would stream in, every morning.

SMIKE. Every morning? Winter too?

KATE. I think . . . I can't remember.

NICHOLAS. I suspect that it was always summer here. (*Smike has been looking at "the tree".*)

SMIKE. Is it the same. As when. Is it the same. (*Kate and Nicholas look at each other.*)

NICHOLAS. Things look a little different, Smike. The tree looks smaller. And the garden has become a little overgrown. But still—it is the same. (*Smike goes towards the tree.*)

SMIKE. You climbed up there. (*Kate, Nicholas and Smike move round the stage.*)

NARRATOR. And from the house they walked on to the churchyard, where their father lay, and where Kate and her brother used to run and loiter in the days before they knew what death was, let alone its meaning.

NICHOLAS. Once, Smike, Kate was lost, and we searched for an hour, and we couldn't find her, and at last we found her here, beneath that weeping willow, fast asleep. And so our father, who was very fond of her, picked up her sleeping body in his arms, and said that when he died he wanted to be buried here, where his dear, little child had lain her head. Do you remember, Kate?

KATE. I've heard it told so often, I don't know.

SMIKE. You lay down here?

KATE. (*Smiling.*) Yes. So they say. (*Kate wanders a little away. Smike takes Nicholas' hand.*)

SMIKE. Please promise me.

NICHOLAS. What promise? If I can, you know I will.

SMIKE. Please, if I can, may I be buried near—as near as possible—to underneath that tree?

NICHOLAS. Of course. Yes, yes, you will. (*Kate turns back from her wander. She puts out her arms and spins round.*)

NARRATORS.

And in a fortnight, Smike became too ill to move about. And he would lie upon an old couch, near the open doors that led into a little orchard.

(*Two actors set a couch upstage.*) And Nicholas and Kate would sit with him and talk for hours and hours together.

Till the sun went down, and Smike would fall asleep. (*Smike on the couch. It's sunset. Kate and Nicholas leave Smike and walk downstage. During the scene, it grows darker, and we can no longer see Smike through the dusk.*)

KATE. Nicholas.

NICHOLAS. Yes, what?

KATE. What is it?

NICHOLAS. I was thinking about those we left behind.

KATE. One person, in particular? (*Pause. Nicholas turns to Kate.*)

NICHOLAS. It is, I suppose . . . I love her, Kate.

KATE. I know. Your feelings are as obvious to me, as mine must be to you. (*Pause.*)

NICHOLAS. Oh, Kate. Oh, both of us. Has he—

KATE. He has proposed.

NICHOLAS. What did you say?

KATE. I said—that it was very painful for me, very difficult. But, still, I had to tell him, no.

NICHOLAS. And why?

KATE. Because—you know why.

NICHOLAS. Tell, me, Kate.

KATE. Because—of all the kindness of the brothers, to you, and to all of us. Because—Frank's rich, and we are poor, and it would look as if, we'd taken gross advantage of . . .

NICHOLAS. There's my brave Kate. (*Pause.*) You've no idea, how much your strength in making your, this sacrifice, will help me making mine.

KATE. But Nicholas, it's not the same.

NICHOLAS. It is the same. For Madeline is bound to our two benefactors with ties just as strong—and she too has a fortune. (*Pause.*)

KATE. So—we shall stay together.

NICHOLAS. Yes. And when we're staid old folk, we will look back, on these times, and wonder that these things could move us so. And, even, who knows, we might thank the trials which bound us to each other, and which turned our lives into a current of such peace and calm. (*Pause.*) We'll always be the same.

KATE. Oh, Nicholas. I cannot tell you how, how happy I am, that I've acted as you would have had me.

NICHOLAS. And you don't, at all, regret . . .

KATE. I don't regret. At least. Perhaps . . . No, no. I don't regret. (*Slight pause.*) And, yes, I hope and pray we'll never change. (*Smike stands there.*)

SMIKE. Who calls? Who calls so loud? (*Nicholas and Kate look at Smike. Kate to go towards Smike, but Nicholas stops her with a touch. Smike, insistent.*) Who calls so loud? (*Nicholas a step towards Smike.*)

NICHOLAS. Come hither, man. I see that thou art poor. Hold, there is forty ducats. Let me have—

SMIKE. Such mortal drugs I have, but Mantua's law Is—is—

NICHOLAS. Oh, Smike—

SMIKE. Is death to any he that utters them. (*Prompting.*) Art thou so bare—?

NICHOLAS.
    Art thou so bare and full of wretchedness,

And fearest to die? Famine is in thy cheeks,
Need and oppression starveth in thy eyes.
Contempt and—
SMIKE. No. No, I don't fear to die. My will consents. (*Nicholas turns to embrace Smike, who throws his arms round Nicholas' neck to stop himself collapsing.*) You know, I think, that if I could rise up again, completely well, I wouldn't want to, now. (*Smike looking over Nicholas' shoulder at Kate.*) For nothing—can be ill, if she be well.
NICHOLAS. Then she is well, and nothing can be ill. (*Pause.*) Her body sleeps in Capel's monument. (*Pause.*) But her immortal part with angels lives. (*Nicholas lifts Smike up into his arms.*)
SMIKE. Is it. E'en so. I see a garden. Trees and happy children's faces. And her body sleeps. Light on the faces. Living with the angels. Dreamt my lady came and found me dead. Such happy dreams. (*He pulls himself up to whisper in Nicholas' ear. Then, out loud, to Kate:*) I'm going home. Who calls. Who calls so loud? (*Smike is still. Nicholas realises he is dead. He turns to Kate. He is crying.*)
NICHOLAS. He said—I think you know. (*Pause. Kate can say nothing.*) And then he said he was in Eden.

Scene Four

Lambeth. Two adjacent attic rooms, represented simply by the people in them. On one side, Squeers sits, on a wooden box, with a candle, drinking. On the other side—presently in darkness—Peg Sliderskew sits, surrounded by rubbish.

NARRATORS.
It was a dark, wet, gloomy night in autumn—

An obscure street in Lambeth, muddy, dirty and deserted—

A mean and miserable house—

A bare and wretched attic chamber—

And a grotesque, one-eyed man.
SQUEERS. Well. Here's a pretty go. Uncommon pretty. Here have I been—what is it—six weeks—a-following up this blessed old dowager —and the Academy run regular to seed the while. Hm. It's the worst of getting in with an audacious chap like Nickleby. You never know when

he's got done with you. You go in for a penny, find that you're in for a pound. (*Slight pause. He grins.*) A hundred pounds. (*He takes another drink.*) I never saw a file like that old Nickleby. To see how sly and cunning he grubbed on, day after day, a-worming and a-plodding and a-tracing and a-turning, and a-twining of himself about, until he found out where this precious Mrs. Peg was hid, and cleared the ground for me to work upon—creeping and crawling, gliding—out of everybody's depth, he is. (*Slight pause.*) Well. So. (*He looks at a letter.*) The pigs is well. The cows is well. The boys is bobbish. Young Mobbs has been a-winking, has he? Well, I'll wink him when I'm back. And Cobbey would persist in sniffing while he was a-eating of his dinner, saying that the beef was so strong as it made him. Well, then, Cobbey, see if we can't make you sniff a little without beef. Oh, and Pitcher was took with another fever—so he would be—and fetched by friends, he died the moment he got home. Of course he did, to aggravate us. An't another chap in all the school but that boy would arrange to die exactly at the quarter's end. If that's not spite and malice, then I do not know what is. (*He puts the letter away. Standing.*) Well, so. It's pretty nigh to time, to wait on the old woman. Pretty sure, that if I'm to succeed at all, I shall succeed tonight. So one quick glass to wish myself success, and put myself in spirits. (*He pours the drink and raises it.*) Mrs. Squeers. Young Wackford. Fanny. Here's your health. (*Squeers drinks. Then he turns and goes out of his room and into the other room.*) Well, my Slider!

PEG. Huh? That you?

SQUEERS. It is. It's me. And me's first person singular, the nominative case, agreeing with the verb "its," governed by "Squeers" understood. And if it isn't, you don't know any better.

PEG. Wha? What's that?

SQUEERS. (*Coming over to her.*) This. Is a bottle, Peg. You see?

PEG. O' course I see.

SQUEERS. And this here is a glass. And see, I fill the glass, and I say "Your health, Slider" and I empty it—(*He does so.*) I fill it once again, and hand the glass to you.

PEG. (*Takes the glass and drinks.*) Your health.

SQUEERS. That's right, that's right. You understand that, anyways. Now, Peg, how's the rheumatics? (*Squeers filling Peg's glass.*)

PEG. Ooh, they're better. Ooh, much better, thank'ee, sir. (*She drinks.*)

SQUEERS. You look a great deal better, Peg, than when I first came here.

PEG. Och, well . . . you frightened me.

SQUEERS. I did?

PEG. Och, aye. You knew me name. And where I'd ganged from, and the reason why I'se hiding here. (*Slight pause.*) Nae wonder. I was frightened. Eh? (*Squeers pouring Peg another drink.*)

SQUEERS. Oh, well, Peg, yes, I understand. But see, there's nothing of that kind takes place that I don't know about. See, I'm a sort of lawyer, Peg, of first rate standing, and of understanding, too; I'm the intimate and confidential friend of nearly everyone as has got themselves into a difficulty by being a bit nimble with their fingers. See, I'm a—what's the matter, Peg? (*For Peg has been chuckling for a few moments, and is now cackling.*)

PEG. So he weren't married after all.

SQUEERS. No, Peg. He wasn't. No.

PEG. And some wee lover came and carried off the bride, eh? From beneath his very nose.

SQUEERS. That's right, Peg, yes. (*Peg becoming very affectionate with Squeers.*)

PEG. So. Tell me it again? Will ye? Tell it me again, beginning at the beginning, now, as if you'd never told me. Tell it again, and then, who knows, I might show you the paper, you'se so keen to see. (*Pause.*)

SQUEERS. Oh, might you, Slider?

PEG. Och, I might. But only if you tell me how the old goat lost his dainty bride. (*Pause. Peg caressing Squeers.*) Go on.

SQUEERS. Well, certainly, I will. But after you've shown me the paper, Peg. (*He pours her another drink.*) And then, we'll drink the health of Arthur Gride. (*Peg cackles with pleasure, and stands, and potters off into the gloom.*)

PEG. Och, aye, then. But only if you tell me the tale. If you promise. Will you?

SQUEERS. Of course I will, Peg, course I will. (*Peg comes back with the deed.*)

PEG. Then here you'se are. Right! (*Squeers eagerly opens the deed.*) He said it was his beauty. Well, he's lost his beauty, now. Lost both of 'em. (*Squeers reading.*)

PEG. So, then. What's it say?

SQUEERS. "To Madeline". "To come of age or marry". "The said Madeline . . ." That's it. This is the go! (*Squeers stands, to go out.*)

PEG. Uh? Where you'se going?

SQUEERS. (*Too quietly for Peg to hear.*) Out. I've finished with you, Peg.

PEG. Wha's tha' you're saying? I can't hear.

SQUEERS. (*Shouts.*) I'm going, Mrs. Sliderskew! (*Peg bobbling across the room after him.*)

PEG. But wha' about the tale! And toasting Arthur Gride! You canna just get up an' leave me! Hey! (*Squeers gets to the "door", and finds two Officers, Frank Cheeryble and Newman Noggs.*)

SQUEERS. What's this?

NOGGS. That's him.

OFFICER. You're Mr. Squeers?

PEG. (*Stumbling to the door.*) Hey!

NOGGS. And that's her.

SQUEERS. What's this? What's going on?

OFFICER. I have a warrant, issued on advice from these two gentlemen. (*Slight pause. Neighbors, including a Young Woman appear.*)

PEG. The polis?

SQUEERS. Yes, Peg, yes.

NOGGS. That's right.

PEG. Hey—it's the lunatic!

SQUEERS. Huh—so it is. (*The officers grabbing at Peg, who waves the bottle wildly.*)

PEG. Hey! Get your hands off me! (*The attention of the officers on Peg, as Squeers makes a run for it. Frank notices.*)

FRANK. Hey, stop! Stop that man! (*Many neighbours now watching, as Frank and an officer chase Squeers round the stage, and, if possible, round the audience as well. Finally, Squeers finds a little hiding place and his pursuers rush past him. Everyone is thus shouting and pointing in an opposite direction when Mr. Squeers appears, takes off his hat, brushes it, and attempts to sneak off unnoticed. Newman Noggs, however, has spotted him, and brings a metal tray down firmly on his head. Squeers collapses.*)

NOGGS. Hey, not so much of the lunatic! Not so much, Mr. Squeers and Mrs. Sliderskew! Eh! Eh?

FRANK. (*Putting his hand on Noggs' arm.*) Now, Mr. Noggs, we must go home, and tell my uncles what has happened. (*The officers take out Squeers and Sliderskew. Noggs and Frank, with the deed, follow.*)

Scene Five

Ralph's room; and his run round London. A large number of Narrators form a semi-circle round Ralph Nickleby, who stands in what we imagine to be his dining room.

NARRATOR. And on the next day, half-way through the morning, Ralph Nickleby sat alone, in the solitary room where he was accustomed to take his meals.

RALPH. What is this, that hangs over me, and I can't shake it off? I'm never ill, I've never moped, and pined—but what can any man do without rest? (*Slight pause. The sound of a bell.*) Night after night goes by, I have no rest. I sleep, and I'm disturbed by constant dreams. I wake, I'm haunted by this heavy shadow of—I don't know what. (*Slight pause. The sound of a bell.*) One night's unbroken rest, and I should be a man again. (*Ralph suddenly aware that the bell has been ringing.*) Noggs! Noggs! (*Silence. He picks up his watch.*) What? Noon? Where is he? Noggs! (*No answer. The bell. Ralph turns and goes to the "wall" of people, two of whom step aside to form a door. A Messenger stands there.*) Yes? Who are you?

MESSENGER. Is this the residence of Mr. Nickleby?

RALPH. I am that man.

MESSENGER. A letter, sir. (*He takes the letter.*)

RALPH. Thank you. (*Ralph turns back downstage, and the wall closes behind him. He reads the letter.*) What is this? "It's most urgent", "Matters come to light". "We will explain it". "Dreadful news". What are the old fools mad? Or is this, from its wildness, just another waking nightmare? Sent to haunt me? (*The wall splits up and becomes the bustling streets of London.*)

NARRATORS.

    And like a haunted man, without his hat or coat, Ralph stumbled through the door, into the street.

    At first he drifted aimlessly, a sleepwalker, but then his pace grew brisker, and he almost ran . . .

    The streets and people swirled around him, and the sounds of London merged into a single roar, as Ralph sped on, he scarcely could tell why, towards a house in Somers Town.

(*The actors have now formed into three lines, facing Ralph, their arms straight up in the air, like the gables and rooves of houses. Ralph bangs on the floor.*)

RALPH. Door! Door! Where are you, Snawley? Door! (*Snawley's Wife pokes her hand between two of the actors, as opening a door a little way. She looks terrified.*)

MRS. SNAWLEY. Who—oh—

RALPH. I wish to see your husband, ma'am.

MRS. SNAWLEY. He's not in. Gone away.

RALPH. Do you know who I am?

MRS. SNAWLEY. Oh, yes, I know, but still, he's gone away.

RALPH. Tell him I saw him, through the window-blind above. Tell him that I must speak to him, most urgently.

MRS. SNAWLEY. There's nothing that he wants to say to you. Except that, wasn't him that forged the letter. You or schoolmaster did that, so don't you try to lay it at this door.

RALPH. He sets me at defiance, does he?

MRS. SNAWLEY. Yes, he does. And so, sir, so do I. (*And she withdraws, and the "door" closes behind her. The wall of actors breaks up again, and swirls around Ralph.*)

NARRATORS.

And so Ralph turned again, and hurried back,

Through different streets across the city,

To another house,

Whose windows were closed shut,

Whose blinds were drawn,

All silent, melancholy and deserted. (*And the three-line wall has formed again, but, this time, with the hands of each of the back two lines placed over the eyes of the line in front. Ralph knocking.*)

RALPH. Gride! Gride! (*Gride stands on a chair behind the lines, as if at an upper window.*)

GRIDE. What? Who's that?

RALPH. Gride, let me in.

GRIDE. Hush. Hush, no. Go away.

RALPH. Come down!

GRIDE. I won't. Don't speak to me, don't knock . . . Don't call attention to the house—Just go away.

RAPLH. I'll knock, I'll shout, I'll sweat, till I have all your neighbours up in arms, if you don't tell me what you mean by lurking there!

GRIDE. I mean—I mean—it isn't safe. Please, please, don't talk to me. Just go away. (*Gride disappears behind suddenly raised hands, as if he had slammed his shutters closed.*)

RALPH. How is this? They all fall from me and shun me like the plague! How have they changed! These men who used to lick the dust from my feet. I *will* know what it is. I must, at any cost. (*The wall breaks again, and swirls, and reforms as a long single line of backs, from upstage centre to downstage left.*)

NARRATORS.

And so Ralph set off once again,

And crossed the river,

And determined now to hazard everything, came to the meagre house in Lambeth where his tried auxiliary the schoolmaster had lately lodged. (*Ralph runs downstage along the line. A Young Woman—clearly a Prostitute—appears at the end of the line.*)

YOUNG WOMAN. Hallo. What can I do for you?

RALPH. (*Breathless.*) Old woman. Old, and wizened. Deaf. Top floor.

YOUNG WOMAN. You what?

RALPH. And a man. Short, stunted. With a leer. One eye.

YOUNG WOMAN. Oh, yur. I know them people. What d'you want?

RALPH. I want to know where they are now.

YOUNG WOMAN. They're gone.

RALPH. Gone where?

YOUNG WOMAN. Gone with the constables. The Police-Office, I think.

RALPH. Where is the police office?

YOUNG WOMAN. (*With a shrug.*) Now, that—I know. (*Ralph takes the Young Woman's arm and hurries her back upstage along the line. The line of breaks, obscuring the set-up of the next scene, and then forming a new semi-circle upstage.*)

Scene Six

The Lambeth Police Office. Wackford Squeers is revealed, sitting on a bench, with a bandaged head. He is drunk.

NARRATORS.

And in the Lambeth Police-Office there was a kind of waiting room, and Ralph was shown to it, and told to wait:

And shortly afterwards an officer admitted him to Mr. Wackford Squeers. (*The semicircle breaks, as a door for Ralph to come to Squeers.*)

SQUEERS. Hm. I say, young feller, you have been and done it now.

RALPH. You have been drinking.

SQUEERS. Hm. Well, not *your* health, I can assure you, my old codger.

RALPH. Why did you not send to me? (*Squeers sits. Not answering the question.*)

SQUEERS. With me locked up here hard and fast, and you all loose and comfortable.

RALPH. It's only for a few days. They will give you bail. They cannot hurt you, man.

SQUEERS. Well. S'pose that's right. If I explain it all. (*Slight pause.*) "Prisoner", he says, the powdered head, "You have been found in company with this old woman; as you were apprehended in possession of this document. In absence of a satisfactory account, I shall detain you." (*Slight pause.*) Well, then, what I say now is, that I *can* give a satisfactory account. I can hand in my card, and say, "I am the Wackford Squeers as is therein named, sir. Whatever's wrong's no fault of mine. I'm merely an employee of a friend—my friend Ralph Nickleby, of Golden Square."

RALPH. What documents?

SQUEERS. *The* document. The Madeline Whatsit document. The will.

RALPH. Whose will? How dated? Benefitting whom? To what extent?

SQUEERS. I can't remember. In her favour, all I know. (*Pause.*)

RALPH. I tell you once again. That they can't hurt you. We'll devise a story for you; if you need a thousand pounds security, you'll have it. All you have to do is keep your wits about you, and keep back the truth.

SQUEERS. Oh, that's it, is it? That's what I'm to do? Well, I tell 'ee, Mr. Nickleby. That what I do, or say, is up to me, what serves me most, and if I find it serves me to reveal your part in this, then reveal it's what I'll do. (*Slight pause.*) My moral influence with them lads, is tottering to its basis. (*Slight pause.*) The images of Mrs. Squeers, my daughter Fanny, and my son, all short of victuals, is perpetually before my eyes. All other thoughts just melts away and just vanishes in front of 'em. (*Slight pause.*) In short, the only number in arithmetic I knows of as a husband and a father, now, is Number One. In this most fatal go. (*Ralph looks at the wall. A door forms, and a Police Officer stands there. But Squeers hasn't finished.*) A-double-L. All. Everything. A cobler's weapon. U-P, up, an adjective, not down. S-Q-U-double-E-R-S. Squeers, noun substantive. (*Pause.*) In sum total. It's All Up With Squeers. (*And the wall closes round in front of Squeers, and Ralph appears in front of it again.*)

RALPH. So. This fellow turns on me as well. They are all struck with fear, while, yesterday, was all civility, compliance. But they shall not move me. I won't budge an inch. (*The wall dispersing.*)

NARRATORS.

And so, then, finally, with a reluctant, grudging step, Ralph Nickleby set course towards the City.

He had not eaten or drunk anything all day, he felt sick and exhausted, and his every sense was numb, except for one of weariness and desolation. (*The wall has gone. The next scene is revealed.*)

Scene Seven

The Cheerybles' house. One chair, beside a small table with a lamp on it. Ralph approaches Mr. Charles, Mr. Ned and Tim Linkinwater.

RALPH. So—which is Mr. Charles?

MR. CHARLES. I am.

RALPH. You sent me this, this morning, asking me—demanding that I come here to your house at half past seven o'clock. Well, it is only shortly after. I am here. (*Slight pause.*) As no-one bids me to a seat, I'll take one for I am fatigued with walking. (*Ralph sits.*) And now, if you please, gentlemen, I wish to know, I demand to know, I have the right to know—what you have to say to me which justifies the tone you have employed. (*Waving the letter.*)

MR. CHARLES. Very well, sir. Brother Ned. (*Mr. Ned goes out and returns with Newman Noggs.*)

RALPH. Oh—this—this is a good beginning. Oh, yes, you are candid, honest, open-hearted and fair-dealing men! To tamper with a fellow such as this, who'd sell his soul for a drink, whose every word's a lie—oh, this is a beginning!

NOGGS. I will speak.

RALPH. Oh, yes, I'm sure you'll—

NOGGS. I *will* speak. And ask, who made me "a fellow such as this"? (*Slight pause.*) If I would sell my soul for a drink, why wasn't I a thief, a swindler, a robber of pence from the trays of blindmen's dogs, rather than your drudge and packhorse? If my every word was indeed a lie, why was I not a pet and favourite of yours! A liar! When did I ever fawn and cringe to you? (*Slight pause.*) I served you faithfully. You were talking just now about tampering. Who tampered with the Yorkshire schoolmaster? Who tampered with a jealous father, urging him to sell his daughter to old Arthur Gride, and tampered with Gride too, and did so in a little office *with a closet in the room? (Ralph a sharp gesture.)* Aha! You mind me now! And what first set the drudge to listening at doors, and watching close and following? The master's cruel treatment of his flesh and blood, his vile designs upon a young girl, which made the miserable and drunken hack stay on in service, in the hope of doing her some good, when he might have otherwise relieved his feelings by pummelling his master soundly, and then going to the Devil. I'm here now because these gentlemen thought it best. When I sought them out—as I did, there's no tampering with me—I told them that I wanted to help to find you out, to track you down, to finish what I had begun, to help the right; and that when I'd done it I would burst into your room, and face you man to man, and—like a man. And now I've done it. Now I've had my say. Let anybody say theirs. I've done. *(Pause.)* At last. *(Pause. A general gesture.)* So—fire away!

RALPH. Hm. *(Pause. A little wave.)* Go on, go on.

MR. CHARLES. It is, sir, simply told. *(He waves to Mr. Ned.)*

MR. NED. We knew about the deed, and how Gride had acquired it, and we heard, from neighbours, of the great to-do Gride made when it was gone.

MR. CHARLES. Our dear friend Mr. Noggs acquainted us with Squeers' visit to you, and as you and he pursued Peg Sliderskew, we in our turn followed you, and then the schoolmaster, and found the house in Lambeth, and procured a warrant to arrest them for possession of a stolen document.

MR. NED. Which then was done. The woman, and the schoolmaster, and most of all, the deed, are now in police possession.

MR. CHARLES. Now, sir, you've heard it. How far you are implicated in this matter, you best know. But we would not—would not see an old man like you disgraced or punished.

RALPH. Sir, you have not the man to deal with that you think you have. *(Pause.)*

MR. NED. What's this?

RALPH. Oh, merely, that I have not heard a word of proof of any o: these wild allegations; that I spit on your fair words and your false dealings; and that there is law, still, to be had, and I will call you to account. Take care, sir, you have said enough already. I'd advise you, say no more.

MR. CHARLES. Then we've not said enough. *(He looks at Mr. Ned.)*

MR. NED. No, no, indeed.

MR. CHARLES. Sir, what would you say if we said that this man Snawley had confessed?

RALPH. Snawley? Then I'd reply that Snawley is a frightened coward, and that this "confession" was most likely forced from him.

MR. CHARLES. And if we told you that the boy was dead? (*Pause.*)

RALPH. You mean—the simpleton—

MR. NED. Is dead, indeed. (*Pause. Ralph laughs.*)

RALPH. Oh, gentlemen, then I forgive you everything. For this news, I am in your debt, and bound to you for life.

NOGGS. Oh, you. Oh, how can—it's unnatural.

MR. CHARLES. It is. (*He nods to Mr. Ned who goes out.*)

RALPH. What's this? Another? Have you dredged my nephew up, to add to all these lies? (*Re-enter Mr. Ned with Brooker.*) What? Him? D'you know, this is a felon, a convicted criminal?

MR. NED. You asked, sir, for our proof that broken boy was not the son of Snawley.

RALPH. Yes, I did. Well—

MR. NED. Our proof is not concerned with papers, or confessions. It is that we know the poor boy was another's son.

RALPH. Another's? Whose?

BROOKER. Yours. (*Pause. Ralph presses the palms of his hand against his temples.*)

RALPH. What? (*Pause.*)

BROOKER. Do you remember? About, oh, what, a quarter of a century ago? A family in Leicestershire? A father and a daughter? A father that you'd wound into your net, you'd cheated, like you cheated me? But a daughter who had grown attached to you, because, of, he was young, then, charming in his way, and she could not believe he was not their family's benefactor? And who fell in love with you, Ralph Nickleby. And married you. (*Pause.*) But, of course, it had to be a secret, from the father. He was rich. And if he'd known, the daughter would have lost a great inheritance. And that would never do. Oh, would it. So, a secret wedding. And a little secret son. Put out to nurse. A long way off. So not to interfere. (*Pause.*) And then, as time went on, began to see her less and less. Stayed up in London, making money. And your wife, a young girl, alone, in a dull old country house. And eventually, she couldn't bear it any more. Could she? (*Pause.*) And so she ran off? Didn't she? (*Pause.*) And you ordered me to fetch the boy, to keep him from her—didn't you? (*Pause.*) And you had used me ill. And cruelly. The boy was hidden in an attic, and neglect had made him sickly, and the doctor said that he must have a change of air or else he'd die. You went away. Six weeks. When you returned, I told you that the child was dead. (*Pause.*) And you—I think—realised—you missed him. When he'd gone. You missed someone who thought well of you. He brightened up your house, and made a little laughter in your halls. And you missed him. Didn't you? (*Pause.*)

MR. CHARLES. So the boy was not, then, dead.

BROOKER. Sirs, I offer no excuses for myself. You could say, I was harshly treated and driven from my real nature. But, I'm guilty. (*Slight pause.*) Yes, I stole the boy. And took him to a Yorkshire school. And paid his fees, for six years. And then went away. (*Pause.*) But then . . . came back. And went to look for him. I couldn't find him, there, he'd gone. So—came to London. And confronted him. No use. But then, a month, six weeks ago, I saw the boy. He was sitting in a garden. Knew his face. And he, I think, knew mine. (*To Ralph.*) The school was run by my friend, Mr. Wackford Squeers. I gave the boy a name. Do I need to tell you?

RALPH. Smike. (*Pause. Throughout Brooker's speech, it has been growing steadily darker. Now the only source of light is the lamp on a table near Ralph.*)

MR. NED. Unhappy man. Unhappy man.

MR. CHARLES. But doubly, trebly, ten times more unhappy must *you* be, Ralph Nickleby. (*Pause. Then, like a reptile's tongue, Ralph's hand shoots out towards the lamp. It crashes and there is darkness.*)

Scene Eight

In the darkness, the wall forms again. Lights, and Ralph is running along it, parallel to the front of the stage.

NARRATORS.

Creeping from the house, and slinking like a thief . . .

Groping like a blind man . . .

Ralph Nickleby went from the city, and took the road to his own home.

(*The wall is forming into a cloud, hands stretching out towards Ralph.*)

And there was one black, gloomy mass that seemed to follow him,

Not hurrying in the wild chase with the others,
But lingering, sullenly, behind, and following him.

(*The wall reforms. At the back, a line of people, at crazy angles, like bent and broken iron railings; in front, a pile of bodies, forming hideous shapes.*)

He passed a poor, mean burial ground,

A rank, unwholesome spot, where the very grass and weeds appeared to tell that they had sprung from paupers' bodies, and Ralph peered in through the iron railings . . .

(*And the railings become a group of drunks, careering round in front of the bodies, one actor playing a pipe.*)

And then there came towards him, full of shouts and singing, a group of fellows full of drink, in high good humour,

And a member of their company, a little, weazen, humpbacked man, began to dance . . .

(*And indeed a little man does dance, to the music of the pipe, and Ralph joins in the clapping, until he is swallowed up and disappears. And suddenly, everything stops, and the Narrators stand there, still.*)

And Ralph came home.

He could hardly make up his mind to turn the key and open up the door.

And when he had—

And closed it, with a crash behind him—

He felt as if he had shut out the world.

(*The Narrators dispersing now. One Narrator appears, with a single chair.*)

There was no light. How dreary, cold and still it was.

He groped his way towards the stairs, and climbed, up to the very top—

To the front garret—

Which was now a lumber room.

(*If there is a trap, Ralph appears through it. If not, he enters. The last Narrator places the chair carefully.*)

LAST NARRATOR. Here Ralph remained. (*The Narrator goes. Ralph stands there. We see he is holding a piece of rope.*)

RALPH. I know this room. This room was where he slept. I was his father. But he didn't die here. And he didn't die with me. He died—elsewhere. (*Pause.*) But if he hadn't . . . If he'd grown up here. Might we have been—a comfort to each other. And might I—have been a different man. A man more like my nephew. Or my brother. Nicholas. (*He begins to tie the rope into a noose.*) But now. To be held up in the most repulsive colours. And to know that he was taught to hate my very name. "Ralph Nickleby". (*Pause.*) "To wound him, through his own affections. Oh, to strike him through this boy . . ." (*Pause.*) "All love is cant and vanity". (*A knocking on the door downstairs.*)

RALPH. What's that? (*We hear Tim's voice.*)

TIM. (*Off.*) Is that—Ralph Nickleby?

RALPH. What do you want with him?

TIM. (*Off.*) I'm from the Brothers. They want to meet with you tomorrow.

RALPH. Yes, yes. Tell them, they can come tomorrow.

TIM. (*Off.*) At what hour?

RALPH. At any hour! What time they like. (*Pause.*) All times will be alike to me. (*Ralph looks up.*) That hook. Big, black one, in the ceiling. Never noticed it before. (*Slight pause.*) Perhaps he noticed it. Perhaps it frightened him. (*Slight pause.*) It frightens me. (*Slight pause.*) But it would hold me. (*He looks round the room where his son had slept.*) Outcast. A noun. Cast out. And homeless. (*Long Pause.*) Me. (*Ralph quickly puts the noose round his neck and raises it above him. A dummy on a rope falls from the flies, down through the trap. The light just catches Ralph, swaying, as if from the rope. Darkness. A moment. Then light. Ralph has gone. The rope has fallen through the trap. Mr. Charles, Mr. Ned and Tim Linkinwater stand there.*)

MR. CHARLES. And in the morning, they went round, and knocked, and knocked again.

MR. NED. And eventually, they broke a window, and went in, and searched the house.

TIM. And they found the body of Ralph Nickleby, and cut it down. (*Blackout.*)

Scene Nine

The Cheerybles' house. Just two chairs represent it. Narrators:

NARRATORS.

And some weeks passed, and the first shock of these happenings subsided.

Madeline was living in the house of friends of the Mr. Cheerybles;

Young Frank was absent;

And Nicholas and Kate were trying, in good earnest, to stifle their regrets, and to live for each other and their mother.

And there came one evening,

Per favour of Mr. Linkinwater,

An invitation from the Brothers Cheeryble for dinner on the next day but one,

An invitation comprehending not just Nicholas, his mother and his sister

But their great friend Miss La Creevy, too—

Who much to the astonishment of Mrs. Nickleby,

Was most particularly mentioned. (*And the Nicklebys and Miss La Creevy are greeted by Mr. Charles, Mr. Ned and Tim Linkinwater.*)

MR. CHARLES. Now, we took the liberty, dear friends, of naming one hour before dinner, as we had a little business to discuss, which would occupy the interval. I wonder, Tim, if you would be so kind as to escort dear Mrs. Nickleby and Miss La Creevy too—to show them something of the house, perhaps, and p'raps to tell them something too.

TIM. It would be my great pleasure. Ma'am. And Ma'am. (*Pause. Mrs. Nickleby, Kate and Nicholas in their different ways, looking bemused.*)

MRS. NICKLEBY. Well, certainly, I—

MR. NED. (*His finger to his lips.*) Not another word. (*And, with as much grace as she can muster, Mrs. Nickleby allows herself to be escorted out by Tim, Miss La Creevy following, a little smile on her face.*)

MR. CHARLES. Now, Kate, my dear. Tell me. Have you seen Madeline since your return to London?

KATE. No, sir. And I have not heard from her.

MR. CHARLES. Not heard from her? What do you think of that, Brother Ned? Is that not sad?

MR. NED. Oh, very, Brother Charles. Yes, very sad. The whole thing's so upsetting, that you will forgive me if, for just a moment, I withdraw myself into another room. (*Much winking between the Brothers: Mr. Ned withdraws.*)

MR. CHARLES. Poor Brother Ned, as I've remarked to you before, sir, often, always such a prey to his emotions. Now. We were engaged, I think, upon the topic of Miss Madeline, who, as you know, becomes entitled, on her marriage, to a certain sum of money.

NICHOLAS. Yes, we know that, sir.

MR. CHARLES. In fact, a sum amounting to twelve thousand pounds, from the will of Madeline's maternal grandmother. One could say, quite a dowry. Hm? (*Pause.*)

NICHOLAS. You did receive our letter, sir?

MR. CHARLES. Yes, yes, we did. You both explained your feelings— yours for Miss Madeline, and Kate's for nephew Frank. You had resolved, despite those feelings, to reject all thought of love and matrimony—and to live, instead, just for each other.

NICHOLAS. Yes, sir. That is our resolve.

MR. CHARLES. A noble sentiment. But still, perhaps, a selfish one.

NICHOLAS. What, selfish? Why?

MR. CHARLES. Because of other people's feelings. For an instance, those of Brother Ned and I.

NICHOLAS. I'm sorry. I don't understand. (*Mr. Ned has appeared. Behind him, unseen by Nicholas and Kate, are Frank and Madeline.*)

MR. NED. You don't? You don't see why *we* are offended? To have it thought that we were such mean judges of two persons' characters. To think that we'd consider for a moment that your love for Madeline, or

Kate's for Frank, had anything to do with money? Come, how could you think so!

KATE. We—we did not think so, sir.

MR. CHARLES. And worse than that. Much worse. To think that you yourselves would be corrupted and debased, by marrying the people whom you've set your hearts upon?

NICHOLAS. Sirs, I had thought we'd made it plain. We have—my sister and I have—learnt nothing in our journeyings so strongly as we've learned what happens to the kindest, and the noblest and the gentlest people, when their souls are tainted by the touch of money.

KATE. We have seen our father, and our uncle, sirs, the one who was most dear to us, the other, one who should have been, destroyed; one in the want of money; and the other by the having it, and loving it too much.

FRANK. Oh, Kate. Oh, Nicholas. How can you be so blind? They stand in front of you!

MR. NED. Now, Frank—

FRANK. No, no, you cannot say it, Uncle Ned, you cannot say it, Uncle Charles; but I can: that you see before you, Nicholas and Kate, two men who walked barefoot to London, penniless and hungry, and who have made their fortune, and have they been tainted or debased? Have they been made ignoble, or ungentle, or unkind? You see them, Nicholas.

KATE. Frank. Back.

MR. NED. Yes, yes, returned most unexpectedly, without so much as a presentiment.

MR. CHARLES. As is his wont.

MR. NED. And with him, someone else whose feelings, we might take into account. (*Nicholas sees Madeline.*)

NICHOLAS. Oh, Madeline. You've heard, all this?

MADELINE. Yes, yes. I've heard.

NICHOLAS. And you—they've told you, everything, I—

MADELINE. Yes they have. (*Nicholas is completely thrown.*)

NICHOLAS. This is—I told you, sirs, in confidence, my feelings for Miss Madeline, I . . . I have no idea, of course, if they, if she—what feelings she has entertained, I— do you understand?

MADELINE. I understand what I have understood since we first met. And I understand that, since then, you have changed.

NICHOLAS. Oh, no—

MADELINE. And that you cannot see me any more, but only my inheritance. (*Pause. Madeline takes Nicholas's hands.*) Oh, Nicholas. That

someone who has been through what you've been through, who has
striven as you've striven, who has learnt what you have learnt, could
think that it is right to sacrifice our happiness for such a superstition, to
believe that there are any barriers between us that we can't surmount.

NICHOLAS. Our happiness.

MADELINE. Oh, Nicholas. How could you ever think that I felt otherwise? (*Pause. Nicholas turns to Kate.*)

NICHOLAS. We're over-ruled. (*Kate to Frank.*)

KATE. So it would seem.

MR. CHARLES. And so it is.

MR. NED. And so it is. (*We hear Mrs. Nickleby approaching.*)

MRS. NICKLEBY. Oh, Mr. Linkinwater, this is too extraordinary.

MR. NED. Quick, quick, everyone away . . . and talk among yourselves,
if you've got anything to talk about . . .

MR. CHARLES. Yes, hurry, all out, everyone—(*Nicholas, Madeline,
Kate and Frank go apart as:*)

MRS. NICKLEBY. (*Approaching.*) Now, of course it's very pleasant, if it
is true, but I assure you, if it isn't, it's a most cruel . . . Mr. Cheeryble.
(*And Mrs. Nickleby, Miss La Creevy and Tim are now back in the
room.*)

MR. NED. Yes, Mrs. Nickleby?

MRS. NICKLEBY. Can this be true?

MR. CHARLES. Not only can, but is. (*Slight pause.*)

TIM. Hm. Didn't keep 'em in suspense as long as said you would. Impatient, what I call it.

MR. CHARLES. What, d'you hear that, Brother Ned, from Tim, who has
been wearying us from morning until night—

MR. NED. It's true, Charles, it's all true, the man's a wild young fellow,
he must sow his wild oats, and then perhaps he'll come in time to be a
respectable and normal member of society—(*The Brothers taking the
arms of Mrs. Nickleby.*)

MR. CHARLES. I'm sure that Mrs. Nickleby agrees, dear brother—(*The
Brothers leading Mrs. Nickleby out.*)

MRS. NICKLEBY. (*With a desperate look back at Tim and Miss La
Creevy.*) Well, I . . . I mean, if I am asked my view . . . Uh—oh—
(*And they are gone. Tim and Miss La Creevy left alone. Miss La
Creevy sitting. Tim moves the other chair closer, and sits.*)

TIM. Well, isn't it a pleasant thing. To people like us, to see young
folks we are so fond of brought together.

MISS LA CREEVY. Yes, it is. Indeed.

TIM. Although—although it makes one feel, oneself, quite solitary. Almost cast away. I don't know, if you feel . . .

MISS LA CREEVY. Well, certainly, that's true; I mean, it's true, that I don't know.

TIM. It's . . . almost something that would make one think of getting wed oneself. Now isn't it?

MISS LA CREEVY. Oh, nonsense, Mr. Linkinwater.

TIM. Now, is it? Is it nonsense? Really? (*Pause. Miss La Creevy holding her breath.*)

MISS LA CREEVY. Now, Mr. Linkinwater, you are mocking me.

TIM. No, no, I'm not.

MISS LA CREEVY. Why think—how we'd make people laugh.

TIM. Well, let 'em. We'll laugh back.

MISS LA CREEVY. And, think, as well: what would the brothers say?

TIM. Why, Miss La Creevy, bless your soul! You don't suppose I'd think of such a thing without their knowing it? Why, they left us here on purpose!

MISS LA CREEVY. Oh, I can never look them in the face again.

TIM. Now, come. Let's be a comfortable couple. We shall live in this old house; we'll sit and talk, or sit and sit, quite calm and perfectly contented. Oh, let's be a comfortable couple, let's, my dear.

MISS LA CREEVY. Oh, Mr. Linkinwater, since you put it in that—most affecting fashion—yes. (*They kiss. Then they look up to see, behind them, Frank, Kate, Madeline, Nicholas, Mr. Charles, Mr. Ned and Mrs. Nickleby.*)

MRS. NICKLEBY. Oh, Miss La Creevy! (*Tim stands up.*)

TIM. There is not, I swear, another woman like her in the whole of London. I just *know* there ain't.

MRS. NICKLEBY. And—Mr. Linkinwater! (*A knock at the outside door. Mr. Ned slips out, as:*)

MR. CHARLES. Mrs. Nickleby, I wonder, might I be granted the incalculable pleasure of escorting you to dinner?

MRS. NICKLEBY. (*Vaguely.*) Yes, of course . . .

MR. CHARLES. And, everyone, and everyone . . . (*And Mr. Charles and Mrs. Nickleby, Kate and Frank, Tim and Miss La Creevy, go into dinner, followed by Nicholas and Madeline, the last. As they are going, re-enter Mr. Ned, followed by Newman Noggs.*)

MR. NED. Uh, Mr. Nickleby. Forgive me. (*Mr. Ned takes Madeline's arm.*)

NICHOLAS. Yes, of course, I—

NOGGS. Nick. (*Nicholas to Noggs, as Mr. Ned takes Madeline out. Noggs is "genteelly dressed in black".*)

NICHOLAS. Oh, Newman. Newman.

NOGGS. Yes, it's your own Newman. Nick, my dear boy, I give you—

everything. All health, all happiness, and every blessing. I can't bear it, it's too much—it makes a child of me!

NICHOLAS. Where have you been? How often have I asked for you, and been told that I should hear before long!

NOGGS. I know, I know. They wanted all the happiness to come together. I've been helping 'em. I—I—look at me, Nick, look at me!

NICHOLAS. (*"In a tone of gentle reproach".*) You'd never let *me* buy you such a suit. I offered to.

NOGGS. I didn't mind, then. Couldn't have the heart to put on clothes like these. They'd have reminded me of old times, made me miserable. But now—I am another man, Nick—Oh, my dear boy, I can't speak, please don't do anything—you don't know what I feel today; you can't, and never will.

NICHOLAS. I can. I think I do. But, come, let's go to dinner. (*And as Nicholas takes Noggs' arm, Mr. Ned, Mr. Charles and Kate re-appear.*)

MR. NED. And never was there such a dinner since the world began.

MR. CHARLES. And at the end of all the toasts and speeches, Nicholas took Kate apart—

NICHOLAS. And whispered to her that, in all his happiness, there was still one dark cloud, and that his joy could never be complete until it was dispelled. (*The scene breaking.*)

KATE. And so the two of them set forth, the next afternoon, to book Nicholas a place on the coach for Greta Bridge in Yorkshire.

NARRATORS.

And on their way back to the Strand, as luck would have it, they passed by a little theatre,

On which was displayed a boldly-printed bill,

Announcing that tonight would be the positively last appearance of the celebrated company of Mr. Vincent Crummles, and his wife and family.

Scene Ten

The stage door of a theatre. Enter Crummles, dressed as a Bandit, to Nicholas and Kate.

CRUMMLES. My dear young man! My dear young man!

NICHOLAS. Oh, Mr. Crummles. This is—a most happy chance. May I introduce my sister?

CRUMMLES. (*Pumping Kate's hand.*) It's a pleasure. It's a double pleasure, meeting you, Miss Johnson. (*Kate a look to Nicholas, who shrugs.*) I'm delighted, sir, I'm quite delighted, with this chance to say goodbye.

NICHOLAS. Goodbye? Why, are you going? Where?

CRUMMLES. Oh, haven't you seen it, in the papers?

NICHOLAS. No.

CRUMMLES. Well, that's a wonder. It was there, in the varieties. Ah, look. (*Producing a cutting.*) I have it here.

NICHOLAS. (*Reads.*) "The talented Vincent Crummles, long favourably known to fame as a country manager and actor of no ordinary pretensions, is about to cross the Atlantic"—!—"on a histrionic expedition. Crummles is to be accompanied, we hear by his wife and gifted family. Crummles is quite certain to succeed." (*Handing the cutting back.*) America!

CRUMMLES. That's right, sir.

NICHOLAS. With—with all the company?

CRUMMLES. Well—no. In fact, sir, I must own our numbers have been much depleted since we saw you last. Finances, sir, the main cause—always, sir, finance. But there have been departures, too: old Fluggers joined the church, by reasons of his years of practising; and Tom Folair defected to a company that mounts spectaculars hard-by the bridge at Waterloo: attracted by the glitter, sir, and promises of quick and easy fame. Well, he'll find out, of course . . . and even, this may well upset you rather more, Miss Snevellicci left us—

NICHOLAS. Oh?

KATE. Miss Snevellicci.

CRUMMLES. Yes, to marry the good-looking young wax chandler who supplied the candles to the Portsmouth theatre . . . but apparently, deliriously happy.

KATE. Ah.

CRUMMLES. So, we thought . . . We have a fair start—The Americans are much devoted to grand gesture and the melodrama, and I've heard, on quite the best authority, that they'll pay anything . . . and then, who knows, we might buy that little plot of land, support ourselves in our old age . . .

NICHOLAS. I think, as always, you have acted wisely, sir.

CRUMMLES. But, see—it is herself approaching! (*Mrs. Crummles sailing over, with the Master Crummleses and the Infant Phenomenon, all in costume.*)

MRS. CRUMMLES. Mr. Johnson! What an unexpected joy! And—Mrs. Johnson?

KATE. Miss.

MRS. CRUMMLES. Sir, here are two you know. And another. (*Nicholas is kissed by the Phenomenon. He shakes hands with the Master Crummleses.*)

NICHOLAS. I'm very pleased to see you once again. I'm very pleased— to see—see everyone.

MRS. CRUMMLES. So are you coming—to tonight's performance? It is positively, quite unalterably, the last.

NICHOLAS. I know. But sadly, I regret—

MRS. CRUMMLES. Regret? That's all that I remember of you, Mr. Johnson. All the time, regretting.

NICHOLAS. I have, unfortunately, to be up at dawn, for a journey of my own. And in fact—have such preparations to complete . . .

MRS. CRUMMLES. And if not regretting, then farewelling, Mr. Johnson. (*Pause. Something in Nicholas's tone has deflated the bombast.*)

NICHOLAS. Yes, I am afraid . . . (*A smile.*) Yes, yes. (*He shakes Crummles's hand.*)

CRUMMLES. We were a happy little company, Johnson. You and I never had a word. I shall be very glad tomorrow morning to remember that I saw you once again, but now I almost wish you hadn't come. (*Slight pause.*)

KATE. (*Out front:*) And Mr. Johnson submitted to another hug with even better grace than before, if that were possible; and waving his hat as cheerfully as he could, took farewell of the Vincent Crummleses. (*The Crummleses go out.*)

Scene Eleven

The journey to Yorkshire; Dotheboys Hall. The Narrators, as the stage grows darker and darker:

NARRATORS.

And the next morning, Nicholas began his journey. It was now cold, winter weather,

And sometimes, he would recognise some place which he had passed on his journey up to Yorkshire, or on the long walk back,

And as night fell, it began to snow, and everything became as he remembered it, and it was easy to believe that everything which had since happened had been but a dream, and that he and Smike were plodding wearily along the road to London, the world before them. (*Very early morning gloom. We can hardly see. A scrape, a scuffle—someone running, others running after. Some of the boys are chasing Young Wackford. It is a slow, stumbling, dark kind of chase.*)

JACKSON. Hey, Wackford, Wackford—

COATES. Where's your pa then, Wackford?

BOLDER. Where's he be? (*Slight pause.*)

WACKFORD. Dunno. (*A violent scuffle as the Boys follow Wackford's voice. Three or four boys find Wackford and pinion him against a wall.*)

JACKSON. Dunno? Come on, now, Wackford. Summat's happened. We know that.

SNAWLEY SNR. We heard your man cry, through the parlour window.

JACKSON. Heard your sister, screaming in the night.

JENNINGS. Tell us what happened, Wackford.

BOLDER. Or we'll. . . .

JACKSON. There's no telling what we'll do.

WACKFORD. My ma—

JACKSON. Yuh? What?

WACKFORD. My ma said—

SNAWLEY SNR. Yuh?

WACKFORD. Pa's gonna be transported to Australia. And some old lady with him. And one man he worked for's going to jail. And another one's gone and hanged hisself. What else d'you want to know? (*Slight pause.*)

JACKSON. Right, then. (*The heavy noise of footfall. The Boys quickly push Wackford away. All the Boys now on stage. Enter Mrs. Squeers, Fanny, Phib and a small Boy who has become the New Smike, carrying the brimstone-and-treacle bowl. Mrs. Squeers carries the spoon.*)

MRS. SQUEERS. What's going on? Where's Wackford? (*Wackford hurries to his Mother, looking nervously at the Boys.*) It's brimstone-and-treacle morning! Every boy on line. Quick! Quick! What are you thinking of? First boy! (*The boys get into line.*)

TOMKINS. First boy. Tomkins. Twelve. A cripple.

COBBEY. Second boy. Cobbey. Thirteen. Another cripple.

PETERS. Third boy. Peters. Seven. Blind.

GRAYMARSH. Fourth boy—(*And he is interrupted by Jackson, who pushes himself forward, through the line, and past Jennings.*)

JACKSON. Jackson.

MRS. SQUEERS. What's this?

JACKSON. (*Grabbing the spoon.*) Johnny Jackson. (*Bolder, pushing his way through the line.*)

272

MRS. SQUEERS. Boy!

BOLDER. Fifth boy. Bolder. (*He grabs the bowl from the New Smike.*)

MRS. SQUEERS. Right, then, Bolder—(*She lifts the cane. It is grabbed by Coates.*)

COATES. Sixth. Coates. Eat.

MRS. SQUEERS. Have you gone mad?

JACKSON. Said—eat. (*Jackson, Coates and Bolder push Mrs. Squeers to her knees, helped by the others. Jackson forces the spoon into Mrs. Squeers' mouth.*)

JACKSON. Eat.

MRS. SQUEERS. You—little—(*But she is forced to eat the brimstone.*)

BOLDER. There. What now?

JACKSON. It's the end of term. It's break-up. So, let's break up. Break it all up. Break it all up—now. (*And a few boys start to chant. And the chant grows louder. And, as it grows, the bigger boys, followed by the smaller Boys, start to rush about, smashing everything they can see, pushing at Mrs. Squeers and Fanny, and dipping Wackford's head in the brimstone bowl.*)

BOYS. Break—up. Break—up. Break—up. Break—up. (*And in the general melee, Mrs. Squeers manages to escape, pulling Wackford after her, but Fanny and Phib are pinioned, pinched and prodded by groups of Boys, while the others continue to smash up Dotheboys Hall. The chant louder and faster.*)

BOYS. BREAK—UP BREAK—UP BREAK—UP BREAK—UP BREAK—UP (*And as the chant and the smashing-up build on, until they can grow no faster and louder, and John Browdie, Tilda and Nicholas burst in.*)

JOHN. Stop! Stop! Hey, all of 'ee—ye lads—stop! STOP! (*And everything stops.*) What's happening? What's going on here, eh? (*Pause. A little voice.*)

SNAWLEY SNR. Please sir. Squeers is in prison, sir, and going to be transported, sir, and—

COBBEY. And we're breaking out.

BOYS. Break-up—break-up.

JOHN. Well, I'll not stop ye. But—don't hurt the women, eh? Where's Mrs?

GRAYMARSH. Run away, sir.

JOHN. Little fat one?

TOMKINS. Gone with her.

JOHN. And Fanny? (*Fanny and Phib are allowed to come to John.*) Right, then. So—that's it. (*Pause.*)

BELLING. Can we—go now, sir?

NICHOLAS. (*Suddenly.*) Yes. Yes, go. Go, run away. As far as possible. Don't hurt them, don't hurt anyone, but still—yes, break it all up, then go. Go! Go! (*And cheering, the Boys run out, some confidently, some tearfully, some fast, some slowly, reluctantly, taking everything with them.*)

FANNY. Well, Mr. Browdie. And your friend as well. Excited all our boys to run away. But we will pay you out for it, even if our pa's unfortunate, and trod down by his enemies, we'll pay you out, I promise, you, and him, and Tilda!

JOHN. No, tha won't. I tell thee, Fanny, that I'm glad the old man's been caught out at last, but you'll have enough to suffer from without me crowing. More than that, tha'll need a friend or two to help thee get away, and here we are, and ready to lend thee a hand. So, are tha coming? (*Fanny turns away, arms folded.*)

TILDA. Come on, Fanny, please. (*Fanny turns back. She's crying. Tilda takes her arm, and she, Fanny and Phib go out. John and Nicholas left there for a moment.*)

JOHN. Well, then. Bloodshed. Riot. Eh? (*Pause.*)

NICHOLAS. Thank God—at least—it's over. (*And as they go, Narrators:*)

NARRATORS.

And for some days afterwards, the neighbouring countryside was over-run with boys.

And some were found crying under hedges, frightened by the solitude; (*We see a Boy wandering on from some hiding place. He holds the brimstone bowl and spoon.*)

One was discovered sleeping in a yard nearby the building; (*We realise the Boy is the New Smike.*)

And another wandered twenty miles, lost courage, and lay down in the snow, and slept. (*And the Boy sits, at the very front of the stage.*)

And in the course of time the Hall and its last breaking up began to be forgotten by the neighbors,

Or only spoken of as among things that had been. (*And the stage is empty now, except for the New Smike, sitting alone at the front of the stage.*)

Scene Twelve

Devon at Christmas. The New Smike, in the loneliness and silence, begins to sing what he can remember of a Christmas carol.

THE NEW SMIKE. God—rest ye, merry gentlemen—Let—uh—uh—you, dis-play (*Pause.*) For uh-uh-uh, our uh-uh-uh, Was born on, Christmas Day—(*Pause.*) To la-la-la from Satan's power When—Uh, uh gone astray—(*Pause.*) Oh, oh, uh, uh of comfort and joy—(*Slight pause.*) Comfort and joy . . . (*Pause.*) Oh, oh, tidings of comfort and joy. (*And the New Smike is still. And then, very faintly, we can hear the tune of the carol, being hummed. And more voices join, and we are in Devon, at Christmas. And the Families enter, to form a pleasant, almost photographic tableau: Nicholas, Kate, Mrs. Nickleby, Madeline, Mr. Charles, Mr. Ned, Frank, Tim, Miss La Creevy and Newman Noggs. And during their final narration, the carol grows behind them.*)

MADELINE. And when her term of mourning had expired, Madeline gave her hand and fortune to Nicholas.

KATE. And on the same day and at the same time, Kate became Mrs. Frank Cheeryble.

MR. CHARLES. And it had been expected that Tim Linkinwater and Miss La Creevy would have made a third couple on the occasion,

MISS LA CREEVY. But they declined,

TIM. And two or three weeks afterward went out together one morning before breakfast,

MR. NED. And,

KATE. Coming back with merry faces,

MR. CHARLES. Were found to have been quietly married that day.

NICHOLAS. And the money which Nicholas acquired in right of his wife he invested in the firm of the Cheeryble Brothers, in which Frank had become a partner.

FRANK. And before many years elapsed, the business began to be carried on in the names of "Cheeryble and Nickleby",

MRS. NICKLEBY. So that Mrs. Nickleby's prophetic anticipations were to be realised at last.

TIM. The twin brothers retired.

FRANK. Who needs to be told that they were happy?

KATE. They were surrounded by happiness of their own creation, and lived but to increase it.

NICHOLAS. The first act of Nicholas, when he became a rich and prosperous merchant, was to buy his father's old farm;

MADELINE. And soon, he and his wife were blessed with a group of lovely children.

FRANK. And within a stone's throw was another such retreat, enlivened by children's voices, too,

KATE. And here lived Kate, with many new cares and occupations,

NICHOLAS. But still, the same true loving creature and the same gentle sister, as in her girlish days.

MRS. NICKLEBY. And Mrs. Nickleby lived sometimes with her daughter and sometimes with her son,

MADELINE. And spent much time relating her experience,

MRS. NICKLEBY. Especially on the matter of the management and bringing up of children,

KATE. With much importance and solemnity.

MR. CHARLES. And there was one grey-haired,

MR. NED. Quiet,

MR. CHARLES. Harmless gentleman,

NOGGS. Who lived in a little cottage hard by Nicholas' house, and in his absence, attended to the supervision of affairs.

MADELINE. His chief delight and pleasure was the children,

NOGGS. With whom he became a child himself, and a master of the revels. The little people could do nothing without dear, old Newman Noggs.

KATE. And, as time went on, the house in which young Nicholas and Kate had spent their childhood was enlarged and altered, to accommodate the growing family.

NICHOLAS. But no old rooms were ever pulled down,

KATE. No old tree was rooted up,

NICHOLAS. Nothing with which there was the least association of old, bygone times and childhood days was ever cut down,

KATE. Or removed,

NICHOLAS. Or even—changed. (*And all the Company are singing now, and John and Tilda run in to join the Families, who are shaking each others' hands, and talking and moving from person to person, and embracing: the happiest of Christmases.*)

COMPANY.

    Now to the Lord Sing Praises
    All you within this place,
    Like we true loving brethren,
    Each other to embrace. (*And Nicholas, a little apart, looks down-*)

stage, as if out of a window, and sees the Boy, sitting outside in the snow.)

For the merry time of Christmas
Is drawing on apace—(*And, unnoticed, Nicholas slips away, and trudges over to the still boy.*)

And it's tidings of comfort and joy,
Comfort and joy,
And it's tidings of comfort and joy. (*Nicholas has reached the Boy. He touches him. The Boy does not move. Kate and Madeline notice that Nicholas has gone.*)

God bless the ruler of this house
And send him long to reign, (*Nicholas turns back to the house. He sees his wife and his sister appear. They look at him. Upstage of them, the party is going on.*)

And many a merry Christmas
May live to see again . . . (*Nicholas takes a step back towards the house. But he can't leave the boy. A despairing look at Kate and Madeline.*)

Among our friends and kindred
Let's sing with mickle main . . . (*And, as the carol builds up to its climax, with descants and the organ coming in, Nicholas turns back to the Boy and picks him up in his arms, looking at his wife and sister.*)

Oh, it's tidings of comfort and joy,
Comfort and Joy—(*And then he turns to us, and stands there, holding the boy in his arms.*)

Oh, it's tidings of comfort and joy,
Comfort and joy,
Comfort and joy. (*Darkness.*)

THE END